IMAGES OF THE DIVINE

STUDIES IN THE HISTORY
OF
CHRISTIAN THOUGHT

EDITED BY

HEIKO A. OBERMAN, Tucson, Arizona

IN COOPERATION WITH
HENRY CHADWICK, Cambridge
JAROSLAV PELIKAN, New Haven, Connecticut
BRIAN TIERNEY, Ithaka, New York
ARJO VANDERJAGT, Groningen

VOLUME LIV

AMBROSIOS GIAKALIS

IMAGES OF THE DIVINE

IMAGES OF THE DIVINE

THE THEOLOGY OF ICONS AT
THE SEVENTH ECUMENICAL COUNCIL

BY

AMBROSIOS GIAKALIS

WITH A FOREWORD BY

HENRY CHADWICK

E.J. BRILL
LEIDEN · NEW YORK · KÖLN
1994

This book has been published with the generous financial support of Mr Manolis Sarantos.

The paper in this book meets the guidelines for permanence and durability of the Committee on Production Guidelines for Book Longevity of the Council on Library Resources.

Library of Congress Cataloging-in-Publication Data

Giakalis, Ambrosios.
    Images of the divine : the theology of icons at the Seventh Ecumenical Council / by Ambrosios Giakalis ; with a foreword by Henry Chadwick.
        p.   cm. — (Studies in the history of Christian thought, ISSN 0081-8607 ; v. 54)
    Revision of author's thesis (Ph. D.)—University of Cambridge, 1988.
    Includes bibliographical references and indexes.
    ISBN 9004099468
    1. Council of Nicaea (2nd : 787) 2. Icons—Cult—History of doctrines—Middle Ages, 600-1500. 3. Image (Theology)—History of doctrines—Middle Ages, 600-1500. 4. Iconoclasm. 5. Orthodox Eastern Church—Doctrines.   I. Title. II. Series.
    BR240.G53   1993
    246'.53'09021—dc20   93-31993
                                                                    CIP

Die Deutsche Bibliothek - CIP-Einheitsaufnahme

Giakalēs, Ambrosios:
Images of the divine : the theology of icons at the Seventh Ecumenical Council / by Ambrosios Giakalis. With a foreword by Henry Chadwick. - Leiden ; New York ; Köln : Brill, 1993
    (Studies in the history of Christian thought ; Vol. 54)
    ISBN 90-04-09946-8
NE: GT

ISSN 0081-8607
ISBN 90 04 09946 8

For my mother and teacher:
the Orthodox Church of Greece

CONTENTS

FOREWORD

The iconoclast controversy is one of the more arcane debates within the Byzantine Church, yet its importance for Eastern Christians can scarcely be overstated. Its outcome confirmed the veneration of icons as an essential aspect of the theology and devotional life of Orthodoxy. Rooted in a natural desire to make the holy tangible and accessible, the use of icons goes back at least to the fourth century. There were even then, however, some rumbles of disapproval from a few of the Greek Fathers, but the crisis came to a head only in the eighth century, when a series of military defeats at the hands of the Arabs, which threatened the loss of the empire's heartland of Asia Minor, led to a characteristic bout of theological introspection. If God was punishing the Romans, they needed to address their sins, and there was ample biblical precedent, particularly in the Old Testament, for regarding idolatry as the chief sin which offended God.

It was an easy step to identify idolatry with the 'worship' of icons. The suppression of icon-worship by Leo III and Constantine V was accompanied by a significant improvement in the military fortunes of the Byzantines, which served to reinforce iconoclast opinion. The iconophiles reacted instinctively to defend the relics and images of much-loved saints without which they felt themselves denied the intimacy which they had enjoyed with their heavenly patrons. The persecution of the iconophiles was directed personally by Leo III and his successors. As the later iconoclast emperors moderated their zeal, however, the forces of tradition regrouped. Under the patronage of the iconophile Empress Irene, a high civil servant Tarasius was elected patriarch to implement the policy of restoring unity through a general council of the Church. By 787, the date of the Seventh Ecumenical Council, the iconophiles were not only politically in the ascendency but had honed their arguments well. Iconophile refugees in Italy had made the Papacy sympathetic to their cause. Tarasius' programmatic declarations promised harmony with the West.

Father Ambrosios discusses in detail in successive chapters the major themes of the council. Arguments from tradition dominated a large part of the debate as each side sought to prove its case by appealing to the Bible and the Fathers. The iconoclasts relied largely on Johannine texts, notably the injunction to worship God in Spirit and truth, on Epiphanius of Salamis, the celebrated fourth-century hammer of heretics, and on Eusebius of Caesarea, the church historian. The iconophiles countered their arguments with a wealth of material from the Old Testament and from the Fathers, particularly Athanasius, the Cappadocians and Cyril of Alexandria. One testimony to which both sides appealed (the iconophiles with better reason), a letter of the ascetic Neilus to the early fifth-century prefect Olympiodorus, has the historical importance of being the oldest surviving description of a church's decorative scheme. On the philosophical level the arguments revolved around the concept of the relationship between prototype and image. In this respect the iconophiles drew on a tradition going back to Athanasius and Basil of Caesarea which used the analogy of the veneration of the imperial portrait. The fourth-century Fathers had made use of the analogy in the context of trinitarian theology. The iconophiles applied it to images of Christ and the saints. The veneration of the image, they claimed, is relative, the honour paid to the image ascending to the prototype. On the christological level the iconoclasts took their stand on the principle that the icon was an idol if it did not represent Christ as he really is. They held that anyone who venerates the icon of Christ divides him into two because only one of his two natures, the visible human nature, is being venerated. The iconophile's answer was that through the visible character our minds are caught up to the invisible divinity. The inability of the iconoclasts to accept the iconophile account of the relationship of prototype to image, however, made this argument less than compelling for them.

Father Ambrosios shows that one of the chief underlying assumptions of the council was the espousal or rejection of the concept of uncreated grace. This was not made a topic of discussion yet it pervades every aspect of the debate. The doctrine of uncreated grace, which was first adumbrated by the Cappadocians, was a solution to the problem of how God could remain utterly transcendent and yet at the same time be active in an intimate way in the material world. For the iconophiles God, who is holy by nature, is present as a deifying energy in every human saint and as a sanctifying energy in the saint's image. Veneration by the faithful ascends through the icon of the saint or of Christ to the prototype; sanctifying grace descends through the icon to the venerator. For the iconoclasts the fundamental problem concerning the veneration of icons was the idea of participation in the divine energies. They held that the immense gulf between the material and the spiritual, the created and the uncreated, could not be bridged by any sanctified matter apart from the Eucharistic body of Christ. This suggests that they could not admit a real distinction between divine essence and divine energy. The iconophiles, for their part, rejected the Eucharist as an icon because it could not then be the real body and blood of Christ.

The iconoclasts belonged to a tradition which held what might be considered a one-sided doctrine of divine transcendence. The victory of the iconophiles was a victory for the accessibility of the holy. A lay and monastic piety triumphed in the council over a clerical approach — one of the factors which was to account for the difference of ethos between East and West which has endured to the present day.

HENRY CHADWICK
Peterhouse,
Cambridge

PREFACE

The purpose of this study, which originated as a doctoral dissertation submitted to the University of Cambridge in 1988, is to
elucidate the theological significance of the Seventh Ecumenical
Council from the documents which record its decisions.

The theological evaluation of the council is still a matter of
dispute. Eminent scholars have expressed negative views on the
council and have overlooked its contribution to Christian theology
in general. Characteristic in this respect are the dismissive remarks
of E.J. Martin: "The Council of Nicaea is one of those events, trivial
in themselves, which are great crises in the history of Christianity."[1]
H.-G. Beck expresses himself in even stronger terms: "The Seventh
Ecumenical Council contains nothing of theological importance."[2]
Happily, there have also been scholars such as P.J. Alexander who
have perceived the theological significance of the council and have
described it in a positive way as "a most important council".[3]

Hitherto there has been no systematic exposition of this "importance", a lack which the present work attempts to remedy. The
background and historical development of the crisis which led to
the council are the subject of many specialist studies and are only
dealt with here in a summary fashion. My particular concern is
to examine the theological conceptions which shaped the dominant
themes of the council. These themes have been isolated because
they permit the student to enter into the theological mentality of
the age. Such themes, decisive for the entire development of the
question, are constituted by ideas concerning (1) the person of
Jesus Christ, (2) the presence in the world of the uncreated energies
of the Triune God, (3) the meaning of reality and its distinction
from non-reality, (4) the meaning of the worship of God "in spirit
and truth" and of its concrete application, (5) the way in which
the tradition of the Christian past is to be understood, and (6)
the educational ideals of the period and the theological means of
their application in the practice and life of the Church. Around
these fundamental axes, on which the iconoclast struggle is centred,

---

[1] *A History of the Iconoclastic Controversy*, London 1930, p. 109.
[2] *Geschichte der orthodoxen Kirche in byzantinischen Reich (Die Kirche in ihrer Geschichte)*,
Gottingen 1980.
[3] *The Patriarch Nicephorus of Constantinople*, Oxford 1958, p. 20, n. 1.

revolves an analysis of the theological criteria of the opposing sides.
My conclusions reveal the deeply irreconcilable views which are
evidence of two mutually exclusive interpretations of Christianity.
There are also important points of agreement, however, which are
worth recording.

The following sources form the basis of this study:

1. *The acta of the council* (Mansi, vols 12 and 13).
2. *Against Constantine Caballinus* (*PG* 95, 309–344).
3. *The Inquiries of Constantine* (ed. H. Hennephof).
4. The letters of Germanus of Constantinople (*PG* 98, 156B–193D).
5. The treatise of John Damascene *On the Holy Images* (*PG* 94, 1232A–1492B = Kotter, vol. iii).
6. *The Nouthesia Gerontos* (ed. B.M. Melioransky).
7. The works of Theodore of Studius (*PG* 99).
8. The works of Nicephorus of Constantinople (*PG* 100).
9. Photius' *Epistulae et Amphilochia* (ed. Laourdas-Westerink) and *Homilies* (trans. C. Mango).
10. *The Synodikon of Orthodoxy* (ed. J. Gouillard).
11. Lives of Germanus, Theodore of Studius, etc.
12. Iconoclast poems and their refutation by Theodore of Studius (*PG* 99, 436–477).

For the better understanding of what was said at the Seventh Ecumenical Council, these need to be supplemented by the additional
sources listed in the Bibliography. Modern works deal with the
theology of the icons only in passing; those that treat the historical
aspect of the controversy are much more numerous and are noticed
in the Bibliography. It should be noted in particular that on account
of the wealth of iconophile texts in relation to the poverty (in bulk
rather than in content) of iconoclast texts, it was unavoidable that
the iconophile arguments should be set out more extensively than
those of the iconoclasts. This does not express any partiality in this
study towards the iconophiles. It merely reflects the nature of the
extant sources.

My researches were pursued in difficult circumstances. I owe my
deepest debt of gratitude to the Revd Professor Henry Chadwick,
who was a constant source of encouragement and inspiration at
times when ill health threatened to bring my studies to a premature
close. Father John Romanides has likewise been a tower of strength.
To him I owe a valuable new perspective on the theological issues
debated at the coucil. I also owe many helpful suggestions to Bishop
Kallistos of Diokleia and Bishop Rowan Williams, who read the

manuscript at more than one stage. I must also record my gratitude to Miss Constance Babington-Smith, whose practical support during my stay at Cambridge was invaluable, and to Dr. Nicholas Gendle who gave freely of his advice.

I could not have completed my studies without the generous financial help provided by Charles Anthony, Costas Carras, Dimitrios Panagopoulos, Antony Polyviou, the Hellenic Foundation and the Holy Synod of the Church of Greece. To all these I express my heartfelt gratitude.

Finally, I should like to thank Manolis Sarantos, who not only encouraged me to turn my thesis into a book but provided the funds with which this could be done, Dr. Norman Russell, without whose editorial help I could not have prepared the work for publication and Professor Heiko A. Oberman, editor of *Studies in the History of Christian Thought*, for accepting this volume as part of the series.

Ambrosios Giakalis
Athens

CHAPTER ONE

INTRODUCTION

The Origins of the Iconoclast Controversy

Nearly twenty years ago Peter Brown complained that the iconoclast controversy was "in the grip of a crisis of over-explanation".[1] Some scholars held that the origins of the controversy lay in the secular programme of reform of the first two Isaurian emperors, Leo III (717–41) and Constantine V (741–75), whose zeal in ordering the military and agricultural affairs of the empire spilled over into ecclesiastical matters as they sought to relieve the Church of lands which could otherwise be made more productive.[2] Others held the causes to be primarily religious, the decision being taken to purify the empire of idolatry in order to propitiate the divine anger made so clearly manifest in the defeats suffered by imperial forces at the hands of the new religion of Islam.[3] To a third group the mutual antagonism between the Eastern and the Graeco-Roman spirits seemed to offer an explanation, the aniconic art of the East on the one hand and the Graeco-Roman tradition of plastic art on the other being held to have come into conflict with each other in Asia Minor.[4] Inquiry focussed on the "iconophobe" fringe of Asia Minor, the homeland of Leo III and Constantine V, where Greek, Iranian, Jewish and Arab influences were thought to have

---

[1] "A Dark Age Crisis: Aspects of the Iconoclastic Controversy" in *Society and the Holy in Late Antiquity*, London 1982, p. 254.

[2] S. Zampelios *Byzantinai Meletai. Peri pigon Neoellinikis Ethnotitos*, Athens 1857, p. 246ff; P. Uspenskii, *Istorija vizantijskoij imperii*, St Petersburg 1913, vol. ii, pp. 22–53, 89–109, 157–74; K. Paparrhegopoulos, *Istoria tou Ellinikou Ethnous*, Athens 1932, vol. iii, 2, pp. 25ff; cf. the same author's *Epilogon tis Istorias tou Ellinikou Ethnous*, Athens 1877, p. 179 (Paparrhegopoulos regards the iconoclast movement as a precursor to the French revolution — see his *Histoire de la civilisation hellénique*, Athens 1878, p. 194); C. Diehl — G. Marcais, "Le monde oriental de 395 à 1081", *Histoire general, Histoire du Moyen Age*, Paris 1936, vol. iii, pp. 262–3; M.V. Levtchenko, *Byzance des origines à 1453*, Paris 1949, p. 136, takes a Marxist view, seeing iconoclasm as a pretext under which certain social groups fought for their politico-economic class interests.

[3] A. Lombard, *Constantine V. Empereur des Romains (740–775)*, Paris 1902, pp. 105, 124, 127, 128; *DACL*, vol. vii, 1 (1926), col. 234; E. Ludwig, *La Mediteranée*, New York 1943, vol. i, p. 313; A.A. Vasiliev, *History of the Byzantine Empire 324–1453*, Madison 1952, vol. i, p. 252; G. Ostrogorsky, *History of the Byzantine State*, Oxford 1956, p. 160ff.

[4] D. Zakythinos, *Vyzantini Istoria 324–1071*, Athens 1971, p. 197.

encountered one another.[5] The accusation of the iconophiles that their opponents were "Jewish-minded" and "saracen-minded" lent weight to this, as did the suspicion that the iconoclasts were tainted with the thought of the Manichees, the Marcionites and the Paulicians.[6] A suggestion that Monophysite influence might have played an important role enjoyed a vogue for a while but has since been shown to be without foundation.[7]

The reason for such a diversity of views is that the lack of satisfactory first-hand iconoclast sources and the fragmentary char-

[5] The iconophiles accused the iconoclasts of being under the influence of Islam, which rejected every human representation as an idol. The epithet "Saracen-minded" is characteristic of them. See, e.g., Germanus, *Ad Thomam*, Mansi 13, 109DE; Theophanes, de Boor, p. 410; Mansi 13, 357D, 157E etc. For the position of Islam on the icons and its influence on the iconoclast controversy, see also the following: C.H. Becker, "Von Werden und Wesen der islamischen Welt", *Islamstudien*, Leipzig 1924, vol. i, pp. 432–44; H. Lammens, "L'attitude de l'Islam primitif en face des arts figurés", *Etudes sur le siècle des Omayyades*, Beirut 1930, pp. 351–89; G. Marcais, "La question des Images dans l'art musulman", *Byzantion* 7 (1932), pp. 161–83; K.A.C. Cresswell, "The Lawfulness of Painting in Early Islam", *Ars Islamica* 11–12 (1946), pp. 159–66 (with a full bibliography); A.A. Vasiliev, "The Iconoclastic Edict of the Caliph Yazid II, A.D. 721", *DOP* 9/10 (1956), pp. 23–47; L. Breyer, *Bilderstreit und Araberstums in Byzanz. Das 8 Jahrhundert (717–813) aus der Weltchronik des Theophanes*, Graz 1957; A. Grabar, *L'Iconoclasme byzantin*, Paris 1957 (esp. ch.V, "Hostilité aux images: chrétiens d'Asie, Juifs, Musulmans"); G.E. von Grunebaum, "Byzantine Iconoclasm and the Influence of the Islamic Environment" *History of Religions* 2 (1962), pp. 1–10; M.G.S. Hodgson, "Islam and Image", *History of Religions* 3 (1963–4), pp. 220–60; S. Gero, *Byzantine Iconoclasm during the Reign of Leo III, with particular Attention to the Oriental Sources*, Louvain 1973, (chapter: "Contemporary Muslim Iconoclasm and Leo"); L.W. Barnard, "Byzantium and Islam", *Byzantinoslavica* 36 (1975), pp. 25–37, and the relevant chapter in his *Graeco-Roman and Oriental Background of the Iconoclastic Controversy*, Leiden 1974, pp. 10–33; P. Crone, "Islam, Judeo-Christianity and Byzantine Iconoclasm", *Jerusalem Studies in Arabic and Islam* 2 (1980), pp. 59–95.

[6] The charge of "Judaising" is already found in the sources of the iconoclast period: Germanus is categorical on this (Mansi 13, 198BD), as is the *Nouthesia* (p. xiii). On this see J.B. Frey, "La question des images chez les Juifs à la lumière des récentes découvertes", *Biblica* 15 (1934), pp. 265–300; J. Starr, *The Jews in the Byzantine Empire 641–1204*, Athens 1939; A. Grabar, *L'Iconoclasme byzantin*, pp. 116–20; A. Sharf, *Byzantine Jewry from Justinian to the Fourth Crusade*, London 1971, pp. 6ff; S. Gero, *Leo III*, p. 59ff; J. Gutmann, "Deuteronomy: Religious Reformation or Iconoclastic Revolution?" in *The Image and the Word. Confrontations in Judaism, Christianity and Islam* (ed. J. Gutmann), Missoula 1977; P. Crone, "Islam, Judeo-Christianity and Byzantine Iconoclasm". On the relationship between Paulicianism and the iconoclast movement L. Barnard sees two parallel religious movements which are not mutually dependent ("The Paulicians and Iconoclasm" in *Iconoclasm* (edd. Bryer and Herrin) pp. 75–82).

[7] On the relationship between the Monophysites and the iconoclast controversy, see G. Ostrogorsky, *Studien zur Geschichte des byzantinischen Bilderstreites*, Amsterdam 1964; M. Mundell, "Monophysite Church Decoration" in *Iconoclasm*, pp. 59–74; S. Brock, "Iconoclasm and the Monophysites" in *Iconoclasm*, pp. 53–7. Brock rejects Monophysite influence on the genesis of the iconoclast movement.

acter of those sources which do exist have led scholars to view the controversy largely through the eyes of the iconodules. In the literature of the victors of the struggle iconoclasm is presented as a deviation from the age-old tradition of the Church. Many of those who took this perspective for granted sought to account for iconoclasm as an aberration, as a break in a smooth tradition which needed to be explained by reference to external, non-hellenic factors. Modern research, however, has tended to reject outside influences and see the controversy as the result of a crisis within Byzantium, as a domestic reaction to the shock of the Muslim invasions of the seventh century.

The Muslim successes left the Byzantines reeling. Seeing themselves as the people of God, the true Israel, they naturally looked to the Old Testament for guidance. When the Israel of the Old Testament was faced with the success of its enemies, it purified itself of idolatry. It followed that the empire too should purify itself of idolatry as a means of propitiating the anger of God.[8] But why were icons chosen as the scapegoat? A number of scholars have accurately traced the progress of the controversy and the various reforming measures taken by the iconoclast emperors.[9] The social function of icons was first examined by Brown who asked the questions, "Why were icons considered so vulnerable in the eighth century?" and "Why had they achieved sufficient prominence to have drawn attack upon themselves?"[10] The Arab invasions had left Asia Minor devastated with cities in ruins and populations displaced. Until that time the Byzantine empire had been a "commonwealth of cities" with a large degree of autonomy being exercised by each community. As part of the work of reconstruction and resistance to further attacks greater control had to be exercised by the centre. Iconoclasm was part of a centipetal reaction to the invasions. In Brown's view icons became victims of this reaction for two reasons: on the one hand they were associated with the cult of civic saints who had been discredited through the destruction of their cities; on the other they were an alternative source of power deriving their efficacy not through official ecclesiastical rites but through the holiness of the person they depicted.

---

[8] G. Ostrogorsky, *History of the Byzantine State*, pp. 160ff; S. Gero, *Leo III*, passim.
[9] Most notably, G. Ostrogorsky, *History of the Byzantine State*, Oxford 1956; A. Grabar, *L'Iconoclasme byzantin*, Paris 1957; P.J. Alexander, *The Patriarch Nicephorus of Constantinople*, Oxford 1958; S. Gero, *Leo III*, Louvain 1973, and *Constantine V*, Louvain 1977. On the history of the icon, see also C. Mango, *The Brazen House. A Study of the Vestibule of the Imperial Palace of Constantinople*, Copenhagen 1959.
[10] P. Brown, "A Dark Age Crisis", p. 287.

The rise of the icon to prominence as well as its vulnerability in the sixth and seventh centuries are connected intimately with the rise of the holy man, or *geron* as he is called in Greek. Ever since his appearance in Syria in the fourth century, the lone Christian ascetic had been a figure endowed with power. People flocked to him for healing and counsel because his ascetic feats were evidence that he had the ear of God. He was an intercessor, a healer of the sick and a potector of the weak. He was also an arbiter of Church discipline whose ability to communicate God's forgiveness of sins did much to lighten the burden of the Church's rigorous rules. He was a living icon of God's power and love. When he died his image was put up to perpetuate his presence. Indeed sometimes he became the protecting saint of a city.[11]

In the sixth century there was a new resurgence of civic patriotism which found visible expression in the icon of the saint who interceded on behalf of his community. St Demetrius of Thessalonica and St Nicholas of Myra are two prominent examples. Such holy patrons encouraged a warm personal piety because they made the austere majesty of the divine accessible to the humble believer. In Brown's memorable phrase they were "the backstairs government of that awesome throne".[12] But when the city was destroyed the protecting saint was in some degree discredited. His icon, moreover, was deprived of its local "constituency"; when it was brought to Constantinople it did not have the backing of a local cult. Iconoclasm was in some measure a rebuttal of civic saints, of local autonomy. But it went much deeper than simply lending weight to the claims of central authority against local government. Fundamentally it was a debate about the locus of the holy. For holiness was not just a matter of personal piety; it was closely connected with the exercise of power in society. The legitimacy of material images as such was never a point at issue. The controversy revolved around *which* images could be regarded as vehicles of the holy. For the iconoclasts the holy was mediated to the people through material things consecrated by the clergy — the basilica with its liturgy, the Eucharist, the symbol of the cross. To have the holy mediated by a myriad icons seemed to them to dilute it to the

---

[11] The seminal study on the social role of the holy man is P. Brown, "The Rise and Function of the Holy Man in Late Antiquity", JRS LX1 (1971), pp. 80–101. On the biblical background and patristic understanding of the holy man, see J.S. Romanides, "Jesus Christ: the Life of the World" in *Xenia Ecumenica*, Helsinki 1983, pp. 232–75 and *Christ, Cross and Resurrection. A Pauline Approach*, Rhodes 1988.

[12] P. Brown, "A Dark Age Crisis", p. 283.

point at which it ceased to be efficacious. The iconophiles, by contrast, sought through the icon to enable the holy to permeate the material world.

The purpose of these vehicles of holiness was to enable human beings to have access to God through participation in the divine life. On the deepest theological level the iconoclast controversy was about deification. Much of the debate was centred on the person of Christ, on whether his portrayal in colours on wooden boards did equal justice both to his human and to his divine natures. But Christ's human nature, although distinct, is inseparable from his divine nature. It is not just his humanity but his deified humanity which is represented in icons. A broad tradition going back through St Maximus the Confessor to Athanasius and Clement held that that which Christ is by nature the believer can become by grace. In the Eastern tradition such assimilation to Christ through participation in uncreated grace is called deification. Only by participating in the divine energies can man have real communion with God. The iconoclasts sought to restrict such access to deifying grace to the ecclesiastical channels represented by the clergy and the Eucharist. The iconophiles had what we might call a more "charismatic" approach. The monk, the holy man, the icon, the wonder-working relic — these were also channels by which divine grace filled the ordinary faithful so that they became "gods by grace", empowered to take their place after death in the court of heaven.

The Outbreak and Intensification of the Controversy

According to the *Narratio* of John of Jerusalem, which was read at the second session of the Seventh Ecumenical Council (787) a Jewish Magus called Tessaracontapechys promised the Caliph Yazid II (720–4) a thirty-one year reign if he ordered the destruction of the icons in his realm.[13] Yazid complied and his edict was executed "by the lawless hands of Jews and Arabs". By the grace of Christ, however, and through the mediation of the Theotokos and the saints, as Theophanes tells us, he died prematurely "without most people having heard of his satanic decree".[14] The icons were restored and Yazid's son, Walid, ordered the false prophets to be put to death. Theophanes insists that Leo III "inherited his baneful doctrine" from Yazid, having adopted the "Arab way of thinking".[15] In Theophanes' view, the licentious and uneducated Bishop

---

[13] Mansi 13, 197–200; cf. Theophanes, de Boor, p. 402.
[14] Theophanes, ibid.
[15] Theophanes, ibid. On the edict, see A.A. Vasiliev, "The Iconoclastic Edict

Constantine of Nacoleia agreed with Yazid; the *Narratio* of John of Jerusalem likewise says that Constantine imitated the "lawless Jews and impious Arabs".[16]

Constantine of Nacoleia is one of the three bishops of Asia Minor who acted as leaders (whether in a planned way or not is not known) of the movement against the icons. The other two were Thomas of Claudiopolis and John of Synada. From the correspondence of the Patriarch Germanus (715–30) with these and from his work *De Heresibus et Synodis* we learn that when they came to Constantinople they probably had contact with Leo III, whom they encouraged to take action against the icons.[17] We are also told that their theological argument was that through the worship of icons the Church had fallen into idolatry. Germanus, citing a good many scriptural precedents for the use of images in the Church, maintained that the worship of the icons was an ancient custom of the Church. Rejecting the accusation of idolatry, he stressed that the Incarnation of Christ frees Christians from "all idolatrous errors and impieties".[18]

In my view neither Yazid's decree nor the anti-iconic movement of the three Anatolian bishops exercised any decisive influence on Leo III in his action against the icons. Yazid's decree was no more than a parallel and coincidental iconoclastic act. And it is difficult to believe that the "collarless figure" of Constantine of Nacoleia and the other two bishops could have played such a great historical

---

of the Caliph Yazid II, A.D. 721", *DOP* 9/10 (1956), pp. 23–47; A. Grabar, *L'Iconoclasme byzantin*, pp. 103–112. The influence of the decree on Leo III has been disputed by P. Lemerle, *Le premier humanisme byzantin*, Paris 1971, pp. 32–3; and S. Gero, *Leo III*. H. Glykatzi-Ahrweiler, "The Geography of the Iconoclast World", in *Iconoclasm*, pp. 21ff, disputes the influence of eastern elements in general on the origins of iconoclasm.

[16] Theophanes, de Boor, p. 402; Mansi 13, 200A.

[17] J. Herrin, *The Formation of Christendom*, Oxford 1987, pp. 331–3. On Germanus, see L. Lamza, *Patriarch Germanos I von Konstantinopel*, Würzburg 1975, and V. Grumel, "L'iconologie de saint Germain de Constantinople", *EO* 21 (1922), pp. 165–75. Germanus's letters to John of Synada, Constantine of Nacoleia and Thomas of Claudiopolis are printed in Mansi 13, 100B–105A, 105BE and 108A–128A, repectively. For a detailed analysis see D. Stein, *Der Beginn des Bilderstreits und seine Entwicklung bis in die 40er Jahre des 8 Jahrhunderts*, Munich 1980, pp. 1–88. For the importance of the letters see G. Ostrogorsky, "Les débuts de la querelle des images", in *Mélanges Charles Diehl*, vol. i (1930), pp. 235–55. The *De Heresibus*, written after Germanus's dethronement in 730, is printed in *PG* 98, 77–80. The influence of the movement of the three bishops on Leo is accepted by G. Ostrogorsky, *History of the Byzantine State*, p. 162, and P. Lemerle, *Le premier humanisme byzantin*, pp. 34–6. It is rejected by P. Brown "A Dark Age Crisis", p. 255, and especially by S. Gero, *Leo III*, pp. 85–93.

[18] *PG* 98, 169C; cf. 172C–173C.

role.[19] I believe that S. Gero is right when he says that "the key to understanding the origin of Byzantine iconoclasm is still in the person of the emperor Leo himself" and that "in the final analysis, Byzantine iconoclasm . . . was not Jewish, Muslim or Anatolian, but indeed an imperial heresy, born 'in the purple' in the royal palace".[20]

Leo first "began to speak about the destruction of the holy and venerable icons" ten years after ascending the throne in 726.[21] The final stimulus to the outbreak of the iconoclast movement in an official sense came from a severe earthquake which created a new island in the Aegean Sea between the volcanic islands of Thera and Therasia. The emperor interpreted this phenomenon as a manifestation of divine anger at the use of icons.[22] The first icono-clastic act of Leo may be regarded as the removal by an officer of the icon of Christ which was set over the Chalce gate of the palace.[23] The people were outraged and killed the emperor's emis-sary on the spot, whereupon a riot ensued.[24]

At a silentium, or council of state, called by the emperor on the 17 January 730, the Patriarch Germanus refused to support the iconoclast policy of Leo by signing the relevant decree. Unable to comply with the pressure brought upon him, he was forced to resign. He was succeeded by his "pupil and syncellus", Anastasius, who signed the decree.[25] The persecution began at once with monks as the main target.[26] In his *De Haeresibus et Synodis* Germanus speaks to us of the destruction of icons, altars and veils, and of the defilement of sacred things and the burning of holy relics.[27] *The Fount of Knowledge* also mentions the destruction of portable icons

---

[19] S. Gero, *Leo III*, p. 91.
[20] S. Gero, *Leo III*, p. 131.
[21] On the exact year of the beginning of official iconoclasm, see G. Ostrogorsky, "Les débuts de la querelle des images", and S. Gero, *Leo III*, pp. 94–5.
[22] Theophanes, de Boor, p. 404; Nicephorus, *Breviarium*, de Boor, p. 57, 21.
[23] Theophanes, de Boor, p. 404.
[24] Theophanes, de Boor, p. 405. The general revolt of the thematic forces in Hellas and of the fleet of the Cyclades (Theophanes, de Boor, p. 405; Nicephorus, *Breviarium*, de Boor, p. 57) in 727 is no longer regarded as having any connection with Leo's iconoclast measures; see Th. Korres, "To kinima ton 'Helladikon'", *Byzantiaka* 1 (1981), pp. 39–49. The burning of the "Ecumenical School" at Leo's instigation, mentioned by George the Monk in his *Chronikon* (written under Michael III, 842–67), de Boor, p. 1904, II, p. 742, seems to be pure fiction; cf. P. Lemerle, *Le premier humanisme byzantin*, pp. 89–94.
[25] Theophanes, de Boor, pp. 408–49; G. Ostrogorsky, "Les débuts de la querelle des images", p. 238ff.
[26] Germanus, *De Haeresibus et Synodis*, *PG* 98, 80B. See also *The Fount of Knowledge*, *PG* 94, 773A, and the anonymous eleventh-century Bruxelles chronicle, ed. F. Cumont, *Anecdota Bruxelliensia* I, Ghent 1894, pp. 31, 20–2.
[27] *PG* 98, 80BC.

and wall-paintings.[28] Theophanes mentions furthermore the burning of holy relics "condemned" by Leo: "he maintained that the
veneration of idols and the unlawful honouring of 'dead bones'
was not right."[29]

Pope Gregory II (715–31) in letters to Leo III protested vigorously.[30] His successor, Gregory III (731–41) called a council (1
November 731) which anathematised those who destroyed or
blasphemed the sacred icons.[31] Leo, taking his revenge on the pope,
imposed burdensome new taxes on Calabria and Sicily (the
Patrimonia Petri) and, removing these territories from his jurisdiction along with Illyria, assigned them to the jurisdiction of the
patriarch of Constantinople.[32]

The iconoclast crisis reached its climax under Constantine V
(741–75), who besides being an able general and administrator,
was also an intelligent iconoclast theologian who attempted to
construct the dogmatic presuppositions and foundations of iconoclasm, transferring the polemics onto the christological level and
introducing Christ as a person incapable of being represented in
iconic form.[33] We have knowledge of his theological conceptions
from surviving fragments of his works and from indirect testimonies
in iconophile literature.

Desiring to give his iconoclast theses the strongest possible force,
he conceived the idea of calling an Ecumenical Council. The calling
of the council was preceded by an intensive propaganda campaign,
during which public meetings were held in which leading sup-
porters of the iconoclast party delivered speeches to the people
or disputed with their opponents on terms favourable to them-

---

[28] *PG* 94, 774AB.
[29] Theophanes, de Boor, p. 406; *Acta Martyrum Constantinopolitanorum, AASS,*
Aug. 11 (1935) 437C. For the details of the persecutions, see S. Gero, *Leo III,*
pp. 97–101.
[30] First letter, Mansi 12, 959A–974A; second letter, Mansi 12, 975–982B. The
authenticity of the letters is discussed below.
[31] See L. Brehier and R. Aigran, "Grégoire le Grand, les états barbares et
la conquête (590–757)", in Fliche et Martin, *Histoire de l'Eglise,* vol. v, Paris 1947,
p. 455ff.
[32] See V. Grumel, "L'annexion de l'Illyricum oriental, de la Sicile et de la
Calabre au patriarcat de Constantinople", *RSR* 40 (1952), pp. 191–200; M.V.
Anastos, "The Transfer of Illyricum, Calabria and Sicily to the Jurisdiction of
the Patriarchate of Constantinople in 732–733", *SBN* 9 (1957), pp. 14–31.
[33] See G. Ostrogorsky, *Studien zur Geschichte des byzantinischen Bilderstreites,* pp.
2–3, 226; P.J. Alexander, *The Patriarch Nicephorus,* p. 148; P. Brown, "A Dark Age
Crisis", p. 254, n. 13; M.V. Anastos, "Ekklisia kai Politeia kata tin periodon tis
Eikonomachias", in *Eucharisterion,* Athens 1958, p. 15; S. Gero, *Byzantine Iconoclasm
during the Reign of Constantine V, with particular Attention to the Oriental Sources,*
Louvain 1977, esp. pp. 37–52, 143–51; J. Travis, *In Defense of the Faith,* Brookline,
Mass., 1984, p. 1.

selves.[34] At the same time the emperor entered the fray as an author, composing the *Inquiries* with an appended patristic florilegium.[35]

The council, which met in 754 at the palace of Hiereia, was an important milestone in the iconoclast movement.[36] Three hundred and thirty eight bishops took part with Theodosius of Ephesus presiding, the patriarchal throne of Constantinople having been vacant from the end of 753.[37] Its proceedings lasted from the 10 February to the 8 August 754. Neither the pope nor the eastern patriarchs were present, as a result of which Hiereia was mockingly called "the headless council".[38] Sissinius of Perge (called Pastillas) and Basil of Pisidia (called Trikkakabes) also stayed away.[39] We do not know if any monks were present. At the last session (8 August) in the church of the Blachernae in Constantinople the emperor presented Constantine of Sylaeum as his choice for the patriarchal throne of Constantinople.[40] He was duly acclaimed and on the 27 August the *Definition* (*Horos*) of the council was published and the excommunications announced of Germanus of Constantinople, George of Cyprus and Mansur (= John Damascene).[41]

In the formulation of its decisions the council took as its model

---

[34] Theophanes, de Boor, p. 427; a picture of these meetings is given in the *Nouthesia Gerontos*; on this, see S. Gero, *Constantine V*, pp. 25–36.

[35] John of Studius reports that the *Inquiries* were thirteen in number (*AASS*, April 1, XXVII). These have not survived except for a few fragments from two of them quoted by Nicephorus (*Antir.* I, *PG* 100, 205–238D and *Antir.* II, *PG* 100, 329A–373) in his attempt to refute them. The Greek text has been published by G. Ostrogorsky, *Studien zur Geschichte des byzantinischen Bilderstreites*, pp. 8–11; H. Hennephof, *Textus byzantini ad Iconomachiam pertinentes*, Leiden 1969, pp. 52–55. Ostrogorsky's text is reprinted by H.-J. Geischer, *Der byzantinische Bilderstreit*, Gutersloh 1968, pp. 41–3. The florilegium has been preserved by Nicephorus and published by J.B. Pitra, *Spicilegium Solemesne Sanctorum Patrum*, I, Graz 1962, pp. 371–503, from four Greek manuscripts (Par. gr. 910, 911, 1250 and Coisl. 93). Perhaps the florilegium was compiled with the help of the theologians of the council.

[36] Theophanes, de Boor, p. 427.

[37] Mansi 13, 232E; Theophanes, de Boor, p. 427; Nicephorus, de Boor, p. 65.

[38] Theophanes, de Boor, p. 427; see *Adversus Constantinum* (*PG* 95, 331CD). It appears that the Eastern patriarchs had already before 754 written "denunciatory letters" against the emperor (*Vita Stephani*, *PG* 100, 1117D–1120A).

[39] Mansi 12, 1010D; 13, 400A. According to Nicephorus (*Breviarium*, de Boor, pp. 65, 30–61, 1), Theodosius of Ephesus left the council. On their names, see S. Gero, *Constantine V*, p. 55, n. 10.

[40] Mansi 13, 209D. Theophanes, de Boor, p. 428; Nicephorus, *Breviarium*, de Boor, p. 66.

[41] The Greek text of the *Horos* is in Mansi 13 and also in H. Hennephof, *Textus Byzantini*, pp. 44–53, with some part omitted. A full English translation of the *Horos* is given in S. Gero, *Constantine V*, pp. 68–94. For a full translation of the acta of the Council see J. Mendham, *The Seventh Ecumenical Council*, London 1849, and D. Sahas, *Icon and Logos*, Toronto 1987. C. Mango, *The Art of the Byzantine Empire 312–1453*, New Jersey 1972, pp. 165–8, gives a translation

the emperor's treatise, which had set the christological problem
at the centre of the debate and maintained the impossibility of
the iconic representation of Christ. Veneration, says the *Definition*,
is only due to God. It censures the honouring of icons as a practice
leading to idolatry, as not consonant with the supremely spiritual
worship of Christianity, as diminishing and insulting the glory of
the saints through representing them in "common and dishonour-
able matter" as a result of "the mindless contrivance of the wretched
painter for lamentable, sordid gain."[42] The council condemned the
honouring of the icons as idolatry on the grounds that it was
opposed to Scripture and holy tradition and not authorised by the
first ecumenical councils.[43] It censured the iconic depiction of
Christ as leading to the heresy of Nestorianism or of Monophysitism.
Since the divinity and the humanity have been united in Christ
in one person without confusion or division, anyone who confesses
Christ as a person depicted pictorially either takes him to be a
mere man or confuses the two natures and presents the divine
nature and the divine hypostasis as circumscribed. Anyone who
confesses Christ as depicted pictorially in his humanity divides the
two natures and presents the human nature as subsisting in its own
right.[44] The only true icon of Christ given by God is the bread
of the Eucharist.[45]

The council did not follow Constantine in his theses concerning
the Theotokos, the saints and holy relics. On the contrary, it
declared with reverence: "The making of icons or their setting up
in churches or private dwellings, or their secret retention is for-
bidden. Transgressions will be liable to penalties under the imperial
laws."[46] The emperor demanded an oath from all present that there
would be no more "iconolatry".[47]

After this a persecution broke out which reached its peak in the
760s, when severe measures were taken against the recalcitrant.
Nicephorus asserts that the destruction of icons and churches and

---

of portions of the *Horos*. See also the excellent study on the *Horos* in M.V. Anastos,
"The Arguments for Iconoclasm as Presented to the Iconoclastic Council of 754",
in *Late Classical and Medieval Studies in Honor of A.M. Friend Jr* (ed. K. Weitzmann)
Princeton 1954, pp. 177–88. The excommunications are mentioned by Theo-
phanes, de Boor, p. 428 and Nicephorus, *Breviarium*, de Boor, p. 66.
    [42] Mansi 13, 221C, 229DE, 248E, 269C, 280DE, 324D.
    [43] Mansi 13, 217A, 232E, 237D, 240C, 245E, 268C, 280DE, 292D, 324CD.
    [44] Mansi 13, 252A, 256AB, 256E–257A, 257E–260B.
    [45] Mansi 13, 261D–264C.
    [46] Mansi 13, 272AB, 272D, 276D, 277CD, 328C.
    [47] *Adversus Constantinum, PG* 95, 337C; *Vita Stephani, PG* 100, 1112A; Nicephorus,
Breviarium, de Boor, p. 73; Theophanes, de Boor, p. 437.

the persecution of iconophiles, especially monks, began after the council of 754.[48] The monks, as the more zealous of the iconophiles, were Constantine's chief target. "He stigmatised and dishonoured the schema of the monks in the Hippodrome."[49] The emperor believed that only when monasticism was crushed would the war against icons be brought to a close. The monks resisted with the epistolary encouragement of the Eastern patriarchs.[50] The Martyrology was enriched with new martyrs, the earliest monastic victim being St Andrew "the Calibite".[51] The great figure of this period, however, was Stephen the Younger.[52] Under Leo III he fled to a safe place together with his family. At the age of sixteen he came to Mount Auxentius in Bithynia, and in his thirty-first year became abbot of his monastery. Under Constantine he was arrested and thrown into prison in Constantinople, where a further 342 monks were kept in harsh conditions. In November 765 Stephen was severely beaten by an enraged mob in the streets of Constantinople. Having survived this experience, he advised many monks to retire to places of refuge. Many of them "hastened to safe retreats", the Black Sea, the Crimea, Italy, Cyprus and (Muslim-ruled) Syria-Palestine.[53] As the persecutions became more intense, the governor of the Thracesion theme, Michael Lachanodromon, emerged as a real scourge. He put before the monks the choice of either renouncing the monastic habit and marrying or being blinded and exiled to Cyprus.[54] There was such pressure from the governor "that not a single monk was left within his jurisdiction". Moreover, sytematic inquiries in the army and the court brought secret icon-worshippers to light whom Constantine "handed over to various punishments and the most severe scourging".[55]

Constantine V was succeeded by his son Leo IV (775–80), whose short reign may be described as a transitional period from the harsh iconoclastic policy of his father to the restoration of icons under

---

[48] Only the *Vita Stephani* refers to anti-iconophile activity prior to 754; see S. Gero, *Constantine V*, pp. 111–14. On the removal of the icon of the Milion, see *PG* 100, 1172AB. According to S. Gero, *Constantine V*, p. 114, before 754 persecution was sporadic.

[49] See S. Gero, *Constantine V*, p. 121, n. 37.

[50] Theophanes, de Boor, p. 437.

[51] Theophanes, de Boor, p. 432ff.

[52] Theophanes, de Boor, p. 436; Nicephorus, de Boor, p. 72; *Vita Stephani*, *PG* 100, 1067–1188.

[53] *PG* 100, 1120B; 1117CD.

[54] Theophanes, de Boor, p. 446.

[55] Theophanes, de Boor, p. 437.

Irene.[56] The harsh legislation against the veneration of icons, although not repealed, was allowed to slacken. Leo thus behaved as "a friend of the Theotokos and the monks", who returned from exile, the more distinguished of them succeeding to the great episcopal sees.[57] Leo, in my opinion, abandoned his father's view that the destruction of monasticism was a necessary precondition for the victory of iconoclasm. He ceased to persecute the monks but remained a consistent iconoclast and when necessary did not hesitate to persecute and pillory any court officials who were regarded as iconophile.[58] Smitten by a high temperature, Leo died quite suddenly, having reigned for only five years.

The Seventh Ecumenical Council (787)

The premature death of Leo IV brought his son Constantine VI to the throne at the age of ten. Irene assumed the regency, exercising supreme power as her son's guardian.

After dealing with certain difficulties caused by conspiracies of court officials against her and her son in favour of the Caesar Nicephorus, brother of Leo IV, Irene, who was a convinced iconophile, began carefully to prepare for the restoration of the icons.[59] The victories of the iconoclast emperors against the Arabs and Bulgars and the diplomatic successes of the engagement of her son to Rothrude, the daughter of Charlemagne, provided the positive prerequisites for this.[60]

On the 21 August 784 the Patriarch Paul resigned on conscientious grounds and, retiring to the monastery of Florus, assumed the monastic habit.[61] Irene, desiring to give the election of the patriarch the character of a popular vote, summoned "all the people" to the Magnaura palace, where they shouted unanimously that the only worthy candidate for the patriarchal throne was the palace secretary, Tarasius. Irene agreed with "all the people" and

---

[56] See G. Ostrogorsky, *History of the Byzantine State*, p. 175; E. Martin, *A History of the Iconoclastic Controversy*, p. 86.
[57] Theophanes, de Boor, p. 449.
[58] Theophanes, de Boor, p. 453.
[59] Theophanes, de Boor, p. 454.
[60] Theophanes, de Boor, p. 455.
[61] Theophanes, de Boor, p. 457. The Patriarch Paul IV (780–4) explained "with much lamentation" to the empress when she went to the monastery of Florus to meet him that he regretted accepting election as patriarch of a Church "subject to tyranny and separated from the other catholic thrones". He repeated this to the "patricians and leading men of the Senate" and proposed the calling of an Ecumenical Council, showing clearly that he continued to be repentant. The application of direct or indirect pressure on the patriarch, however, to force him to resign cannot be ruled out.

Tarasius, after a certain amount of hesitation, accepted the election on the condition — as he said in his address to the people — that an Ecumenical Council should be convened which would settle definitively the question of icons and would establish peace and unity in the Church and the empire.[62] On Christmas day 784 Tarasius, who had been "numbered among the laity", was ordained patriarch of Constantinople in the church of Hagia Sophia.[63] Thus the way was made clear to the calling of an Ecumenical Council.

The summoning of the council was preceded by an exchange of correspondence between the Patriarch Tarasius and other patriarchs. Through these "synodical letters" the newly elected patriarch reviewed the whole situation, demonstrated the necessity of calling an Ecumenical Council and invited the patriarchs to take part. Letters were also exchanged between the imperial couple and Pope Adrian I (771–795). This correspondence was important because through it communion was established between the Church of Constantinople and the other Churches and the foundations were laid (parallel, I believe, to other behind-the-scenes operations) for the success of the work of the council.

The documents exchanged were:-

(i) The letter of Patriarch Tarasius to Pope Adrian I. This is no longer extant. We know, however, that it was sent from information supplied by Theophanes, from Adrian's reply and from the observation of the papal legates that the pope had received "letters of this kind".[64]

(ii) The letter (*Divalis sacra*) of the Emperor Constantine VI and Empress Irene to Pope Adrian I. Only the Latin translation of Anastasius the Librarian is extant. In this letter, which was probably sent in August 785, the pope was invited to attend the council either in person or through representatives.[65]

(iii) The reply of Pope Adrian I to Constantine VI and Irene, sent on 27 October 785, of which a Greek translation is also extant. According to the testimony of Anastasius the Librarian the Latin original was edited with the consent of the papal legates in the course of its translation.[66] This happened because the original

---

[62] Theophanes, de Boor, p. 458; see also Tarasius's homily in Theophanes, de Boor, pp. 459–60; Mansi 12, 986D–990A.

[63] Theophanes, de Boor, p. 460.

[64] Mansi 12, 1127A; cf. Grumel, *Régestes*, 351. On the bearers of the letter, Leo the Apocrisiarius, Theodore, bishop of Catania, and the deacon Epiphanius, see Hefele, *A History of the Councils*, vol. v, p. 349.

[65] Mansi 12, 984E–986C; Dölger, *Regesten*, 341, 343. On the problem of the chronology, see Hefele, *A History of the Councils*, vol. v, p. 348.

[66] Mansi 12, 1073.

version contained certain expressions which were displeasing to the
Patriarch Tarasius and could have caused offence. In the acta of
the council the text of this Greek translation is found parallel to
the Latin original. The letter was read out at the second session.
In it the pope expresses his joy at the restoration of orthodoxy
and the decision to call a council. He repeats his statements on
the papal primacy. The strongly iconophile line of his predecessors
is stressed and the veneration of icons is defended with biblical
texts and passages from the Fathers. He makes it known that he
will take part in the council through his legates and requires the
condemnation in their presence of the Council of Hiereia (754).
He asks for the return of the patrimony of Peter and protests at
Tarasius's use of the title "Ecumenical Patriarch" and the ascent
of a layman to the throne of Constantinople.[67]

(iv) The reply of Pope Adrian I to the Patriarch Tarasius. This
letter is undated but Hefele believes that it was sent at the same
time as the letter to the emperor and empress.[68] Anastasius tells
us that this letter, too, was edited. The original and the translation,
however, agree in the sources. Furthermore, he asserts that he
found the original in the Roman archives.[69] In this letter, which
was read at the second session of the council, the pope reproaches
Tarasius for his direct transition (*per saltum*) from the lay state to
the patriarchal throne. He defends the primacy of Rome. He
expresses his joy at the orthodoxy of Tarasius, without which he
would not have recognised his ordination and would not have
received his synodical letters. He adduces biblical and patristic
testimonies on behalf of the icons. He makes it known that he
will take part in the council through legates and seeks the
anathematisation of the Council of Hiereia in their presence.[70]

(v) The letter of the Patriarch Tarasius to the patriarchs of the
East. In this letter, which was read at the third session of the council,
Tarasius seeks the patriarchs' co-operation in the burdensome work
which he has undertaken. He goes on to make a confession of
faith and to condemn the Council of Hiereia. Finally, he requests
the despatch of representatives to the Ecumenical Council which
is about to be called.[71]

(vi) The reply of the "hierarchs" of the East, Politianus of
Alexandria (787–801), Theodore of Antioch (757–797) and Elias II of

---

[67] Mansi 12, 1055A–1072C.
[68] Hefele, A *History of the Councils*, vol. v, p. 354.
[69] Mansi 12, 1081.
[70] Mansi 12, 1078C–1083D.
[71] Mansi 12, 1119D–1127A.

Jerusalem (770–797), to the Patriarch Tarasius. In this letter, which was read out at the third session, the patriarchs express their joy at the restoration of orthodoxy in Constantinople and the reconciliation of the ecclesiastical and imperial powers for the well-being and unity of Christians. They go on to explain that for reasons of security they prevented Tarasius's emissaries from coming to meet them in order to avoid provoking Arab suspicions that the Christians were entering into negotiations with Constantinople, which would have had serious consequences for their hard-pressed communities. The views of the Eastern patriarchs, they said, would be represented by a letter compiled by certain "hierarchs". This letter would be brought by the syncelli Thomas (of Alexandria) and John (of Antioch), who would also bring the synodical letter of the dying Patriarch Theodore of Jerusalem (735–70), which the patriarchs of Alexandria and Antioch had received. They go on to censure the Council of Hiereia and to express the opinion that the unavoidable absence of the Eastern patriarchs on account of adverse circumstances should not hinder the calling of an Ecumenical Council. Besides, they had not been present at the Sixth Ecumenical Council (680–1) for the same reasons without this having called its validity into question. The Roman pope had similarly given his assent and had been present through representatives.[72]

Irene summoned the council to convene at the church of the Holy Apostles in Constantinople on the 17 August 786. According to Tarasius the council was preceded by conspiratorial movements and factional meetings of the iconoclast bishops who were already in Constantinople. "A large number" of laypeople who maintained that there was no need for a council also took part in these meetings, which came to the notice of Tarasius, who informed the conspirators that Constantinople had a bishop and that the holding of rival meetings would be punished according to ecclesiastical law by deposition.[73] At the church of the Holy Apostles Irene followed the proceedings with her son Constantine from the place reserved for catechumens. After the reading of a number of conciliar documents it was stated that an Ecumenical Council could not be called "without the agreement of the rest of the most holy patriarchs". This was a direct blow at the validity of the Council of Hiereia. At this juncture a large body of imperial guards loyal to the memory of Constantine V burst in, either "at the instigation

---

[72] Mansi 12, 1127E–1135B (letter of Eastern patriarchs); 1135C–1146C (letter of Theodore of Jerusalem).
[73] Grumel, *Régestes*, 354.

of one of the heretical bishops of the council" according to the
acta, or "at the instigation of their own officers, who clung to the
teaching of their wicked tutor (viz. Constantine V)" according to
Theophanes, and caused complete pandemonium, threatening to
kill the patriarch and the iconophile bishops and monks.[74] The
attempt of the emperor and empress to restore calm failed and
the council was dissolved. A number of iconoclast bishops "opposed
to the truth" mingled with the crowd, shouting, "we have won"
and acclaiming Hiereia as the Seventh Ecumenical Council. The
first attempt at convening an Ecumenical Council thus ended in
disorder, choked by violence and the clash of wild passions.[75]

Irene was not dismayed. After replacing the iconoclast units of
the imperial guard with iconophile troops from Thrace, she convened the council anew at Nicaea in Bithynia, where the First
Ecumenical Council (325) had been held. The proceedings took
place in the cathedral of Hagia Sophia from the 24 September to
the 13 October 787. Seven sessions were held at Nicaea and
the final eighth session at the Magnaura palace in Constantinople.
The emperor and empress were not present in person. They were
represented by two high dignitaries, the patricius and ex-consul
Petronius and the imperial ostiarius (chamberlain) and logothete
(head of the military chancery) John. Pope Adrian I was represented by Peter, Archpriest of the holy church of the Apostle
Peter in Rome, and Peter, priest and abbot of the monastery of
St Sabbas. The two oriental priest-monks, John and Thomas,
represented the apostolic sees of the East but, as we have seen,
were not sent personally by the patriarchs. Consequently, their
presence at the council was not strictly in order. There is no doubt,
however, that the Churches of the East were in favour of the icons
and consequently their viewpoint was correctly represented. The
number of bishops or their representatives at the council fluctuated
between 330 and 367.[76] Moreover, there was a significant number

---

[74] On the role of the army in iconoclasm, see W. Kaegi, "The Byzantine Armies
and Iconoclasm", *Byzantinoslavica* 27 (1966), pp. 48–70, and the same author's
"The Byzantine Thematic Armies in the First Iconoclastic Period (728–787)",
in his *Byzantine Military Unrest*, Amsterdam 1981, pp. 209–243.

[75] On these events, see Theophanes, de Boor, pp. 461–2; Mansi 12, 990–1,
990–1002; P. Speck, *Kaiser Konstantin VI*, vol. i, Munich 1978, pp. 153–6.

[76] Photius (*De Synodis*, quoted by Mansi 13, 491D) computes the number of
bishops or representatives at the Council to be 367. The number of monks given
by Nicodemus of the Holy Mountain (*Pedalion*, p. 314) is 136. On the number
of participants in the council, see J. Darrouzès, "Listes episcopales du concile
de Nicée (787)", *REB* 33 (1975), pp. 5–76; J.A. Munitiz, "Synoptic Greek Accounts
of the Seventh Council", *REB* 32 (1974), pp. 147–86.

of heads of monasteries (archimandrites and hegumeni) as well as "a crowd of monks". Primacy of honour was accorded to the papal legates; they were the first to sign the acta and their names were placed at the head of the list of those present. In practical terms, however, the council was presided over by the Patriarch Tarasius.

At the first session (24 September) Tarasius, at the instigation of the Sicilian bishops, proclaimed the opening of the proceedings of the council in a short address in which he referred to the unsuccessful attempt to convene a council in the previous year, underlined the imperial concern for the unity and peace of the Church — though not at the cost of any innovation — and called on the vociferous iconoclast participants of the previous year to come forward and express their opinions freely.[77] An official imperial letter (*sacra*) was then read which stressed the deep concern of the emperor and empress for the peace and unity of the Church and guaranteed freedom of expression in the council. After this three former iconoclast bishops, Basil of Ancyra, Theodore of Myra and Theodosius of Armorium, came forward, sought pardon from the assembly and read an orthodox confession of faith in favour of the icons. They were forgiven and deemed acceptable to the council by a unanimous vote. Seven other bishops, Hypatius of Nicaea, Leo of Rhodes, Gregory of Pessinus, Leo of Iconium, George of Pisidia, Nicolas of Hierapolis and Leo of Carpathus, accused of having been the instigators of the disturbances of 786, attributed their error to ignorance and to bad teachers of bad doctrine.[78] Their sincerity was doubted and they were examined rigorously. Finally, thanks to the excellent administration of Tarasius, extreme solutions were avoided and the suspect bishops were deemed acceptable. They took their places in the council, however, only at the third session.

In the second session (26 September) the case of the formerly hard-line iconoclast, Gregory of Neocaesarea, was examined.[79] Criticism of him was severe. He was finally pronounced acceptable and was asked to return at the next session with the relevant libellus. The letters of Pope Adrian I to the Emperor Constantine VI and the Empress Irene and to the Patriarch Tarasius (which have already been mentioned) were also read. Tarasius noted that Pope Adrian had confirmed the ancient traditions of the Catholic Church,

---

[77] Mansi 12, 991E–1051A.
[78] "Ignorance": Mansi 12, 1018B; "bad doctrine": Mansi 12, 1019A.
[79] Mansi 12, 1051A–1111E.

which the East also observed, including the veneration of icons, true worship (*latreia*) belonging to God alone.[80]

At the third session (28 September) Gregory of Neocaesarea and the seven bishops who had recanted before him were pronounced acceptable.[81] Then the synodical letters of Patriarch Tarasius to the patriarchs of the East were read, together with the reply of the "hierarchs" of the East and the synodical letter of Patriarch Theodore of Jerusalem, who by now had died. The papal legates observed that the oriental patriarchs' understanding of icons was in harmony with the teaching of Pope Adrian I and the Patriarch Tarasius. By the close of the third session it had become clear that Constantinople had finally established relations with the other Churches. This work, which had been begun behind the scenes, was crowned by the work of the council.

The fourth session (1 October) was dedicated to proving the legitimacy of the worship of icons on the basis of Holy Scripture and the Fathers.[82] Six biblical texts were presented for consideration and about thirty patristic texts, to which should be added a number of reports of wonder-working icons. Finally, the correspondence between the Patriarch Germanus and the iconoclast bishops of Asia Minor, which we have already discussed, was read out. The value of this evidence is uneven. Some testimonies — many of those referring to wonder-working icons — bear witness to an engaging naivety.

The council then went on to pronounce anathemas on those who were against the icons and to confess the orthodox faith, which was signed by the participants headed by the papal legates, the Patriarch Tarasius and the legates of the thrones of the East.[83] Twenty-eight priests or monks were present as representatives of bishops. One hundred and thirteen abbots and ten monks represented the monastic order, with Sabbas, abbot of the monastery of Studius, at their head.[84]

At the fifth session (4 October) other testimonies on behalf of the icons were read.[85] Some members of the council brought books containing arguments in favour of icons and asked that they should be read, but the Patriarch Tarasius observed that a sufficient number had already been read. Then it was announced that books

---

[80] Mansi 12, 1086B.
[81] Mansi 12, 1114A–1154E.
[82] Mansi 13, 1A–156E.
[83] Mansi 13, 129A–133A.
[84] Mansi 13, 133B–156E.
[85] Mansi 13, 157A–201E.

on the icons by iconoclasts should be systematically destroyed. The monk John, representative of the Eastern patriarchates, finally read a text relating to the real origin of the attack on the images.[86] John attributed the beginning of iconoclasm to the edict of the Caliph Yazid II against the icons, and to Constantine, the iconoclast bishop of Nacoleia and chief adviser to the Emperor Leo III.

The sixth session (6 October, or, according to the translation of Anastasius, 5 October) was dedicated to the reading of the *Definition* (*Horos*) of the Council of Hiereia (754) and its refutation.[87] The formerly prominent iconoclast bishop, Gregory of Neocaesarea, was called upon to read the *Definition*, not in order to humiliate him personally but because his reading of it would guarantee its authenticity.[88] The refutation, read by the deacons John and Epiphanius of Constantinople, is an anonymous work. It is attributed by some to the Patriarch Tarasius and by others to the deacon Epiphanius of Catania, the representative of Bishop Thomas of Sardinia.[89]

The seventh session (13 October), at which the *Definition* of the council was read by Bishop Theodore of Taurianum, was of special importance.[90] The author of the *Definition* is unknown.[91] It is not impossible, however, that it was the product of a joint enterprise. The council proclaimed that it remained faithful to tradition, following the six Ecumenical Councils and neither adding anything nor taking anything away. The creed of Nicaea-Constantinople was recited. Arius, Macedonius and their followers were excommunicated. The council confessed that Mary was truly the God-bearer, as the Third Ecumenical Council of Ephesus (431) had declared. It proclaimed with the Council of Chalcedon (451) its belief in two natures in Christ. It anathematised with the Fifth Ecumenical

---

[86] Mansi 13, 197A–200B.

[87] Mansi 13, 204A–364E.

[88] For the content of the *Horos*, see above, pp. 9–10.

[89] Tarasius is favoured by H.-G. Beck, *Kirche und theologische Literatur im byzantinischen Reich*, Munich 1959, p. 489 and G. Ostrogorsky, *History of the Byzantine State*, p. 179. Tarasius seems to have had a good theological and philosophical education (Ostrogorsky, op. cit., p. 177). C. Mango, *The Empire of New Rome*, London 1980, p. 137, regards Tarasius (d. 806), the later Patriarch Nicephorus (758–828) and Theodore of Studius (759–826) as examples of educated men of their age who had connections with the civil service and "without being profound scholars, possessed nevertheless a conventional rhetorical training and some acquaintance with philosophy". For the attribution to Epiphanius, see D. Sahas, *Icon and Logos*, p. 40, n. 188 and p. 41, n. 194.

[90] Mansi 13, 354E–413A.

[91] Hefele, *History of the Councils*, vol. v, p. 374, accepts the authorship of Tarasius.

Council (533) the teaching of Origen, Evagrius and Didymus (it did not mention the Three Chapters). It condemned with the Sixth Ecumenical Council (680–1) Sergius, Honorius, etc., proclaiming two wills in Christ. It accepted the written and unwritten traditions, amongst them the traditions relating to the images. It concluded that the cross and representations of Christ and the saints may be depicted on the walls of churches in order to stimulate the remembrance of the prototypes, and that these may be venerated with lights, incense and kissing, but not with the true worship (*latreia*) that belongs to God alone.

The council then anathematised the Council of Hiereia (754), those who had taken part in it and those who accepted its teaching. It anathematised the three leading iconoclasts, Theodosius, Sissinius (or Pastillas) and Basil and the three iconoclast patriarchs, Anastasius (730–53), Constantine II (754–66) and Nicetas (766–80). It condemned Antonius and John "as Manes, Apollinaris and Eutyches", Theodore of Syracuse, John of Nicomedia and Constantine of Nacoleia.

A conciliar letter was sent to the Emperor Constantine and the Empress Irene concerning the decisions of the council, and also to the priests and clerics of the principal churches of Constantinople.[92]

The eighth and final session (23 October) was held in the Magnaura palace in the presence of the emperor and empress.[93] Cordial addresses were exchanged between Tarasius and Irene (which are no longer extant). The *Definition* of the council was read and signed by the emperor and the empress. The anathemas and part of the patristic arguments from the fourth session were read in the presence of the people and the army. Twenty-two canons were also promulgated,[94] four of which (canons 7, 9, 13 and 16) were of direct relevance to the problem of the icons. The others dealt with the subjects of episcopal dignity, local synods, the reception of converts from Judaism and problems concerning priests, monasteries and laymen. The last session came to a close with an address by Epiphanius, the deacon from Catania.[95] The participants acclaimed Irene and Constantine VI and having received rich gifts from them left for home.

The council of 787 was pronounced Ecumenical and was accepted as such in spite of the reservations of Rome and of the

---

[92] Mansi 13, 400C–413A.
[93] Mansi 13, 413Bff.
[94] Mansi 13, 417Bff.
[95] Mansi 13, 442A–458B.

patriarchates of Alexandria, Antioch and Jerusalem on accour
the way in which the latter were represented.[96] In an encyclical
letter (866) and at a General Council in Constantinople (867)
Photius insisted that the council of 787 belonged to those which
were strictly ecumenical.[97] This was also the judgment of the important Constantinopolitan council of 879–80.[98]

The Western Reaction

In the West, partly as a result of a bad translation of the acta,
Frankish theology exercised a negative influence on the acceptance
of the council through the *Libri Carolini*.[99] The Council of Frankfurt
(794) rejected the decisions of the council on the holy icons and
maintained that the latter were simply a decoration of church
buildings for didactic purposes. It accepted, however, the honouring of saints and relics by veneration.[100] The position of the Council
of Paris (823) was similar, confirming the theological mistrust which
henceforth would dominate East-West relations. By 871 — possibly
much earlier — it became known in New Rome that the Franks
took their military successes and the Roman defeats to be God-
given proof that they themselves were orthodox and the Romans
heretics and therefore not Romans but Greeks. Only the papal
states, according to the Franks, constituted the remnant of the Res
Publica Romana and so only the citizens of this tiny empire were
to be called Romans. They were the only remaining orthodox
Romans because God had given them to the Franks to be guided
by them. In his letter of 871 to the Emperor Basil I (867–86) the
Emperor Louis II (855–75) claimed: "We have received the government of the Roman Empire for our orthodoxy. The Greeks have
ceased to be emperors of the Romans for their cacodoxy." This
is why "we received from heaven this people and city (Rome) to
guide and the mother of all the churches of God to defend and
exalt".[101] The military successes of the Franks gave them the
confidence to reject both the authority of the emperor and the
theology of the council of 787.

---

[96] See what was said by Photius in the fifth session of the Council of 879
(Mansi 17, 493C).
[97] See D. Sahas, *Icon and Logos*, p. 41.
[98] On this council, see J. Karmiris, *Ta Dogmatika kai Symvolika Mnimeia*, vol. i,
p. 262.
[99] See J. Herrin, *The Formation of Christendom*, Oxford 1987, pp. 426–8.
[100] See J. Herrin, op. cit., pp. 434–9.
[101] Quoted by J. Romanides, *Franks, Romans, Feudalism and Doctrine. An Interplay
between Theology and Society*, Brookline 1981, p. 18.

CHAPTER TWO

ICON AND TRADITION

The Meaning of Tradition

In the controversy between iconoclast and iconophile a central place was occupied by different interpretations of tradition. "Tradition" for the Church of the patristic age (and indeed later) is a much stronger term than "custom", though of course it may include godly and edifying customs. The concept had not been a matter of contention. In the debate with the iconoclasts what had been done in the past was crucial to argument about the propriety of what was happening or ought to be happening in the present. To the iconophiles their opponents were guilty of "innovation", a term virtually synonymous with heresy for the reason that it implied an individual's (or group's) break with the venerable and sacred community tradition hallowed by devotion in prayer and sacrament. To an iconophile the mind of the iconoclast was not merely mistaken; it was a manifestation of irreverence, even of blasphemy, of wilfully trampling upon the holiness of God's sanctuary in his Church. The iconoclasts were felt by their opponents to have lost respect and trustful affection both for the saints and for their representation in pictures. The critical hostility of the iconoclasts towards generally accepted ways of worship was therefore at best gross impertinence and offensiveness to the praying Church, and at worst brawling in holy places to the hurt of the people of God.

To the iconoclasts, on the other side, the honouring of icons, even if the practice had extended gradually and was not obviously a sudden and aggressive importation into a body whose immunological system was certain to reject it, was nevertheless in principle and in practice a break with the original past, which was one of aniconic purity. It therefore became important to the iconoclasts to prove from earlier texts that the best and most authoritative figures and great lions of orthodoxy had never conceded the legitimacy of such devotions to icons of the Lord, the Mother of God (Theotokos) and the saints. They had to demonstrate that Christian writers who had allowed a role for icons had been persons of precarious and questionable orthodoxy, lacking in authority as a guide and rule for the present.

A similar framework of argumentation was imposed on the

iconophiles. They too had to show that the main texts of the past to which the iconoclasts liked to appeal came from authors who on other grounds were associated with heretical deviation, whether as Arians or Monophysites or Manichaeans or suchlike.

This point concerning the tradition may be illustrated from the retrospective account written by the patriarch Photius in the ninth century. According to Photius, the Seventh Ecumenical Council was summoned to condemn the iconoclasts, who, "accusing us of introducing daring innovations into apostolic teaching", caused confusion in the Church. The Fathers of this council "set up the pillars of orthodoxy" and through a close scrutiny of "the Isaurian and godless belief" restored to the Church "the ancient dignity of her comliness".[1]

From the very beginning of the council it was agreed by all that the authentic criterion of genuine Christianity was fidelity to the words, commandments, deeds and examples of Christ, the prophets, the apostles and their successors, the Fathers. This criterion related primarily to doctrinal matters but was also equally important in more practical questions. It did not relate simply to the antiquity of what had been handed down. It was above all a product of confidence in the sacred persons who had handed it down, rather than in the period in which the tradition had been formulated. The iconoclasts exploited the authenticity of the tradition with the greatest possible acumen, so as to prove that they were in harmony with the Christian past as a whole. In doing so they attached a special significance to the particular aspect of the tradition which, as they thought, vindicated them, that is to say, its antiquity and especially its witness to truth, rather than to the sacred persons who make tradition effective through the centuries. Thus they presented certain saints as hostile to icons by distorting their words and interpreting them in an arbitrary way.

The aim of the iconoclasts was to have the matter decided on the basis of historical rather than theological evidence. They put their whole emphasis on the "when" and pointedly avoided the "why". "Tell me, whoever taught us to venerate and revere things made by human hands?"[2] This question is attributed to the Emperor Leo III at the beginning of the controversy. It is, of course, insidious. It deliberately identifies icons with idols, and appeals to tradition in order to reject them both.

---

[1] C. Mango (Ed.) *The Homilies of Photius Patriarch of Constantinople*, Dumbarton Oakes Studies 3, Homily 17, pp. 286–96.

[2] Mansi 12, 959E. Cf. ibid. 1146B, Nicephorus *Antir.* 3. PG 100, 376C. Cf. also the reply to the question of Leo III in PG 100 380B.

The Evidence of the Bible and the Fathers

The invocation of tradition begins naturally with the Bible, the *locus classicus* being the second commandment of the Book of Exodus, "You shall not make yourself an idol or any likeness" (Exod. 20:4), which the iconoclasts applied to the production of icons: "If you set up a memorial of Christ or of his saints through the painting of icons, you will slip into idolatry."[3] Historical events in the Bible which presented a parallel to their own activities were also pressed into service. For example, King Hezekiah's removal from the Temple of the bronze serpent which had stood there for eight hundred years was likened to Leo III's cleansing of Christian churches from "idols", that is to say, from icons.[4]

From the New Testament they draw arguments which are more theological, quoting Johannine texts such as: "No man has ever seen God" (Jn 1:18); "God is spirit and those who worship must worship in spirit and in truth" (Jn 4:24); "His voice you have heard, his form you have never seen" (Jn 5:37); and "Blessed are those who have not seen and yet have believed" (Jn 20:29);[5] and, even more tellingly, Pauline passages such as: "and they exchanged the glory of the immortal God for images resembling mortal man; and they worshipped and served the creature rather than the Creator" (Rom. 1:23,25); "even though we have known Christ after the flesh, yet now henceforth we know him no more" (2 Cor. 5:16); "we walk by faith, not by sight" (2 Cor. 5:7); and "therefore faith comes by hearing, and hearing by the work of God" (Rom. 10:17).[6]

The iconoclasts also adduce patristic evidence, some of which is spurious. The Council of Hiereia quotes from the text of the "Acts of John" presented in the Manichaean canon of the apocryphal Acts called "The Journeys of the Apostles". That this text was a work of Manichaean origin was correctly claimed by the Seventh Ecumenical Council.[7] In this text St John the Evangelist is presented as censuring the painting of his icon by his disciple Lycomedes — "You have done wrong in making this" — whom he rebukes as one "still living in a pagan fashion".[8] Also adduced as evidence is a fragment from a letter of St Neilus to Olympiodorus, adapted

---

[3] Mansi 13, 284CD.
[4] 2 Kgs 18:4; Mansi 12, 966D.
[5] Mansi 13, 285E.
[6] Mansi 13, 285BC.
[7] Mansi 13, 173C.
[8] Mansi 13, 168E–169B. Cf. R.A. Lipsius - M. Bonnet, *Acta Apostolica Apocrypha*, Leipzig 1891–1903, vol. 2, p. 165,27.

in such a way as to fit in with iconoclastic conceptions.[9] As evidence against the use of icons they refer to passages from Athanasius of Alexandria,[10] Gregory of Nazianzus,[11] Basil of Caesarea,[12] John Chrysostom,[13] Theodotus of Ancyra[14] and Amphilochius of Iconium.[15] Most of these witnesses seem colourless and irrelevant — detached phrases taken out of their original context.[16]

It appears, however, that there are two references "which are of importance and can substantiate a theological thesis".[17] The first is a fragment from a letter of Eusebius of Caesarea to the Augusta Constantia, sister of Constantine the Great, who had asked him for an icon of Christ.[18] The second is a fragment from the *Testament* of Epiphanius of Cyprus.[19]

In the first fragment Eusebius wonders with surprise which icon she means, the true and immutable icon of Christ as Logos or the icon which he assumed when he became incarnate for our sake, that is to say, the form of the Servant. The former, the "form of God", is clearly inaccessible to man, since "only the Father who begot him" knows the Son. The form of the Servant, on the other hand, which Christ assumed through his incarnation, we know after his resurrection "to have been mingled with the glory of his divinity, and that the mortal has been swallowed up by life". If the Apostles were not able to see the glory of the Lord at his transfiguration, "since what they had seen was unbearable", what should be said about him now that, "having put off mortality and having washed away corruption" through his victory over death and his ascension, he has transformed the form of the Servant into the

---

[9] Mansi 13, 36AD.
[10] Mansi 13, 300E. Cf. Athanasius, *On the Incarnation of the Logos*, PG 25, 29A.
[11] Mansi 13, 297AD. Cf. Gregory of Nazianzus, *Poems*, PG 37, 913.
[12] Mansi 13, 300AB.
[13] Mansi 13, 300A.
[14] Mansi 13, 310E–312A.
[15] Mansi 13, 301D.
[16] G. Florovsky, "Origen, Eusebius and the Iconoclastic Controversy", p. 77.
[17] Ibid.
[18] Mansi 13, 313AD. See the full text in PG 20, 1545–1549. It is significant that the Fathers of the Seventh Ecumenical Council did not question the authenticity of this text but dismissed its doctrine on the grounds that it was propounded by an author of doubtful orthodoxy. Such a dismissal was sufficient to deter the later iconoclasts from appealing again to Eusebius, as he was not mentioned at their subsequent council of St Sophia in 815 AD. See also H.J. Geischer, *Der byzantinische Bilderstreit*, Gutersloh 1968, pp. 15–17; H. Hennephof, *Textus byzantini ad iconomachiam pertinentes*, Leiden 1969, pp. 42–44.
[19] Mansi 292DE. Cf. K. Holl, *Die Schriften des Epiphanius gegen die Bilderverehrung in Gesammelte Aufsatze zur Kirchengeschichte*, 11, 2, Tübingen 1928, p. 363; G. Ostrogorsky, *Studien zur Geschichte des byzantinischen Bilderstreites*, Breslau 1929, p. 67; H. Hennephof, *Textus byzantini*, p. 50.

glory of our Lord and God? Now he reposes in the bosom of the ineffable Father". This icon of the glory of Christ cannot be painted "in lifeless colours and lines". In a manner, then, at variance with orthodox christology Eusebius argues that no possibility exists of representing an already glorified Christ iconically, since Christ "transformed the 'form of the Servant' (Phil. 2:7) into the glory of him who is Master and God"; that is to say, he ceased to be man any longer and was only God. It is precisely this glorious and divine status of Christ that cannot be represented in icons.[20]

But the Church Father cited above all by the iconoclasts is Epiphanius, "renowned among the standard-bearers", who in his *Testament* makes the following statement:

"And in this matter, my beloved children, keep it in mind not to set up icons in churches, or in the cemeteries of the saints, but always have God in your hearts through remembrance. Do not even have icons in private houses. For it is not permissible for the Christian to let his eyes wander or indulge in reveries."[21]

The iconoclasts regard all the above biblical and patristic passages as "clear witnesses inspiring us and strengthening our pious aim".[22]

"Having examined these witnesses with much diligence and thought, and having understood them with the help of the all-holy Spirit, we too find on the vital doctrine of our salvation, namely, on the economy

---

[20] Cf. G. Florovsky, "Origen, Eusebius and the Iconoclastic Controversy".

[21] Mansi 13, 292DE. The iconoclastic synod of Hiereia (754) cited only this fragment from Epiphanius but added that the same Father "issued many other statements which stand in opposition to the making of icons and which can be found by those who lovingly seek to learn". Indeed the subsequent iconoclastic synod of St Sophia (815) cited several such statements from an oration "Against those who produce icons in an idolatrous fashion and in imitation of Christ, the Theotokos, martyrs and angels and prophets" and from two Epistles, one "To Theodosius, the king" and another "To John, Bishop of Aelia" (see H. Hennephof, *Textus byzantini*, pp. 44–51). The Seventh Ecumenical Council clearly stated that these publications are not from this Father but from certain Manichaeans (Mansi 13, 293B, 296CE). This view of the Council has been a matter of controversy in modern scholarship and still remains unresolved. It is interesting to note, however, some iconophile works supporting the Council's attitude, such as the *Nouthesia gerontos*, which belongs to the first period of the controversy (ed. by B. Melioransky, St Petersburg 1901) as well as Patriarch Nicephorus's twelve arguments in support of the inauthenticity of these fragments in J.B. Pitra, *Spicilegium Solesmense* IV, Paris 1858, p. 292f. See also L. Ouspensky, *Théologie de l'icône*, Paris 1980, p. 113, n. 34.

[22] Mansi 13, 280D. See also 328C, where "he who dares to make an icon or venerate it" is described as "an enemy of the doctrines of the Fathers and an opponent of the commandments of God". Cf. Theodore of Studius, *Antir.* 2, PG 99, 381B.

of Christ, that the unlawful art of painters is blasphemous and con-
travenes the six holy and ecumenical councils called by God."[23]

And they concluded with the conviction that the "icons falsely so
called" "have no reality in the tradition handed down from Christ
or the Apostles or the Fathers".[24] Moreover, their attempt to refute
the Jewish tradition also becomes intelligible, since it offers support to the iconophiles:

> "Our catholic Christian Church, lying as it does in between Judaism
> and Hellenism, participates in the customary rites of neither, but treads
> a new path of religion and initiation into mysteries handed down by
> God, on the one hand rejecting the bloody sacrifices and holocausts
> of Judaism, and on the other loathing not only the sacrifices but also
> all the idolmaking and idol worship of Hellenism, the originator and
> inventor of this loathsome art."[25]

The diplomatic manner in which the above passage is couched
sheds light on the Achilles' heel of the iconoclasts. Obliged by
their opponents to range themselves against the Jewish tradition,
they censure it on the one hand on points which are irrelevant
to the question at issue and regard Hellenism on the other as the
chief cause of every iconographical tradition. In this way, without
of course intending to do so, they trace the Jewish iconographical
tradition back to the Hellenic! But the attribution of the representational arts exclusively to the Greeks is clearly one-sided,
since it is now well known that even the Jews, let alone other
ancient civilisations, developed representational arts. More impor-
tantly, however, it deliberately ignores a genuine and very ancient
Greek anti-representational tradition, which begins with Heracleitus[26]
and may be traced through Plato[27] and Plotinus[28] to Origen.[29] Accordingly, the anti-Hellenism of the iconoclasts does not seem to

---

[23] Mansi 13, 240C. Cf. 12, 979D: "Why has nothing been said in the six
councils about the icons?" Theodore of Studius, *Refutation of the new heretics John,
Ignatius, Sergius and Stephen*, PG 99, 465AB. The iconoclasts regarded the Council
of Hiereia (754) as the "holy and ecumenical seventh council", Mansi 13, 349E.
[24] Mansi 13, 268C; 12, 1011A.
[25] Mansi 13, 273C. It is now well known to be an illusion to suppose that
no Jewish synagogues had images in the early centuries. Splendid evidence on
this is provided by C.H. Kraeling, *The Excavations of Dura-Europos: The Synagogue*,
Yale 1956; E.R. Goodenough, *Jewish Symbols in the Graeco-Roman period*, vol. ix,
1964.
[26] Heracleitus, Fragm. 5 in H. Diels — W. Kranz, *Die Fragmente der Vorsokratiker*,
Weidmann 1974, I, pp. 151–2.
[27] Plato, *Sophist*, 240b 11, d1, 241e 3, 264c 11, d4.
[28] Plotinus, *Enneads* 1, 8, 3, 3–9.
[29] Origen, *Against Celsus* VII, 64, 65, 66; VIII, 17, 18, 20.

be sincere, and there is clearly a consciousness on their part of this insincerity, since at least the theses of Origen were certainly known to them. Could it not be that they tried to conceal these very theses so that they should not be condemned as Origenists?

In any event, the fidelity of the iconoclasts to the orthodox dogma of the Theotokos remains surprising:

> "If one does not confess the ever-virgin Mary to be Theotokos in a proper and true sense and to be superior to all visible and invisible creation and does not beseech her intercession with sincere faith as of one who has free access to our God whom she bore, let him be anathema."[30]

They also express themselves in a similar way with regard to the saints:

> "If one does not confess that all the saints who have pleased God from the beginning of the age until now, before the law and under the law and in the time of grace, are honourable in his sight in both soul and body, and does not petition them for their prayers, believing that they have freedom of access to intercede on behalf of the world according to the tradition of the Church, let him be anathema."[31]

The Fathers of the Church, moreover, are "inspired by God".[32] And the iconoclasts conclude their confession of faith with the following:

> "This is the faith of the Apostles; this is the faith of the Fathers; this is the faith of the orthodox; this is how all who adored God worshipped him."[33]

From these passages as well as from their concession "to the ancient habit of making icons amongst the Christians"[34] the significance

---

[30] Mansi 13, 345AB. Cf. also 272BD. One might therefore question the historical accuracy of the information of Theophanes (*Chronographia* 1, ed. C. de Boor, Leipzig 1883, pp. 415 and 435), which shows the Emperor Constantine V blaspheming the Theotokos as Christotokos and as one who gives birth to a mere man. It is not impossible that the emperor held these personal convictions. But it does not seem that these constituted the official theses of the iconoclasts. Finally, it is worth noting that the term "theotokos" was introduced into the Church by Origen. See Socrates, *Eccl. Hist.* 7, 32, 17, PG 67, 812B, and the entry "Mary" in the *Oxford Dict. of the Christ. Church*, Oxford 1978, p. 882. See also S. Gero, *Constantine V*, pp. 143–51 and p. 167.
[31] Mansi 13, 348DE.
[32] Mansi 13, 345D.
[33] Mansi 13, 353A.
[34] Mansi 13, 1160.

which they attached to tradition for the justification of their views becomes evident.

According to the iconoclasts the acceptance or not of icons constitutes the criterion by which tradition is judged. The true tradition, as biblical and patristic witnesses reveal, opposes the use of icons, which must then be regarded as the invention of men possessed by demons. By accepting the use of icons the Church has fallen into idolatry. The tradition, then, which accepts the use of icons in the Church is false and consequently cannot possibly find acceptance in the Church.

But the historical data of the Christian tradition, or at least the theological interpretation of these data, are more favourable to the iconophiles, who are in total agreement with their opponents only on this one point, namely, that the Christian tradition, viewed with orthodox theological criteria, has the power to provide a decisive judgment and a correct conclusion on the question of icons. They do not recognise in the iconoclasts, however, the right or even the power to make correct use of any element of tradition, since they had denied the evidence of tradition on the point at issue:

> "The catholic Church...does not need to unite to herself anything that derives from those who think differently from her divinely inspired tradition; for when the Lord was preached to by the demons, he drove them out (cf. Mk 5:6–13). And when they bore witness that Paul the divine Apostle and his companions were men of the Most High God and proclaimed the way of salvation, Paul chased them out (cf. Acts 16:16–18). Similarly in this case, even though they proclaim something that is true, they are nevertheless driven out of the holy catholic Church of God."[35]

The iconophiles themselves are totally convinced of the infallibility of the Christian tradition and have not the slightest doubt that "the ancient tradition of the catholic Church is most excellent" and that

> "we ourselves, having examined the matter from the aspects of biblical evidence, scholarly investigation, logical argumentation and apodeictic proof, and having been instructed by the teachings of the Fathers, likewise have confessed and do confess and will confess and stipulate and insist and confirm"[36] that "the making of icons is not the invention of painters but an approved institution and tradition of the catholic

---

[35] Mansi 13, 345BC. For the same argument from the iconoclast side, see ibid., 277E.

[36] Mansi 12, 1086B. Cf. 13, 21B: "the tradition of the holy icons is legitimate".

Church. And that which excells in antiquity is worthy of respect, according to the divine Basil.[37] And the very antiquity of the practice and teaching of our spirit-bearing Fathers bear witness, for they were glad to see icons in the sacred churches. And they built sacred churches and decorated them with paintings . . . . Therefore the conception and tradition of iconography belongs to them and not to the painter. To the painter belongs the workmanship alone; the commissioning of the paintings clearly belongs to the holy Fathers who built the churches."[38]

Consequently, the iconoclasts struggle against the Church and against truth. They too, then, should have spoken with "the common and undissenting voice and should have supported the ancient tradition", just as all the faithful

"have kept the tradition of the Apostles and Fathers and have confessed it and have not introduced any innovation or diminution into the custom that has prevailed piously amongst us. For what has been handed down in the catholic Church is susceptible neither to addition nor to subtraction, seeing that the greatest punishment is prescribed for anyone who adds or subtracts; for cursed, says Scripture, is he who moves his fathers' boundary marks (Cf. Deut. 27:16–17).[39]

It is precisely for this reason that the defenders of the icons declare that they are guarding "without innovation" all the ecclesiastical traditions, both written and unwritten, "one of which is also the production of pictorial representations", as "the pious custom of the ancients". In this way, "the teaching of our holy Fathers, or tradition of the catholic Church, is strengthened".[40] Here it is clearly

---

[37] *On the Holy Spirit*, 71 (PG 32, 201A).

[38] Mansi 13, 252BC. Cf. 328D. The sharp distinction between art and iconography on which the iconophiles insist clearly constitutes a reply to the charge of their opponents that through the icons they are adopting and introducing into the Church "an alien invention of demonbearing men" (13, 273D), namely, representational art. The vigorous opposition of the iconophiles to this accusation is proof of the fact that they distinguish sharply between the two and consequently regard iconography not as an art but as "a concept, a lawful institution and a tradition" of the Catholic Church which does not aim at the aesthetic improvement or delight of the faithful but has in view a purely spiritual ascent. This sharp distinction between iconography and worldly representational art has a special significance for the correct understanding of the arguments.

[39] Mansi 13, 325E–328A. Cf. also Mansi 13, 128D and 376C: "We neither subtract anything nor add anything but preserve all the integral traditions of the catholic Church." See also 348B: "The painting of the holy icons has been handed down in the catholic Church from the earliest times and is an established practice in the sacred churches. The holy Fathers and the whole company of Christians have both received this practice and handed it on." Also 348E: "For this tradition is truly ancient in the catholic Church and most probably came to be known by us in order to preserve the memory of the prototypes."

[40] Mansi 13, 377BE; cf. 196C.

apparent that for the iconophiles the boundaries of tradition are
the boundaries set by the Apostles and the Fathers. That is to say,
they identify the tradition of the Church with the teaching of the
Fathers.[41] This tradition, however, begins with the Old Testament.
It is there that the earliest biblical foundations for the making and
venerating of icons are to be sought and they prove that the first
images "made by human hands" for the honour of God had already
been produced in such an ancient period:

> "For Jacob raised a stele to God, as a result of which he blessed him
> and promised him gifts beyond those he had covenanted."[42]

The chief argument which the Old Testament contributes to the
iconophile case comes from the narration in Exodus on the sanctuary of the Tent of Witness:

> "And you shall make two cherubim of gold, of hammered work, and
> you shall set them on either side of the seat of mercy between the
> two cherubim that are on the ark."[43]
> "And he heard the voice of the Lord speaking to him from above the
> mercy seat that is upon the ark of the testimony, from between the
> two cherubim."[44]
> "And he brought me to the Temple . . . and on all the walls round
> about in the inner room and in the outer were carved cherubim and
> palms, a palm tree between cherub and cherub. Every cherub had two
> faces, the face of a man towards the palm tree on the one side, and
> the face of a lion toward the palm tree on the other side. The whole
> of the Temple was carved round about; from the floor to the ceiling
> the cherubim and the palm trees were carved on the wall."[45]

Consequently, "objects made by human hands do exist for the
service and glory of God".[46] From the midst of the people of Israel
God chose Bezalel and Oholiab, whom he blessed and sanctified

---

[41] Within the meaning of the comprehensive term "Fathers" are included the
spiritual leaders of the Old Testament (the prophets and the righteous) as well
as the martyrs and apostles of the New. Paul himself, it should be noted, considered
himself a father of the Church (1 Cor. 4:15).

[42] Mansi 13, 8A; cf. Gen. 28:18.

[43] Mansi 13, 4DE; cf. Exod. 25:18–22 and Mansi 13, 5E.

[44] Mansi 13, 5A; cf. Num. 7:89 and Mansi 13, 285AB: "Therefore he brought
them to the knowledge of God through two things, the one being that 'you
shall worship the Lord your God and adore him alone' and the other that 'you
shall make cherubim of molten gold'."

[45] Mansi 13, 5B; cf. Ezek. 41:1, 17–21.

[46] Mansi 12, 962C; cf. 12, 1067D: "every work carried out in the name of God
is good and holy"; and 13, 97C: "even though they were made by human hands
they were called holy of holies . . . every work carried out in the name of the

"that they may produce works made by human hands, but to the glory and service of God". And:

> "God says to Moses: cut tables of stone and bring them to me. And having cut them he brought them. And God wrote with his own finger the ten life-giving and immortal commandments. Then God says: you shall make cherubim and you shall make an altar . . . and you shall make an ark . . . and put your testimony in the ark, as a memorial to your descendants, that is, the tables, the jar, the rod. Are these forms and likenesses made by human hands or not? But they are for the glory and service of God."[47]
> "For if we believe that the Israelite people were saved through looking at the bronze serpent, far be it from us to doubt the holy Fathers or to depart from their tradition . . . . King Solomon made cherubim to the glory of God in the Temple which he built for God and decorated with various colours. Therefore we too and all the orthodox confess our faith and beautify the house of God with various colours and the decorative work of painters."[48]

Unlike the iconoclasts, they also defend the Jewish tradition, distinguishing it sharply from the Greek:

> "That which belongs to the Old Testament, in which the Israelite people had a share, was a tradition from God; that which belongs to the Greeks was a tradition from demons."[49]

Finding such support in the Old Testament, the iconophiles do not have much recourse to the New, which in this matter does no more than confirm the tradition of the Old: "The Old Testament contained divine symbols . . . and the New inherited them from the Old."[50] The citing of Paul, however, in order to develop an argument for the existence of an iconographic tradition already in the period of the Old Testament is striking:

> "What was set forth was set forth for our instruction, the divine Apostle teaches (cf. Rom. 15:4). Therefore these holy and venerable icons and paintings and panels are like a museum for our instruction and zeal

---

Lord in naturally honourable and holy". See also John Damascene, *Imag.* 11, 23.

[47] Mansi 12, 962DE; cf. Exod. 31:1–11, 25; 34:1–29; cf. also 978A: "what are our churches if not made by human hands?" and 1070A: "what is there on earth that has not been made by human hands apart from what is made by God?" and 13, 276C: "the things that are dedicated to God are acceptable to him."

[48] Ibid. 1063DE; cf. Numb. 21:9; 1 Kgs 6:23; see also Mansi 13, 52C.

[49] Mansi 13, 276B.

[50] Mansi 13, 5D (Tarasius commenting on Hebr. 9). Also "If the Old Testament had cherubim overshadowing the mercy-seat, we too will have icons of our Lord Jesus Christ and the holy Theotokos and the saints overshadowing the mercy-seat", ibid. Cf. ibid. 97C.

and example, and were painted as such that we too might show to God the same example and struggle."[51]

Also striking is the assertion that "the Christian Church received (the painting of icons and their installation in churches) from the holy Apostles",[52] the icons being in no way a modern invention. "We are taught this truth by the appearance of the sacred church buildings in every locality."[53] They point to an unwritten tradition: "Among the many unwritten traditions handed down to us, the making of icons has spread throughout the Church from the preaching of the Apostles."[54] This clearly constitutes an ipso facto argument: "The appearance of the holy icons in the churches is so well established because wherever the Gospel has been preached up to this time, there they are to be seen."[55]

Nevertheless, there is also an attempt to appeal to written apostolic tradition through a report that "in the synod of the Holy Apostles at Antioch" it was said that the faithful must no longer stray after idols but instead should make icons (*antikonizein*) of the theandric spotless stele of our Lord Jesus Christ.[56] It is also admitted indirectly, however, that the tradition of icons is a later "superstructure": "And whatever in the course of time seemed good to our fathers of blessed memory to build upon the foundation of the

---

[51] Mansi 13, 20d; cf. Rom. 15:4. This passage comes in the course of an intelligent exploitation of the various meanings of the term "graphe". Cf. another though unsuccessful attempt to exploit the Pauline term to the same end, ibid., 328DE; cf. also 12, 1054C.

[52] Mansi 12, 1014C; cf. 1058A, 1066D, 1143B.

[53] Mansi 13, 217D. The validity of this argument is questionable, given that the decorative programme may well have been added later to churches that were already ancient.

[54] Ibid., 268D; cf. 220B, 377B, 404D; John of Damascus, *Imag.* 1, 12; 11, 16; Nicephorus, *Antir.* 111, PG 100, 385C–389B.

[55] Mansi 13, 328D; cf. 12, 1018D: "We have been informed by the law, the prophets, the apostles and the Fathers that truth and piety consist in this, that the holy and venerable icons should be in the church in accordance with the custom handed down since early times from the holy Apostles". The fact that no attempt is made to support this thesis historically by offering objective proof, e.g. from the ruins of the palaeochristian churches, is a characteristic example of the absence of any archaeological interest throughout the Byzantine period. A unique exception is the *Onomasticon* of Eusebius of Caesarea (ed. E. Klostermann, GCS 11, 1 Euseb. 111, 1, 1966) which is confined to Jewish archeology, focusing on the historic books of the Old Testament. This is in fact the last part of an extensive book on archaeology written by Eusebius, which is lost. However taking into account that Eusebius was considered to be a heretic, this exception proves the rule. See on this point Germanus of Constantinople, *De haeresibus et Synodis* 14, PG 98, 53A.

[56] Mansi 12, 1018C. On this see F.X. Funk, *Didascalia et Constitutiones Apostolorum*, vol. 2, Paderborn 1905, p. 144, can 4.

apostles and the prophets, that we accept."[57] In this way emphasis
is given above all to the role of patristic tradition: "Our Scripture
and our light and our salvation are our holy and God-bearing
Fathers and teachers"[58] who "clothed and adorned"[59] the Church
with icons. From that time the orthodox emperors and clergy with
the whole of the Christian people "according to the ancient tradition of the holy Fathers" not only received but preserved and
still possess the venerable icons as a memorial and aid to compunction.[60] For this reason the iconoclasts are asked: "On this vital
doctrine of our salvation, namely, the economy of Christ, which
of our divine Fathers pronounced the workmanship of painters
wicked? For one cannot bring oneself to condemn that which one
accepts."[61] Conversely, of course: "And most of the holy Fathers
handed on a written tradition on the use of these (= icons) to
the Christian people."[62]

The Chief Patristic Witnesses

A number of Fathers are cited in support of the icons.[63] Many of
these only constitute an indirect witness to the use of icons or are
simply irrelevant citations on the part of the iconophiles. There
are, however, certain genuine patristic testimonia which really do

---

[57] Mansi 13, 328E. Cf. 12, 1071A.

[58] Mansi 12, 962A.

[59] Ibid., 967C.

[60] Ibid., 1059C. Cf. 1014C, 1063D, 1070E–1071A, 1086B. Also 13, 8E, 20E,
128D, 132E, 217D, 252C, 348B, 377CE, 404D, 474C.

[61] Mansi 13, 241A. This important quotation probably implies that apart from
"the vital doctrine of our salvation" the art of painters and presumably the fine
arts in general viewed from such a theological point of view are considered to
be wicked! On this see P. Van den Ven, "La patristique et l'hagiographie au
concile de Nicée de 787" in Byzantium, 25–7, (1955–57), pp. 325–62 passim.

[62] Mansi 13, 268E. Cf. 269A: "All our holy Fathers accepted the making of
icons; and those who say that it is not a tradition of Fathers are lying".

[63] These are Athanasius of Alexandria (Mansi 12, 1067C; 13, 69BC, 325D,
361E, 24E–32A; cf. PG 25, 96 and 120C; PG 26, 332; PG 27, 12045; PG 28, 797–
805; see also L. Wallach, Diplomatic studies in Latin and Greek documents from the
Carolingian Age, Ithaca and London 1977, pp. 102–106); Basil of Caesarea (Mansi
12, 1014E, 1146A, 1066DE; 13, 72A–73A, 80C, 69E, 93C, 268E, 273AB, 277C,
324C 325D, 377E; from these indirect testimonies it appears that the letter of
Basil the Great to Julian referred to in these columns is one which is no longer
extant); Cyril of Jerusalem (Mansi 13, 160B. Cf. PG 33, 421); Gregory Nazianzus
(Mansi 13, 13BC, 268E, 309D, 361D. Cf. PG 37, 737–8; 36, 329A–332A. See P.
Van den Ven, art. cit. p. 352); Gregory of Nyssa (Mansi 12, 1066BC; 13, 9D,
117A, 268E, 324B; cf. 224BC; see also PG 46, 572C; 776A; 46, 796A–D and L.
Wallach, op. cit. pp. 84–8); John Chrysostom (Mansi 12, 1014E, 1019B, 1066E–
1067A; 13, 8D, 9AB, 68E, 93C, 268E, 300D, 324C, 325D. Cf. PG 56, 407; see
also L. Wallach, op. cit. pp. 94–102 and 116–8; PG 50, 516; and John Damascene,

provide proof of iconography as a Christian tradition. These may be listed as follows:

1. A passage of Athanasius the Great (295–373 AD) from his *Third Discourse against the Arians* (and not the Fourth, as the Acta of the Seventh Ecumenical Council say): "Therefore he who venerates the icon venerates the emperor represented in it."[64] Although this is represented simply as an illustration, and although it refers to a secular rather than a Christian icon of the emperor and not to an icon of a saint or of Christ, and although, lastly, this illustration is used by Athanasius to demonstrate the natural identity between Father and Son in the course of the Arian controversy, nevertheless it constitutes together with the identical example of Basil the Great (see below) the fundamental starting-point for the vitally important distinction between prototype and icon on which the whole argumentation of the iconophiles largely rests.

2. The parallel passage in St Basil's (330–379 AD) work *On the Holy Spirit* addressed to Amphilochius:

"For the icon of the emperor is also called emperor but there are not

---

Imag. 11, 61 (ed. Kotter)); Epiphanius of Cyprus (Mansi 12, 1067D; see *Panarion* 65, 8, 10, ed. K. Holl, GCS Epiphanius III, Leipzig 1933, 12 and L. Wallach, op. cit. p. 34; see also John Damascene, *Imag.* 1, 25; Theodore of Studius, PG 99, 388; Nicephorus, PG 100, 837); Cyril of Alexandria (Mansi 12, 1067B; 13, 162B–13A; see L. Wallach, op. cit. pp. 106 and 108; PG 77, 2217–20); Antipater of Bozra (Mansi 13, 13E, 93D, 125D, 268D; cf. PG 85, 1792–3; see also Mansi 13, 177D–180C (PG 85, 172–3); Asterius of Amaseia (Mansi 13, 16B–17D, 308B–309B, 305BC; cf. *Bibliotheca Hagiographica Graeca*, Brussels 1909, p. 623; PG 40, 168B (Homily on Dives and Lazarus) and 40, 336A–337C); Stephen of Bozra (Mansi 12, 1067D–1070D; cf. L. Wallach, op. cit. pp. 35–8); Isidore of Pelusium (Mansi 12, 1018D. Cf. PG 78, 113A); Leontius of Neapolis (Mansi 13, 44A–53C. PG 93, 1597–1609; L. Wallach, op. cit. pp. 134–8, and L. Barnard, *The Graeco-Roman and Oriental Background and the Iconoclastic Controversy*, Leiden 1974, p. 86ff); Neilus (Mansi 13, 36AD; cf. PG 79, 577–80; cf. L. Wallach op. cit. p. 31); Anastasius of Theoupolis (of Antioch) (Mansi 13, 56A–57B, 269A; cf. PG 89, 1405, 1. 6–17 and 1408, 1. 1–12); Sophronius of Jerusalem (Mansi 13, 56A–57B, 269A; see PF 87, 3557–60); John of Thessalonica (Mansi 13, 164D–165D; cf. A. Gallandius, *Bibliotheca veterum patrum antiquorumque scriptorum ecclesiasticorum*, vol. 13 (1979), pp. 196–7; see also L. Barnard, op. cit. p. 86); and from the Western Fathers Gregory I the Great (Mansi 12, 1059C; see L. Wallach, op. cit. pp. 30–1); Ambrose (Mansi 12, 1067C; see L. Wallach, op. cit. pp. 123–39); Jerome (Mansi 12, 1070E; see L. Wallach, op. cit. pp. 38–9 and PG 40, 865CD); and Augustine (Mansi 12, 1066B, see L. Wallach, op. cit. p. 32), these last all being included in a letter of Pope Adrian I which is of doubtful authenticity (Mansi 12, 1055–71; see L. Wallach, op. cit. passim and particularly pp. 13–14, 47–8, 82–4). Anonymous texts are also adduced, such as the *Dialogue between a Jew and a Christian* (Mansi 13, 165E–168C).
[64] Mansi 13, 69BC; PG 26, 332B.

two emperors; for neither is the power divided nor is the glory
partitioned . . . for the honour rendered to the icon passes over to the
prototype."[65]

Here too we are dealing only with an illustration which does
not refer to a religious icon and which is aimed again, like
the above passage of Athanasius the Great, at proving the natural
identity between Father and Son. Nevertheless, it did constitute
for the iconophiles a precise point of reference in support of
their theses.

3. A passage of Gregory of Nyssa (330–395 AD) from his *Com-
    mentary on the Song of Songs*, which in its original form reads
    as follows:

    "He who looks at an icon made by craftsmanship through the use of
    colours does not let his gaze dwell on the colours of the panel but
    looks to the form alone which the draftsman has displayed through
    the use of colours."[66]

    This is clear counsel on the distinction between archetype and
    icon (in which Athanasius and Basil are engaged above) through
    stressing the difference between the matter of the colours and
    the form which is represented by them.

4. A passage of Epiphanius of Cyprus (315–403 AD) from his
    Panarion, which in its original form reads as follows: "For the
    emperors are not two emperors through having an icon but
    are one emperor with his icon."[67] This is a repetition of the
    theses of Athanasius and Basil, most probably taken from them,
    except that it reveals perhaps the theological mentality of
    Epiphanius and his setting in the iconophile mode of thought
    through the distinction between archetype and its icons in, of
    course, a non-suspect time.

5. A passage of Cyril of Alexandria (390–444 AD) from his letter
    to Acacius, bishop of Scythopolis, on the scapegoat:

    "If any one of us desired to see the story of Abraham (the sacrifice
    of Isaac) painted on a panel, how would the painter draw it? Would
    he draw the events in one scene, or would he draw them separately
    and differently, that is to say, in a series of different scenes? . . . But
    it is not a different Abraham that is seen in different attitudes in

---

[65] Mansi 13, 69E; PG 32, 149C.
[66] Mansi 12, 1066BC; PG 44, 776A.
[67] Mansi 12, 1967D; Epiphanius III 12 (ed. K. Holl, Leipzig 1933).

different parts of the picture, but the same Abraham everywhere, the skill of the painter always accommodating the demands of the real course of events."[68]

This concerns a de facto acceptance of the portrayal of sacred persons and biblical events as legitimate and, moreover, defines the general principles of iconography as a skill "always accommodating the demands of the real course of events" and manifesting "the reality to the beholders".[69]

6. A fragment of Stephen of Bozra (7th–8th cent. AD) from his lost work *Against the Jews*, which has been preserved in its original form in the third discourse of John of Damascus (675–749 AD) *On the Holy Images* and reads as follows:

[68] Mansi 13, 12E–13A; PG 77, 217–220; It is striking that the sacrifice of Abraham as an iconographic theme is presented here by Cyril only as a legitimate possibility which has not yet become an established wall-painting, at least in the churches of Alexandria, although as we gather from Gregory of Nyssa it seems already to have been introduced into the churches of Cappadocia or Constantinople. See Mansi 12, 1066BD and below.

[69] On this see also Mansi 13, 305E: "For everything which is received not on account of need but on account of decoration is convicted of vainglory, as the divine Basil said". Cf. PG 31, 1116C. The use of this passage by the iconophiles proves that their perception of icons did not in any way include an aesthetic dimension. Besides, the concept of beauty, as is well known, does not have any value in itself in Orthodox theology, but is identified with the existence of beings (Gen. 1:31) as being partaken by all of them and as "participation in the beauty-producing cause of all that is beautiful" (Dionysius the Aeropagite, *On the Divine Names* VII, PG 3, 701C). On this see E. Kitzinger, "The cult of Images in the age before Iconoclasm", *DOP* 8 (1954), pp. 141–3, n. 251 and 257. Kitzinger, however, in spite of his brilliant and usually felicitous interpretation of the roots and causes of the development of the veneration of icons, insists that Christians ascribed magical properties and powers to the icons (pp. 116, 119, 146) and goes on to believe that icons are considered to be art objets even by the faithful who honour them. See also on this point E.J. Martin. *A History of the Iconoclastic Controversy*, London 1930, p. 120 n. 3. In spite of all this, the early Christian conception of art as deceit was never abandoned or overlooked by the iconophiles. The insistence of the latter on the distinction between icon and idol and on the subjection of representational art so that it becomes a handmaid "to the demands of the real course of events" without any right to an independent inspiration or contribution from the creative imagination of the painter, demonstrates clearly the unbroken continuity between early Christian and iconophile conceptions of art. See Kitzinger, art. cit. p. 150: "What the artist is called upon to create is a shell, limp and meaningless in itself, ready to receive power and life from on high, from the holy Ghost which will overshadow it, from the heavenly persons who will take up their abode in it". See also L. Ouspensky, *Théologie de l'icône*, Paris 1982, p. 22: "l'inspiration divine est le principe même de l'art liturgique. L'Ecriture trace là, une limite entre l'art liturgique et l'art en general." Charles Murray, "Art and the Early Church" in *JTS (N.S.)*. Vol. 28, Pt2 1977, pp. 303–345, where, although adopting a different approach to the concept of Art in the early Church, supports the view of the present study. P.C. Finney, "Antecedents of Byzantine Iconoclasm" in *The Image and the Word*, ed. J. Gutmann, Missoula, Montana, 1977, p. 31.

"We have made the icons of the saints as a memorial of the saints, such as Abraham and Isaac and Jacob and Moses and Elijah and Zachariah and the rest of the prophets and holy martyrs who have been put to death for him, so that everyone who beholds their icons should commemorate them and glorify him who glorified them. Concerning icons, we have confidence that every work executed in the name of God is good and holy. But concerning idols and statues, away with them. For they are evil and perverse, both they and their makers. For an icon of a holy prophet is one thing but a statue or effigy of Kronos or Aphrodite or Helios or Selene is another. For since man was made in the image of God, he may be venerated. But since a serpent is an image of the devil, it is unclean and to be rejected. If you reject what has been made by human hands, tell me, O Jew, what is there on earth that is venerated which was not made by human hands? Was the ark of God not made by human hands? And what of the sanctuary and the mercy seat and the cherubim and the golden jar which contained the manna and the inner tent and everything that was called by God holy of holies? Were not the cherubim, the icons of angels, made by human hands? What do you say? If you call these things idols, what do you say to their veneration by Moses and Israel? Veneration is a symbol of honour. When we sinners venerate, we glorify God with divine worship and worthy veneration and fear him as our maker and provider, but we glorify the angels and servants of God in accordance with the honour of God as creatures of God and his servants. For an icon is a name and a likeness of the person represented in it. Therefore we always commemmorate with letters and engravings the passions of the Lord and the holy prophets which are recounted in the law and the gospels."[70]

This is direct evidence for the painting of icons and is evidently prior to the ascent to the throne of the Emperor Leo III the Isaurian, for it is directed against the Jews and not the iconoclasts. Perhaps it also constitutes indirect evidence of a contribution from Judaism to the beginning of the iconoclast controversy.[71]

7. A striking phrase of Isidore of Pelusium (395–450 AD) from his 73rd letter: "There is no mention of a temple which is not

---

[70] Mansi 12, 1067–1070; PG 94, 1376. On this fragment see G.B. Ladner, "The concept of the image in the great Fathers and the Byzantine Iconoclastic Controversy", *DOP* 7 (1955), p. 74ff. Also H.-G. Beck, *Kirche und theologische Literatur im byzantinischen Reich*, Munich 1959, p. 447, and E. Kitzinger, art. cit. p. 141, n. 250.

[71] It seems that John Damascene made a selection of passages from the work of Stephen of Bozra, omitting certain rather crude theses which came into conflict with his own more sophisticated and more systematic exposition of modes of iconic representation. Thus, for example, a passage from Stephen of Bozra included in the acts of the Seventh Ecumenical Council is omitted by John on the grounds that two forms of iconic representation which are distinct

crowned by a statue."[72] This refers to the mercy seat of the Hebrews' Tent of Witness and has no connection at all with the use of icons. Nevertheless, the absolute and clear way in which he connects the existence of a temple with the need for a sacred sign or "type" within it through which the presence of the divine is made manifest, at least to the initiates, renders the passage an argument in favour of icons, the last being understood precisely as supreme examples of such "types" or signs.[73] Special care is needed, however, in order not to misunderstand the very rich term "statue" (*agalma*), which of course does not carry its usual meaning here but its original, almost etymological, significance.[74]

8.	The fifth discourse *On Behalf of the Apology of the Christians against the Jews and On the Icons of the Saints* of Leontius, bishop of Neapolis in Cyprus (7th cent.), which is not reproduced here on account of its length.[75] Although a long text, the apology seems to be the only complete discourse dedicated wholly to the question of the honour and veneration of the icons of the saints, a subject which most probably also formed the peroration of the lost work. A surprising point is the assertion with which Leontius begins his discourse, namely, that the tradition of the making of icons is Jewish "and not our own" Christian tradition. This is a broad reference to all the Jewish vessels and objects of reverence made by human hands and points to a systematic refutation of the Jewish accusation of idolatry directed against the Christians.

9.	A letter of St Neilus (fl. 430 AD) to the eparch Olympiodorus, which contains important instructions for the decoration of a newly constructed church:

according to John are confused and identified by Stephen of Bozra: the "image, which has been made by God by imitation, that is, man" is confused with the "image for commemoration of events . . . [which] is twofold: through the word written in the Scriptures . . . and through sensible depiction" (*Imag.* III, 20 and 23). Also omitted is the phrase "for we all venerate the rulers and kiss them", evidently because he was writing in the time of Constantine V, but also because he was living under Arab rule without Christian leaders. On this aspect see L.W. Barnard, "The Emperor cult and the origins of the iconoclastic controversy", *Byzantion*, 43 (1973) pp. 13–29.

[72] Mansi 12, 1018D; PG 78, 1133A.

[73] See E. Kitzinger, art. cit. pp. 145–50.

[74] The Greek word "agalma" derives from the verb "agallo" = I glorify, exalt, and especially exult, hence: "agalma" is everything for which one exults, i.e. delight, glory, honour, and hence: a statue or a pleasing place in honour of a god.

[75] Mansi 13, 44A–53C. On Leontius see H.-G. Beck, op. cit. p. 455.

"In the sanctuary on the east wall of the divine precinct mark only a single cross .... By the hand of an excellent painter fill the nave of the saints on every side with narrative scenes from the Old and New Testaments, so that those who are illiterate and cannot read the sacred Scriptures might through looking at the pictures be instructed in the noble deeds of those who have truly served God and might be stirred up to rival their celebrated and famous achievements, through which they exchanged earth for heaven, having preferred what is invisible to what is visible."[76]

This is the oldest surviving description of the decorative scheme of a Christian church in the fifth century, which consisted exclusively of biblical themes. We are surely confronted here with the beginnings of the development of wallpainting and this most probably explains the reason for the request of the eparch Olympiodorus. Moreover, of special significance is the rejection by St Neilus of all the decorative and aesthetic aspects expressive of the mentality of orthodox iconography.[77]

10. A passage by Anastasius I (540–599 AD), patriarch of Antioch, from his discourse *On the Sabbath* addressed to Symeon of Bozra:

"When the emperor is absent, his icon is venerated in the place of his person. But when he is present, it is absurd to abandon the prototype in order to venerate the image. When it is not venerated because of the presence of him on whose account its veneration takes place, however, it should by no means be dishonoured .... When someone insults the icon of the emperor, he receives a just punishment exactly as if he had dishonoured the emperor himself .... Similarly, if someone dishonours the type of a person, the insult is conveyed to the person himself of whom it is the type."[78]

Anastasius of Antioch takes the same theological attitude as Athanasius of Alexandria, Basil of Caesarea, Gregory of Nyssa and Epiphanius of Salamis in distinguishing firmly between archetype and icon. Certainly this is not a fully developed argument in defence of icons, but it is an important indication of an iconophile mentality dominating the Eastern Fathers.

---

[76] Mansi 13, 36AD; PG 79, 580. On St Neilus see Altaner-Stuiber, *Patrologie*, Freiburg-Basel-Wien 1978, p. 334.

[77] Cf. the parallel information on the decoration of the Church of the Saviour in Rome by Constantine the Great with biblical scenes, Mansi 13, 37A and 220A passim.

[78] Mansi 13, 56E–57A; PG 89, 1405. On Anastasius I, Patriarch of Antioch, see Altaner-Stuiber, op. cit. p. 512. H.-G. Beck, op. cit. p. 458. S.N. Sakkos, *Peri Anastasiou Sinaitou*, Thessalonica 1964. G. Weiss, *Studia Anastasiana* I, Munchen, 1965.

11. A fragment of a discourse evidently *Against the Greeks* by John of Thessalonica (7th cent.):

"We make icons of mortal men, of the holy and embodied servants of God, in order to commemmorate them and honour them and we do nothing unreasonable in painting them as they were in life. For we do not express ourselves through art, as you do, nor do we show bodily characteristics of incorporeal beings. And when we venerate them, we do not venerate the icons, as you yourself have said, but we glorify the personages represented pictorially, and then not as gods — God forbid — but as true servants and friends of God who have the ability to intercede for us. We also make icons of God — I mean of our Lord and Saviour Jesus Christ — but we paint him as he was seen on earth and lived amongst men, not as he is conceived of in his nature as God. For what likeness or what form is there of the incorporeal and formless Logos of the Father? For God is spirit, as Scripture says. That is to say, the holy nature of the consubstantial Trinity is spirit. But since God the Father willed it and his only-begotten divine Logos came down from heaven and was made incarnate for our salvation by the Holy Spirit and the spotless Virgin and Theotokos, Mary, we depict his humanity not his incorporeal divinity."[79]

The fragment goes on to argue for the legitimacy of the representation of angels as beings which are not entirely incorporeal. The outstanding significance of this fragment of John of Thessalonica is that a century before the outbreak of the iconoclast controversy it defends the representation of God incarnate in the person of Jesus Christ.[80] If it is borne in mind that the dialogue is conducted with a Greek, the absence of a reference to Christ in the parallel dialogues with Jews becomes intelligible.[81]

12. Finally there is the evidence of Jerome, priest of Jerusalem (7th–8th cent. AD), from an unknown work of his:

"And just as God allowed every nation to venerate things made by human hands and was pleased to let the Jews venerate the tables which Moses had hewn and the two golden cherubim, so too he granted to us Christians to paint and venerate the cross and the icons of noble deeds and to manifest our work."[82]

---

[79] Mansi 13, 164C–165C. On John of Thessalonica see H.-G. Beck. op. cit. p. 458. Also M. Jugie, "Jean de Thessalonique", in *Dictionnaire de Théologie Catholique*, vol. 8, 820–25.

[80] Cf. E. Kitzinger, art. cit. p. 141ff.

[81] On this see L.W. Barnard, *Graeco-Roman and Oriental Background*, p. 88. In the anonymous dialogue, however, between a Jew and a Christian there is also mention of an icon of Christ (Mansi 13, 168AB).

[82] Mansi 12, 1070E; PG 40, 865CD. On Jerome (c. 740 AD) see H.-G. Beck,

The Evidence of the Councils

Besides this specifically patristic evidence, however, the Seventh Ecumenical Council also cites conciliar evidence, either in a general way in such phrases as "the six councils in Christ have handed down to us"[83] and "if they will accept the holy icons, they will follow the catholic Church, since these have been accepted by the six holy ecumenical councils",[84] or else more precisely, such as in the frequent references to the 82nd canon of the Quinisext Council, which bears the title "on not painting a lamb instead of Christ" and reads as follows:

> "In some representations of the holy icons there is drawn a lamb pointed to by a finger of the Baptist, which is taken as a type of grace, prefiguring for us through the law the true lamb, who is Christ our God. Although we treat the old types and shadows with affection as symbols and patters of the truth handed down to the Church, we prefer to honour the grace and truth as we have already accepted it as the fulfilment of the law. Therefore in order to represent the perfect in the sight of all, even though in pigments, we decree that the lamb who takes away the sin of the world, Christ our God, should be painted henceforth in the icons in his human character instead of as the old lamb. In this way we understand the depth of the humiliation of God the Logos and we are led to the remembrance of his life in the flesh, of his passion, of his saving death and of the redemption which resulted from it for the world."[85]

Also cited is the "Apostolic Council" of Antioch, which decreed:

> "Those who are being saved should no longer stray after idols but instead should make icons of the theandric, spotless stele of our Lord Jesus Christ."[86]

The Evidence of Historical Antiquity

The greatest emphasis of the iconophiles, however, falls mainly on an appeal to historical circumstances which show that the icons do not simply constitute an ancient Christian tradition but are a

---

op. cit. p. 448. Cf. also the same text from Jerome which John Damascene presents in a different way in *Images* III, 125. See also L. Wallach, op. cit. p. 38–39.

[83] Mansi 12, 962A. Cf. 13, 220.

[84] Mansi 13, 237AB. Cf. 248A and 12, 979D.

[85] Mansi 12, 1079BC, 1123E–1126A; 13, 40E–41A; 93E; 220CE. Cf. also the seventh canon of the Council of Constantinople of 869, Mansi 16, 401–3, on the attributes of icon-painters.

[86] Mansi 12, 1018C.

living and real presence in the Church of the divine persons thus
represented, who intervene in a supernatural way through healings
and so on in the life of the faithful:

> "In no way has the painting of icons been handed down to us in recent
> years . . . as we are taught in every locality from the very appearance
> of the holy churches and as the holy Fathers have witnessed and as
> the authors of histories relate whose writings are preserved to this
> day."[87]

These historical circumstances may be discerned in simple pieces
of evidence from the period before iconoclasm on the use and
honouring of icons and in the miracles of saints thus represented
which took place or were confirmed by means of their icons.
References to relevant "histories" are traced back to the period of
Christ in the search for the first traces of iconography. Ironically,
the iconophiles draw their oldest historical references from Eusebius
of Caesarea. One of these is

> "the story of the woman with the haemorrhage, of whom it is related
> by various historians that she set up a statue of the Lord and of herself
> touching in accordance with the Gospel narrative the fringe of his
> statue, just as she was when the healing took place. Between her statue
> and the statue of the Lord a herb grew up, touching the feet of the
> Lord's statue, which was a prophylactic against every disease."[88]

This "history" is presented at the beginning of the Seventh Ecumenical Council in a speech of Antipater of Bozra (5th cent. AD)
on the woman with the haemorrhage.[89] It continues with the following
anonymous scholion:

> "Such a divinely inspired erection of a statue should rather be con-
> sidered to pertain to the Mosaic Law, even though grace and truth
> are better than types and preferable to the shadow."[90]

Characteristic here is the indirect but clear censure of the fashion-
ing of statues in honour of Christ and by extension of the saints.
The same story is cited again and is immediately ascribed to
Eusebius with the following comment: "Eusebius himself said
that he ascertained this with his own eyes." A scholion longer than
the previous one follows immediately:

---

[87] Mansi 13, 217D.
[88] Ibid., 268D.
[89] Ibid., 13E.
[90] Ibid., 93D.

"Clearly when the Saviour in his condescension adapted his grace to the faith of the woman, he showed what we have explained above, namely, that the result is not to be examined in a simple way but that the motive of the doer is to be tested. In the same text Eusebius says that he has also seen the icons of the apostles Peter and Paul and of Christ himself which have survived on painted panels. We do not say this ourselves so that we should make it our business to set up steles of bronze but only to show that since the Lord did not reject the pagan custom but was pleased for a considerable time to manifest in it the wonder-working of his goodness, it is not a holy thing to condemn a custom so clearly established amongst us."[91]

This is connected with a much more emphatic censure of the art of sculpture, which had only recently ("for a considerable time") become tolerable by "condescension" because it constituted a "pagan custom". The Council distinguishes its position on this from any general defence of such a "custom" "that we should make it our business to set up steles of bronze" and regards iconography as a "clearly established custom". Evidently a heretical writer such as Eusebius was cited to divert attention from his hostile attitude to icons, which the iconoclasts had made use of. The Seventh Ecumenical Council, however, does not hesitate to set the same Antipater of Bozra against Eusebius, refuting his Apology in defence of Origen and saying among other things:

"I agree and confess that the man (Eusebius) was very learned and was not ignorant of any aspect of ancient literature . . . yet I say that he had not yet arrived at a precise understanding of dogma. Therefore one must defer to his great learning but not to his knowledge of dogma. For we know that precision in this matter came about long after his time."[92]

Another event from Eusebius's *Ecclesiastical History* is referred to without naming its author:

"When Christ appeared in Jerusalem, Abgar, who at that time ruled the city of Edessa as its king, heard of the miracles of Christ and wrote

---

[91] Ibid., 125E–128A. Cf. Eusebius, *Ecclesiastical History* 7, 18 and note 15 above. The significance of this reference to Eusebius becomes more intelligible by taking into account Eusebius' contribution to the cult of the Christian Emperor Cf. F. Dvornik, *Early Political Philosophy*, Washington 1966, II, pp. 616–18. The political message of the iconophiles is clearly: we are not antiroyalists.

[92] Mansi 13, 178E–108A. On Eusebius's Apology in defence of Origen see *Clavis Patrum Graecorum* II, Brepols-Turnhout 1974, p. 268; Cf. Nicephorus of Constantinople, *Antir.* 3, PG 100, 421; *Apologeticus pro ss. imaginibus*, PG 100, 561; *Apologeticus minor pro sacris imaginibus*, PG 100, 848. See also Mansi 13, 317C, where Eusebius is described as a heretic and a theopaschite.

him a letter. And Christ sent to him an answer by his own hand as well as a copy of his holy and glorious face. And you can go and see that picture which was not made by human hands; crowds of people of the East gather there and pray."[93]

In the fifth session of the council Abgar's icon not made by human hands is mentioned again in the context of the miracle it performed during the siege of Jerusalem by the Persians, when it contributed to the destruction by fire of the wooden siege engines and the saving of the city. This narrative is taken from the *Ecclesiastical History* of Evagrius and in this case too Eusebius is not mentioned.[94]

The following are also adduced as historical evidence for the antiquity of the institution of icon-painting: the "painting" of the Apostle Peter in the contemporary church dedicated to him in Rome;[95] the encomium of John Chrysostom on Meletius of Antioch, where it is mentioned that while Meletius was still alive and in exile his likeness was reproduced "in the seals of rings and on cups and bowls and the walls of rooms and everywhere;"[96] the Church of the Saviour in Rome decorated with frescoes by Constantine the Great;[97] the placing of an icon by the same sainted emperor and his mother in the propylaea of their palace in Constantinople, "in which by setting forth the depictions of the Apostles and prophets and by inscribing their messages concerning the Lord, they proclaimed the saving cross as the boast of their own faith";[98] Gregory of Nyssa's discourse *On the Divinity of the Son and the Spirit*, in which he mentions his personal experience of an icon portraying the sacrifice of Abraham and the emotion which it occasioned;[99] Gregory of Nazianzus's poem *On Virtue*, which mentions the case of the converted sinner whose icon inspired such awe even among prostitutes that it caused them to abandon their profession;[100] Asterius of Amaseia's *Description of Euphemia the Martyr*, which describes the icons of the martyrdom of St Euphemia as seen by the author in

---

[93] Mansi 12, 963D. On icons not made by human hands in general, see E. Kitzinger, art. cit. pp. 117–21; E. von Dobschütz, *Christusbilder*, Leipzig, 1899, pp. 277–79 and passim.

[94] Mansi 13, 189E–192C. The testimony of Leo, Lector of the Great Church of Constantinople, is worth noting: "I was in Edessa and saw the sacred icon not made by human hands" (192C).

[95] Mansi 12, 963E–965A.

[96] Mansi 13, 8CD; 269. Cf. PG 50, 516.

[97] Mansi 13, 37A.

[98] Ibid. 124E–125A.

[99] Mansi 13, 9D. Cf. Mansi 12, 1066B; 13, 12A; 117A; 268E; 277C; 324B. See also PG 46, 572.

[100] Mansi 13, 13BC. Cf. 268E and PG 37, 737–8.

her church;[101] a fragment of *The Martyrdom of Anastasius the Persian* in which the martyr learns the doctrines of Christianity from the icons of various martyrs which he saw in the churches before his baptism;[102] a fragment from the *Acts* of Maximus the Confessor which shows him venerating the icons of Christ and the Theotokos;[103] the story from the *Leimonarion* of John Moschus about the recluse under attack from the demon of fornication who promised to cease his attacks if the ascetic would cease venerating the icon of the Theotokos which he kept in his cave;[104] a fragment from the *Life of St Symeon Stylites* by Theodoret of Cyrus, which mentions the setting up of icons of Symeon in Rome "in all the entrances to the workshops . . . as a protection for them and a guarantee for all the products procured from them";[105] a letter of Symeon Stylites of the Wonderful Mountain to the Emperor Justin II (565–578), in which he asks him to see to the punishment of some Samaritans who had behaved impiously towards the icons of Christ and the Theotokos.[106]

The Evidence of Miracles

A significant amount of space is devoted to the cases brought before the council of wonder-working icons or of miracles confirmed through the icons of the saints who had worked them:

1. In the letter of Pope Adrian which was read at the second session of the council and translated from the Latin a fragment of the *Actus Silvestri* is quoted which tells the story of the legendary healing of Constantine the Great from leprosy and his subsequent baptism by Pope St Sylvester after the appearance to him in a dream of the Apostles Peter and Paul, whom he recognised from their icon.[107]

---

[101] Mansi 13, 16D; 20B; 308B–309B. Cf. PG 40, 333A–337C.

[102] Mansi 13, 21A. See also 117B. Cf. H. Usener, *Acta M. Anastasii Persae (1894)*, *Bibliotheca Hagiographica Graeca*, 84, Bruxelles 1909, p. 3.

[103] Mansi 13, 38E–40A, Cf. 269A; 361E; also PG 90, 156AB and 164A.

[104] Mansi 13, 60E–61B; 193AC. Cf. 192DE and PG 87, 2900BD. Both the Seventh Ecumenical Council and John Damascene regard the *Leimonarion* as a work of Sophronius of Jerusalem. See L. Wallach, op. cit. pp. 79–82. See also in Mansi 193D–196C two further examples of wonder-working icons from the *Leimorarion*: an icon of St Theodosia of Scopelos which made water spring from a dry well, and an icon of the Theotokos which kept its lamp burning during the long absence of an ascetic called John (PG 87, 3052).

[105] Mansi 13, 73B. Cf. PG 82, 1473.

[106] Mansi 13, 160D–161E. Cf. PG 86, 3216 and P. Van den Ven, "Les écrits de S. Syméon Stylite le Jeune", *Museon* LXX, 1957, pp. 2–3.

[107] Mansi 12, 1058C–1060B. See Boninus Mombritius, *Sanctuarium seu Vitae*

2. The spurious discourse of Athanasius the Great, *On the Miracle worked in the city of Beirut by the Icon of our Lord Jesus Christ, our True God*, in which is related the welling of blood and water from an icon of Christ when some of the Jews wounded it with a lance in order to mock the person portrayed.[108] Many healings and conversions of Jews to Christianity followed from this.

3. An event from the miracles of Anastasius the Persian in which a woman was healed and subsequently recognised the martyr who had punished her and later healed her from his icon.[109]

4. A letter of St Neilus to the silentiary Heliodorus describing the miraculous intervention of the martyr Plato and his saving of a young monk from enslavement by the barbarians, the monk recognising him "from having frequently seen the likeness of the saint in his icons".[110]

5. An account given to the council by Theodore, bishop of Myra, of the appearance of St Nicholas to his archdeacon, who recognised him from the characteristics of his icon.[111]

6. A fragment from the encomium of Sophronius of Jerusalem on the healing saints, Cyrus and John, who appeared in a vision to a sick man and advised him to anoint himself with oil from a lamp which burned before an icon of Christ situated "in Alexandria, in the great Tetrapylon".[112] When he did this he was immediately cured.

7. Fragments from the miracles of Saints Cosmas and Damian recounting the healing of various sick people through the icons of the two martyrs and their appearances in dreams to them. Particularly striking is the case of the sick woman who was cured by removing a small portion of a wall painting of the saints "with her nails, crushing it to powder with chrism, putting it in water and drinking the mixture, whereupon she was immediately restored to health".[113]

Sanctorum II, Paris, 1910. Cf. L. Wallach, op. cit. pp. 29–30, 153–9, and H.-G. Beck, op. cit. p. 405.

[108] Mansi 13, 24E–32A. Cf. PG 28, 805–12.
[109] Mansi 13, 22C–24D. Cf. H. Usener, *Acta M. Anastasii Persae*, pp. 22–3.
[110] Mansi 13, 32C–33C. Cf. PG 79, 580–1.
[111] Mansi 13, 33D.
[112] Mansi 13, 57E–60B. Cf. PG 87, 3557–60.
[113] Mansi 13, 64B–65D; 68AD. Cf. L. Deubner, *Kosmas und Damian, Bibliotheca Hagiographica Graeca*, 387 (1907) pp. 132–4, 137–8; and 389, 173–4.

8. An account of the healing of Manzon, bishop of Prakanoi, a participant in the council, through the application of the icon of Christ to the affected part and prayer.[114]

9. Two cures of sick people from the *Life of St Symeon of the Wonderful Mountain*, which were effected through his icons, together with the punishment of some people who had tried to tear down an icon of the saint.[115]

10. Two accounts by Constantine, bishop of Constantia and a participant in the council, of people who had insulted icons and had immediately been punished by them.[116]

11. An account of a cure of a man possessed by a demon through an icon of the Theotokos from the *Life of John the Faster*, Patriarch of Constantinople.[117]

12. An account of a miracle of an icon of the Theotokos experienced by Mary of Egypt from her *Life* attributed to Sophronius of Jerusalem.[118]

13. An account from the martyrdom of St Procopius of three icons not made by human hands, which appeared on a cross which had been ordered from a goldsmith by the saint. The craftsman "wished to erase them but was unable to do so, for his hand remained as if withered".[119]

14. An account of two miracles brought about by icons of Christ which were experienced by St Theodore of Sykeon. One was a cure and the other the learning of the whole psalter by heart after prayer. Both are from the *Life* of the saint.[120]

15. Also mentioned as wonder-working over a considerable pe-

---

[114] Mansi 13, 65DE.

[115] Mansi 13, 73C–77B. Cf. Papadopoulos-Kerameus, "Peri tinos syngrapheos Arkadiou Archepiskopou Kyprou mnimonephthisis en tois Praktikois tis Hebdomis Oikoumenikis Synodou", *Vizantijskij Vremennik* I (1894) pp. 606–7, and P. Van den Ven, *Arcadius Constantiensis, La vie ancienne de S. Syméon Stylite le Jeune, Subsidia Hagiographica*, 32, vol. 1, pp. 139–41.

[116] Mansi 13, 77C–80B.

[117] Ibid., 80E–85C. Cf. *Bibliotheca Hagiographica Graeca, 893*, H.-G. Beck, op. cit. p. 459.

[118] Mansi 13, 85D–89A. Cf. PG 87, 3713–16.

[119] Mansi 13, 89BD. Cf. Papadopoulos-Kerameus, *Analekta Hierosolymitikis stachyologias*, vol. V (1898), pp. 5–6.

[120] Mansi 13, 89E–92B. Th. Ioannou, *Mnimia Hagiologika* (1884) *Bibliotheca Hagiographica Graeca*, 1748, pp. 367–8 and 372.

riod of time is "the icon of the immaculate Theotokos in Sozopolis of Pisidia, from whose painted hand flows a stream of myrrh. There are many witnesses of this miracle".[121]

16. Finally, mention is made of the wonder-working icon not made by human hands of the Kamoulianoi.[122]

Accusations of heresy

Furthermore, historical evidence is sought from heretics of earlier times in order to identify the iconophile position with orthodoxy: most of the heretics through the ages had been iconoclasts!

> "We find that the Manichaeans did not accept icons, nor did the Marcionites, nor did those who confuse the nature of Christ, among whome were the heretics Peter the Fuller, Xenias of Hierapolis and also Severus."[123]

Also,

> "our most holy Fathers say that those who denied the incarnate dispensation of Christ our God rejected the holy icons; we refer to the Jews and the Samaritans, Manichaeans and Docetists on account of the holy icons."[124]

Finally,

> "those who join the passion to the Godhead are manifestly Theopaschites and those who participate in this heresy refuse to approach the icons. Such were the impious Severus and Peter the Fuller and Philoxenus of Hierapolis and the entire many-headed and headless hydra that surrounded them. Eusebius also belongs to this gang, as is proved by

---

[121] Mansi 13, 125A. On this icon see R. Cormack, *Writing in Gold*, London 1985, pp. 35, 43, 47, 54, 132.

[122] Mansi 13, 189B. On this see E. Kitzinger, art. cit. pp. 105–6, 117–17, 130–1, 149–50.

[123] Mansi 12, 1031E, Cf. 13, 180E: "For it is not lawful, said Xenias, to give the angels bodies, seeing that they are incorporeal, and represent them as embodied in human form. But neither should one think to assign honour and glory to Christ through an icon produced by painting. One should know that only worship in spirit and in truth is acceptable to him". Cf. Mansi 13, 181E–184B.

[124] Mansi 13, 168D, 196E and 181C. Cf. Ibid., 160D–161E. On Peter the Fuller see H.-G. Beck, op. cit. pp. 285 and 372. Cf. Mansi 13, 357D: "Christians have often been accused by Hebrews and Hagarenes and other unbelievers of such a thing concerning the divine type of the cross and the holy icons and sacred objects dedicated to God, seeing that a Christian has never brought such an accusation against a fellow-believer".

his letters and his historical works; he rejects the icon of Christ like a Theopaschite."[125]

There are testimonies, moreover, to the burning and falsification and destruction of books by both the dissenting factions.[126]

From the above it is evident that the argument from tradition was for both the iconoclasts and the iconophiles the field on which they clashed most bitterly. They were unanimous in attaching the highest significance to tradition as the supreme judge of truth and the source of the correct response and attitude to the question of the icons. It was tradition above all that governed the attitude of the great mass of the faithful, who were unable to participate in any real way in the complicated and erudite theological arguments on behalf of the icons but nevertheless experienced through the icons the presence of God and his saints in their everyday lives.[127]

---

[125] Ibid., 317C. Cf. Ibid., 181B: "Philoxenus taught these things in conformity with the doctrine and put them into practice. For he removed icons of angels from many places and destroyed them. Those of Christ he locked up in storerooms". See also H.-G. Beck, op. cit. pp. 193 and 395, where Philoxenus is identified as an Origenist.

[126] Mansi 13, 176A; 185A, 189BC, 200D.

[127] Cf. P.C. Finney, "Antecedents of Byzantine Iconoclasm", in *The Image and the Word* (ed. J. Gutmann), Missoula 1977, p. 31. E.J. Martin, *A History of the Iconoclastic Controversy*, London, 1930, pp. 130–149, 191–198. P. Alexander, "The Iconoclastic Council of St. Sophia (815) and Its Definition (Horos)", *DOP* 7 (1953) pp. 60–65.

CHAPTER THREE

ICON AS AN AGENT OF TRUTH

Divine truth lies beyond the capacity of the human intellect even at those times when God makes himself known to us through his uncreated energies, which although within our reach and capable of being experienced, nevertheless elude our understanding. Yet "through God we have come to know God, or rather to be known by God", as St Paul has declared (Gal. 4:9). This was to become the central principle of Christian initiation with regard to icons for the Eastern Church Fathers. Two aspects are of particular importance: first that this grace of God's self-revelation is accommodated to the frail capacity of its human recipients, and secondly that in keeping with the principle of the Incarnation, and also of the Bible and the sacraments, it is given to us under sanctified yet tangible and accessible forms.

Education as a Cultural Ideal

The educational ideal of the iconophiles is a continuation of the Greco-Roman tradition on education, without its being identified with this tradition. Education was a "chosen way of life" (*hairesis biou*) for the ancient Greeks. It was not something to be confined to their instruction in their early years. This was expressed in a striking way by Socrates with his famous saying: "I grow old ever learning".[1] Such an approach to education as a process of indefinite duration is the result of deeper anthropological convictions relating to the human desire for learning and the role of the senses, especially of the faculty of sight, in its realisation. The tradition going back to Heracleitus which maintained the superiority of the faculty of sight is summarised by Aristotle at the beginning of the *Metaphysics*:

"All men naturally desire knowledge. An indication of this is our esteem of the senses; for apart from their use we esteem them for their own sake, and most of all the sense of sight. Not only with a view to action, but even when no action is contemplated, we prefer sight, generally speaking, to all the other senses. The reason for this is that of all the senses, sight best helps us to know things, and reveals many distinctions".[2]

---

[1] See Xenophon, *Memoirs*, 4, 4, 5.
[2] Aristotle, *Metaphysics A* 980a 21–7. Cf. Heracleitus, Fragm. 101a; Herodotus,

Here the decisive contribution of sight to learning and to knowledge is clearly apparent. It is precisely this characteristic which is exploited by the Fathers of the Seventh Ecumenical Council when they say: "The icon is greater than the word and this by divine providence took place for the sake of uncultivated people".[3] That which Aristotle ascribes to human nature, the Council ascribes to divine providence. The question of any difference does not arise. What is certain is the fact that the priority of sight — and consequently of the icon — in whatever concerns learning and knowledge is not the result of independent human choice, but exists "by nature" and "by divine providence", inasmuch as the God who provides in this way is also the creator of human nature.

At this juncture the significance should be emphasised of a lifelong education as a Greek cultural ideal which raises man — always according to Greek philosophical conceptions — towards truth. So long as the "desire for knowledge" is natural and thoroughly human, so long as it is based on sight, and so long as it remains unsatiated until the end, what could be more rational for the Greek mentality than seeking to transform human life into a school? The heirs — not mere imitators — of this tradition were the iconophile Fathers of the Church, who "complied with the nature of things".[4] That is to say, they benefited from the infinite possibilities of learning which can become available to us "through the faculty of sight" and they pointed to the figurative tradition of the Gospel and the synaxaries as the supreme "agent of Truth", not of course of scientific truth but of that transforming and saving truth which constitutes the permanent content of the Christian

---

History 1, 8; and Plato, *Timaeus* 45b, 46e, 47a and 47b. Sight is the most acute of the senses: Plato, *Phaedrus* 250d; cf. Aristotle, *On the Senses* 437a.

[3] Mansi 13, 120C. Among ecclesiastical writers sight is elevated above the other senses by Theodoret of Cyrus (c. 393–c. 466), *Historia Religiosa*, PG 82, 1284A and Evagrius (346–399), *Chapters on Prayer*, ch. 150, *Philokalia* vol. 1, p. 189. In Abba Isaac the Syrian (d.c. 700) there is a preference for the teaching of holy men as opposed to simply seeing them, *Ascetic Works*, Oration 5. We encounter a different attitude in the story of Abba Antony's visitor, who on being asked why he remained silent replied: "It is sufficient for me simply to look at you, Father" (*Gerontikon*, Athens, 1970, p. 4). In the iconoclastic period the stress on the superiority of sight over hearing becomes more intense in all the sources. See John Damascene (c. 675–c. 749), *Imag.* 1,17 (Kotter, p. 93); the *Nouthesia Gerontos*, XXIX; Germanus, *Dogmatic Epistles* 2, to John, Bishop of Synada, PG 98, 160B (Mansi, 13, 101E); Theodore of Studius (759–826), *Epistle* 72, to his child Nicholas, PG 99, 1304 (cf. *Antirrheticus* 1, 19, PG 99, 392A); the Patriarch Nicephorus (c. 758–829), *Antirrhesis* 3, 3 (PG 100, 318A), and *Antirrhesis* 3, 5, (PG 100, 384B). Cf. *Apologeticus* 62, PG 100, 748D–749A.

[4] Mansi 13, 325D.

[5] Mansi 13, 249D. In spite of the fact that the Fathers of the Seventh

faith.[5] This content and this alone the Church strives "to impress through vision on the understanding of he beholder", and this imprint constitutes the greatest educational achievement of icons, their most important contribution to the faithful and to catechumens and is regarded as "of all certainly the most sanctifying and salvific".[6]

This fact will be better appreciated if it is borne in mind that an ecclesiastical training is in no way an arid tradition of theological and abstract historical knowledge but is chiefly one's incorporation into an unbreakable communion of people who are being sanctified and saved through the grace of God. The Apostle urges us towards such an incorporation when he says: "Do not be led astray by various strange teachings; for it is good to assure the heart by faith" (Heb. 13:9). The Christian proclamation does not aim simply at persuading the intellect but much more, at assuring the heart "by grace", providing it with the saving and sanctifying experience of the "unanimous" believing community (Acts 4:32 and 2:1). The more the person who undergoes instruction participates in the purifying, illuminating, sanctifying and saving grace and energy of the Holy Trinity, the more "he is assured in his heart". And the more he is assured, the more he is identified with the believing community. This work is not a matter of studying in a school for a short time and following a course of studies which inevitably comes to an end. It becomes a manner of life, a mode of existence, and one grows old always learning and never graduating from the believing community of the Church. We have here a surprising exploitation of the classical Greek educational ideal, which aims not at the simple satisfaction of the natural "appetite for knowledge", but at the salvation of man. For this reason this ideal, soteriologically orientated, found its full and absolute application in a context in which it became consciously the single goal of life, that is to say, in monasticism, which aimed successfully at maintaining intact the cohesion of the protochristian community "assured by grace". Clement of Alexandria called the Church a school

---

Ecumenical Council are in accord with the Aristotelian appetite for "knowing" through the senses, we should not overlook the radical difference that exists when we look at the senses in general from the Christian point of view in relation to the struggle for the purification and perfection of the faithful. In this context the senses are not "loved in themselves" but are mastered and disciplined very harshly (1 Cor. 9:27) for the sake of attaining spiritual perfection. See Athanasius, *On the Councils in Ariminus and Seleuceia*, PG 25, 785B; Thalassius, *Century* 3, 34 (PG 91, 1452A); John Climacus, *Ladder* 1, (PG 88, 633D). Cf. Nicodemus of the Holy Mountain, *On the guarding of the five senses*, Venice 1803, passim, and Isaac the Syrian, the ascetic writings cited by Nicephorus Theotokis, Leipzig 1770, homily 42, p. 175.

[6] Mansi 13, 116A.

(*didaskaleion*), its greatest teachers being the great ascetics and spiritual Fathers, and the supreme schools in due course the hermitages and monasteries.[7]

The Teaching Role of the Icon

Within the framework of such a training and formation, the icon is the supreme educational instrument of universal power, a permanent substitute open book, unaffected by temporal changes and historical coincidences, which never needs revision, which remains always open and immediately accessible to educated and uneducated alike, and which plays, finally, the role of the compass in the "ship of the Church", pointing it unerringly towards supreme truth and reality, an indisputable and enduring guide to truth:

> "There are times when the reading of Scripture is lacking in churches, but the presence of icons in them evening, morning and midday narrates and proclaims to us the truth of what has taken place".[8]

This is the fundamental role of Christian education: to guide one towards saving truth. In contrast with a scientific and rationalistic education, which aims only at the increase of a person's critical capacity and his application to research, the fundamental data of which must always be changing and advancing, the saving truth of Christian faith remains changeless, "yesterday and today the same for ever" (Heb. 13:8), and the conduit of this truth is the icon. It is for this reason that its educational power is so effective, for the divine factor contributes the largest part, that is to say, the uncreated energies which are present in every sacred icon create its effectiveness. In this way the "rapture of the mind", the "awakening" and stimulation of our soul, is brought about that we might imitate the holy personages depicted in the painting.[9]

In view of the didactic significance of icons, it is worth noting the remarks of Cyril of Alexandria which are adduced as arguments on behalf of icons in the second letter of Pope Adrian to the Emperor Constantine VI and Irene. In accordance with these, the

---

[7] Clement of Alexandria, *Paedagogus* 3, 12; cf. Mansi 13, 304DE; 12, 987AB. On monasteries as schools see E. Matsagouras, *The Early Church Fathers as Educators*, Minneapolis 1977, pp. 65–89. It is not a coincidence that in the West the medieval monasteries developed into universities.

[8] Mansi 13, 316A.

[9] Mansi 12, 1062B and 1066D. Cf. Photius, Homily 17 (Image of the Virgin) in *The Homilies of Photius, Patriarch of Constantinople* (ed. C. Mango) DOP 3, 1958, p. 293. See also Germanus, *Dogmatic Epistle* 4, to Thomas of Claudiopolis (PG 98, 1720): and Mansi 13, 113BC, 277C.

earliest form of Christian icons is constituted by the parables of
the Gospels:

> "The parables fulfil for us the function of icons, by putting forward
> the efficacy of what they mean, as if it were accessible to sight and
> to touch, as well as even of those things that may be contemplated
> invisibly in subtle conceptions".[10]

Furthermore, that which animates and literally brings to life in the
eyes of the understanding the saving events and persons of Scripture is faith itself, which St Cyril regards as the primary and most
decisive paintbrush of Christian iconography:

> "For faith depicts the Logos who, being in the form of God, has also
> been brought to God as the redemption of our life, since he has slipped
> into our likeness and become man".[11]

According to this view, the icons which are used by the faithful
are nothing but sacred books "in coarser script", an educational
condescension to the fallen nature of man.[12] Conversely, the same
Holy Scripture may be characterised "a finer" iconography, aimed
at the eyes of the understanding, at least in its historical part,
without of course overlooking in this "representational" approach,
the incomprehensible aspect of the divine mysteries. The only
difference, as we have said, is the immediacy of contact with the
"coarser form" of the icons, the absence of presuppositions for this
contact (such as letters, knowledge, education) and its perpetual
duration. St John Damascene summarised all the representational
advantages in a masterly way in a single sentence: "The icons are
books for the uneducated, heralds that never fall silent but teach
beholders with mute voice and sanctify their sight".[13]

So long as the Christian educational ideal does not aim simply
at the satisfaction of the information-gathering capacity of the
senses, but primarily at the salvation through faith of him who is
being educated, it is understandable that the Church's means of

---

[10] Mansi 12, 1067B. On these fragments of Cyril see L. Wallach, *Diplomatic
Studies in Latin and Greek Documents from the Carolingian Age*, Ithaca and London
1977, pp. 106–107.

[11] Mansi 12, 1967B. Cf. Theodore of Studius, *Epistle to Plato*, PG 99, 505B:
"It should be believed that divine grace enters into it (the icon) and that it
imparts sanctification to those who approach it in faith."

[12] Mansi 12, 1146B.

[13] *Imag.* 1, 47; 11, 43 (Kotter, p. 151). See also Mansi 12, 1059C; Abba Neilus,
Epistle 2 to Eparch Olympiodorus 61, PG 79, 577D–580A; Mansi 13, 36C. "Uneducated persons", according to divine providence, have the possibility of "brief
and compendious instruction" (Germanus, *Dogmatic Epistle 4 to Thomas of*

teaching should not provide simple information but at the same time, and this is most important, should sanctify the organs of sense which receive the divine and saving teaching. With the teaching, then, which is naturally proffered by the sight of the icons "we sanctify hearing with words; for the icon is a reminder or memorial".[14]

It is because of this that the iconophiles believe in the absolute priority of the vision of divine realities, understanding salvation as a vision of truth:

> "The great Moses, seized with fear lest he be deceived in his desire to see the form and likeness, pleaded with God saying: 'Lord, show me yourself plainly, that I may see you;' but God replied: 'If you see me you will die. But go through the hole in the rock and you will see my back'. God showed him in a vision the mystery hidden from the ages and from the generations; but in our generations in the last days he showed himself to us plainly, his back and his front in their entirety".[15]

Nevertheless, the spiritual preparation of the faithful takes place, at least in its first stages, by audio-visual means, as it had been received from the beginning: "And how are they to believe in him of whom they have never heard? And how are they to hear without a preacher?" (Rom 10:14). The claim of the iconophiles lies precisely in this: that colours and forms and shapes could be used to good effect alongside sounds and words so that the Christian message could be rendered more effective. This refers, of course, to a considered use of representational art, just as reason and the expression of language already have a fixed role in the proclamation and never attempt to penetrate the mystery of salvation, or to exhaust it in their formulations, but are content with its necessary and initiatory description.

In this way the icons are shown to be guides to the truths of Christianity and educational means of exceptional influence:

> "Among Christians the icons of holy men who resisted sin even to the shedding of their blood, as the Apostle said, and who served the

---

Claudiopolis, PG 98, 172D; Mansi 13, 113D) in the sacred stories and truths of the faiths, through their pictorial transmission. The sight of the icon leads to immediate contact with saving truths and to knowledge of them. The Fathers of the Seventh Ecumenical Council discern a certain superiority of the icon in relation to the word (Mansi 13, 200).

[14] *Imag.* 1, 17; cf 111, 12. See also Mansi 13, 113D 220E–221A, 232B, 269BC, 348D, 377C.

[15] Mansi, 962E–963A. Cf. Chapter V, p. 111ff.

word of truth. I mean the prophets and apostles, or whoever else were proved to be true servants of God in the piety of their lives and their performance of good works, are nothing other than a pattern of manliness, and a model of virtues and of a splendid way of life, and a stimulus and incitement to the glory of God, whom they pleased in this life. For a discourse which relates the deeds of a good man benefits the hearers and is often invited in order to excite zealous imitation. This would also happen when one gives heed to an icon in a reasonable way. For that which the word of the story presents through the faculty of hearing is that which silent painting shows through imitation, Basil the Great proclaims, saying that those who pay heed are aroused to manliness from both these. For the very representation of each person set down by the painter in the icon becomes for us the beholders a brief and compendious narrative, as one might say, of the exploits attained by that person and so an imitable example just as even in the case of the idols or false gods, their defiled deeds are also in the proper sense exemplified".[16]

The didactic and mystagogic role of the icon is thus made evident. Its effect on every person who beholds it is immediate:

"Such a beholding urges him who has received the deeds of holy men through hearing about them to a remembrance of what he has heard, and prepares him who is ignorant of them to inquire after them and being instructed in them stirs him warmly to the desire for them and praise of God, so that through both of these, those who behold the good works of the saints should praise our Father in heaven".[17]

As has already been noted, the raising of the faithful "to the desire for them and praise of God" — the ascent "with spiritual eyes to the prototype" of every icon, "that the intellect might be furnished with wings through seeing" is regarded as the highest educational ideal.[18]

This raising up has a direct relationship with the salvation of humanity, brings about our repentance, our separation from every erring path, every deceit, and our return to the correct journey towards the true God:

---

[16] Germanus, *Dogmatic Epistle 4, to Thomas of Claudiopolis* (PG 98, 172CD; Mansi 13, 113D). Cf. Mansi 13, 241BD, 116AC, 277C; 12, 1066D. See also D. Tselengidis, op. cit. p. 133, on the characteristic recognition of the icon as a "succinct and compendious narrative".

[17] Mansi 13, 113DE; Germanus, *Dogmatic Epistle 4, to Thomas of Claudiopolis* (PG 98, 173A). Cf. Mansi 12, 978A: "Men and women, embracing ... newly baptised small children and young lads, and those who have come over from paganism, point out to them the stories and thus edify them."

[18] Mansi 12, 114A; 13, 188D; cf. 12, 966B: "they raise the mind and the heart up towards heaven"; also 1014D: "as a compendious narrative, and to stimulate and teach the people, especially the more simple". John Damascene, following Dionysius the Areopagite, accepts the icons as "suitable and natural means of

"For the holy catholic Church of God by various different means draws those who have been born into her to repentance and knowledge of the observance of the commandments of God, and hastens to direct all our senses towards the glory of God who is over all and through hearing and sight works his correction, setting forth the deeds themselves before the eyes of those who draw near: for when she snatches anyone from cupidity and greed, she shows him an icon of Matthew, who became an apostle after having been a tax-collector, abandoned the madness of greed and followed Christ; or of Zacchaeus, who climbed up into a sycamore in his desire to see Christ and through this set aside half of his wealth to provide for the poor and if he had swindled anyone restored it fourfold; and the continual beholding of the representations in the icons becomes a guard against return and a constant reminder, lest one return to one's own vomit. Or again, has she snatched away someone possessed by illicit love? She sets before him the icon of Joseph the chaste, who, loathing fornication and overcoming it with chastity, preserved that which is "in the image", in which those who are lovers of chastity become participants ... and the remembrance of the iconic wall-painting becomes the guardian of the chaste life. Has she snatched away someone who spends his life in luxury and dresses in fine clothes, who wastes what he should give to the poor in such apparel and embraces a soft life? She shows him Elijah wrapped in his fleece and satisfied with frugal nourishment, and John dressed in camel hair and feeding on wild honey ... and along with them Basil the Great and the host of ascetics and monks who hardened their bodies. And not to spin out the discourse ... we have the whole narrative of the Gospel represented in wall-paintings and leading us to the remembrance of God and filling us with joy".[19]

A particularly striking example is the case of the martyr Anastasius the Persian, who was instructed and brought to baptism and, in consequence, to martyrdom by wall-paintings depicting the holy martyrs.[20]

The educational ministration of icons is unlimited:

"For as often as they (the saints and the saving events of the Bible) are seen in iconic representations, in the same degree are those who

---

ascent", since man is unable "to reach up directly to noetic contemplation" (*Imag.* 1, 11, Kotter p. 85). This refers to the necessary "corporeal guide" of Dionysius (*On the Cel. Hier.* 1, 2 PG 3, 121D) or the "uplifting guide" of Nicephorus (*Antirrhesis* 3, 9 (PG 100, 420D). The elevating function of the icon is noted especially in the Dionysian writings: "we ascend through sensible images, as far as possible, to divine contemplation". (*On the Eccles. Hier.* 1, 2, PG 3, 373B). Also: "it is possible through these (i.e. images) to rise up to the immaterial archetypes" (*On the Cel. Hier.* 2, 4, PG 3, 144B. Cf. PG 3, 145B, 377A, 121D). On the significance of the icon as an uplifting power in Dionysius the Areopagite, see esp. D. Koutras, "I ennoia tis eikonos eis ton Pseudo-Dionysion Areopagitin", *EEBS* 35 (1966–7) pp. 256–8.

[19] Mansi 12, 360BE. Cf. Mansi 12, 966A, 1959C; 13, 394E.
[20] Mansi 13, 21B.

behold them stirred to the remembrance of the prototypes and to desire for them".[21]

It may be argued that the sincere placing of oneself before an icon and the extended "communication" which takes place through it between the uncreated, purifying and illuminating energies of the archetype and the beholder who perseveres in faith and prayer, constitutes a guarantee of his salvation:

> "For not only are the sufferings of the saints instructive for our salvation, but so too is the narrative itself of their sufferings, even when represented in icons, as well as their annual commemoration".[22]

Indeed, the icon appears to be for the faithful a pictorial representation of the words and actions of the Logos, both before and after his Incarnation, in his saving and divinising relations with his people and self-communication to them through the prophets and apostles, the lives of the saints and the writings of the Fathers.

The Limitations of the Icon

The icon is used at the first two levels of communication with God (i.e. the levels of purification and illumination) through the Logos and in the Holy Spirit. It is only set aside from time to time, along with the Bible and the doctrines of the Church, during the intervals when glorification/divinisation is experienced which consists in the direct and unutterable vision of the incarnate Logos in the glory of his Father and his Spirit, the glory which he also has by nature as man as a foretaste of the final restoration in the general resurrection.[23]

The icon cannot therefore be considered an accident of historical evolution, since it is an essential extension of the words and actions which have brought the people of God to faith in him and communion with him through his Logos, both before and after the latter's Incarnation by the Holy Spirit, and especially after

---

[21] Mansi 13, 377D; cf. 360C.

[22] Mansi 13, 304A.

[23] In the Apostolic teaching of the Eastern Fathers the same Christ who was revealed in the flesh in the New Testament was at work prior to his Incarnation in the Old Testament. Before his birth from the Theotokos, Jesus Christ in his uncreated person, either as the Angel of God, or as the Angel of Great Council, or as the Lord of Glory, or Lord Sabaoth, or Wisdom of God, is he who appears "in glory" and as the image of God by nature reveals in himself the Father-Archetype to the patriarchs and prophets. The means then by which the prophets knew God was through Christ. So God never becomes known without Christ.

Pentecost when the Church became the body of Christ and was led into all truth (Jn 16:13).

That is why the correct evaluation of icons may be made only within the context of the place of words and concepts about God in the patristic tradition. The classic expression of this is that of St Gregory the Theologian, who says that "to express God is impossible and to conceive of him is even more impossible".[24] This position is founded on the experience of glorification, during which the prophets, apostles and saints have realised that there is no similarity whatsoever between the uncreated and the created and that the human intellect cannot bridge this epistemological gap. It is God who communicates his glory to man so that he may be known in his manifold uncreated energies in creation and redemption, namely, in purification, illumination and glorification. The icon therefore takes its place alongside words and concepts, which are superseded in glorification/divinisation as far as the uncreated is concerned, but nevertheless are used by the glorified to communicate saving truth to the people God has entrusted to them.

Those who attain the state of glorification transcend all created concepts and experience an ineffable contact with God beyond words and concepts. When they communicate their revelation to men, however, they do use words and concepts. These create *"images"* within man which in a paradoxical way do not correspond to tangible realities. For between the human words and concepts on the one hand, and the uncreated realities on the other, there is no similarity at all, and the identification of the two, according to the Fathers, constitutes a sort of idolatry:

> "The divine Logos at the beginning forbids that the Divine be likened to any of the things known by men, since every concept which comes from some comprehensible image by an approximate understanding

---

Athanasius The Great, *Against the Arians* 3, 12–14 (PG 26, 350, 352); Basil the Great, *Against Eunomius* 2, 18 9PG 29, 497); Gregory of Nyssa, *Against Eunomius* 11, 3 (PG 45, 244).

[24] *Theological Oration* 2, 4. St Gregory the Theologian, who had personal experience of glorification, as one "tested and advanced in contemplation" (*Theol. Orat.* 1, 3), attacks the assertion of the Eunomians that man is able to comprehend the essence of God ("the primary and uncompounded nature", *Theol. Orat.* 2, 3). Referring to Plato (probably *Timaeus* 28c) as purportedly asserting that it is difficult for us to conceive of God and impossible to define him or express him in words, he formulates the contrary statement that "it is impossible to express (God) and even more impossible to conceive of him. For that which is conceived reason can probably express, even if not satisfactorily but only dimly . . ." This means that the conception of God, and consequently the attempt to express him, is impossible even for his friends. For even when

and by guessing at the divine nature constitutes an idol of God and does not proclaim God".[25]

Iconoclast Reservations

It may be that the iconoclasts took the higher aspect of the experience of glorification and applied it to icons in its lower aspects without, however, doing the same for the words and concepts contained in the biblical and patristic tradition. This is why the iconophiles detected that the arguments of the iconoclasts against the icons were in reality arguments against the words and concepts about God used by biblical and patristic authors. It is precisely for this reason that the defenders of the icons assert that those who reject them "struggle against both the Church and the truth, for they are not only full of blasphemy, but their speech also has a superabundance of madness and ignorance".[26] It should be said, however, that even the iconoclasts themselves did not dare to deny completely the existence and usefulness of certain icons in the life of the Church.

By accepting the consecrated bread of the divine Eucharist as the unique "true icon of Christ . . . which he who is God and sacred initiator . . . handed down to his initiated as the clearest type and memorial", they also accept in consequence the power which even every "natural" icon contains to become the bearer and channel of a particular message, a particular truth which its maker is attempting to transmit or proclaim: "For what did God in his supreme wisdom devise in this? Nothing other than to show and manifest clearly to us men the mystery realised by him in the dispensation of the economy".[27] In this way, only the divine Eucharist, "sanctified by the overshadowing of the Holy Spirit", constitutes

---

the vision of God has been attained, God remains a mystery. Nevertheless, the glorified friends of God make use of words and images replete with the experience of glorification in order to assist and guide those on the lower stages of the road to perfection.

[25] Those who attain the state of glorification transcend all created concepts and experience an ineffable contact with God beyond words and concepts. When they communicate their revelation to men, however, they do use words and concepts. These create "images" within man which in a paradoxical way do not correspond to tangible realities. For between the human words and concepts on the one hand and the uncreated realities on the other there is no similarity at all and the identification of the two, according to the Fathers, constitutes a sort of idolatry. See Gregory of Nyssa, *The Life of Moses* 2, 165 (SC p. 112); Athanasius the Great, *Against the Arians* 3, 14 (PG 26, 352A); Gregory of Nyssa, *Against Eunomius*, PG 45, 604, 904C.

[26] Mansi 13, 325E.

[27] Mansi 13, 261E, 64A.

"a genuine icon of the natural flesh (of Christ)" in contradistinction to the "so-called icons" of the iconophiles.[28]

Although they admit in this way the function even of the natural icon as supplying a communication of Truth, they would never prefer to portray Christ or the saints in an imitative way but "rather depict their virtues" through "things revealed about them in written documents as if painting living icons in themselves and stirring up from this zeal for emulation".[29] In spite of all this they do not completely exclude the use of icons, at least as didactic and hortatory means with the capacity to suggest saving truths, "saying it is sufficient to have iconic representations only as memorials and not for veneration".[30] It may therefore be said that with regard to the icons in general being either teachers and communicators of truths or else misleading, according to the subject portrayed, there is no disagreement between the iconoclasts and the iconophiles.

The Emotional Response to the Icon

The icons, moreover, conceal a "psychological need" of the faithful. One might be so bold as to assert that they fulfil in a more exalted manner the role which today various mementoes play in our lives, even souvenirs, photographs, tapes and videos. The Seventh Ecumenical Council seems to have been fully aware of the great psychological significance which the didactic "principle of contemplation" exercises in the field of Christian faith:

> "We have believed these to be true through hearing, and we confirm them through pictorial imitation for our greater assurance, for constituted as we are of flesh and blood, we hasten through seeing to make the assurance of our souls more secure".[31]

Here, however, we are dealing not with a simple application of this didactic principle but with a psychological need to give sensible expression to the transcendent certainties of faith, since, as we have already said, conviction does not spring from sensory vision but is supplied "by grace" to the heart of the believer. Consequently, a sign of the "assurance" already given by divine grace to the soul of the believers is the very making of the icon. This means that no one apart from the believer has any right to put up icons of

---

[28] Mansi 13, 264B, 268CD.
[29] Mansi 13, 345D.
[30] Mansi 13, 364B.
[31] Mansi 13, 101E; cf. 44E–45C.

holy persons and the events of sacred history.[32] The use of icons may be compared with modern cable television which only members or subscribers have the right to receive. The painting of icons has the strict intention of fulfilling a function within the believing community. Every other function or use of icons without reference to, or apart from, educating the actual Christian community, "assuring" it and guiding it into all truth, is not simply senseless but may also be considered a profanation of the sacred icons in the thought of the theologians of our period. If this is not expressed explicitly in the sources we have been considering, it is due solely to the fact the Fathers of the Seventh Ecumenical Council and the authors of the period never in practice encountered such a phenomenon.[33] Moreover, this can also be easily deduced from the fact that the iconophiles never appealed to parallel examples of the use of icons outside Christianity, whereas their opponents by contrast appealed precisely to such examples in order to deliver a mortal blow to the authenticity and exclusivity of Christian icons, believing that if they demonstrated something of this kind they would make a decisive contribution to their abolition.[34]

Indeed there is a hint in the iconoclasts' line of argument which indicates that they attribute the use of icons to historical coincidence, etiquette or external influence: "bowing to the authority of imperial edicts".[35] That is to say, they mean that the iconophiles were taught the practice and theory of their stand on icons in some manner which was unconscious or unperceived by them. Such an interpretation, however, is resisted most strenuously by the iconophiles themselves, who did not defend, it seems, the honouring of icons as a simple historical development, or as an ecclesiastical tradition which could equally as well not have happened or been instituted, but as an authentic institution and Christian completion of the original deposit of faith:

---

[32] On this see also the 7th canon of the Council of Constantinople of 869, Mansi 14, 401–3.

[33] In our epoch the Orthodox icon is for most people a sought-after object of high artistic and archaeological-historical significance. For this reason it is exhibited in museums even in Orthodox countries or in an Orthodox milieu, a fact which simply demonstrates the cessation of its ecclesiastical function and its abuse or misuse regardless of whether or not this is done with full awareness. Moreover, the contemporary presentation of the icon as a "work of art" constitutes clear support for the point of view that for the iconophiles the icon is not regarded as a work of art. It appears that the more the liturgical and ecclesiastical exclusivity of the icon is set aside, the more it degenerates into becoming an artistic product of individual skill, and in consequence becomes the object of praise or censure with style as the only criterion.

[34] See e.g. Mansi 13, 277D, 280BC.

[35] Mansi 13, 121D.

"And to say what is essential" — this refers to the letter of Germanus of Constantinople to Thomas of Claudiopolis, which was read during the fourth session of the Council — "in no way do Christians paint the form of their physical relations or their acquaintances and friends and venerate the pictures. Nor do they give them any honour, nor even do they entertain the thought of such a thing as a result of bowing to the authority of imperial edicts".

Is this assertion a direct consequence of a particular use of icons? Does it mean perhaps that real Christians regard as true relations and true friends only those persons depicted in the icons, namely, the saints, and in consequence regard as the only eternal and definitive king not the temporal emperor but Christ and that is why they represent him in this way?[36] Surely the answer to these questions is in the affirmative. Moreover, the iconophiles seem to be anxious to stress that they are taught by God to depict the sacred personages and events and to regard these sacred representations as the most authentic means of edification which the Church has at her disposal. Every attempt to present the icons as the products solely of a historical process is vigorously resisted.

The emotional factor, too, should not be overlooked as an educational means which the icons, especially the wonder-working ones, bring into play. The iconophiles did not leave even this aspect unexploited in their desire to indicate that contact with truth through the icons constitutes for a person his most vivid educational experience. Thus the Seventh Ecumenical Council adduces patristic witnesses who are able to demonstrate the positive contributions of the holy forms to the supply of consolation, courage, hope, endurance, inspiration and generally, all the elevating states of the soul which are indispensable in the life of the faithful. The first witness is St John Chrysostom, who refers to the case of St Meletius of Antioch. Describing the conditions of St Meletius's exile, Chrysostom says that the inconsolable flock of his city began to draw the form of their exiled pastor

"on rings, seals and bowls, on the walls of rooms and everywhere . . .

---

[36] Cf. Mansi 12, 1146A; 13, 45A, 101D; John Damascene, *Imag.* 111, 26, 75–82; 33, 35–37 (Kotter, pp. 135 and 138). See also, Jn 15:14 and John Damascene, *Imag.* 111, 41, 20; 26, 35–37; 1, 14 (Kotter, pp. 142, 133, 87). On the honouring of the emperor's icon as a historical phenomenon which preceded the widespread use of Christian icons and iconoclasm, see L.W. Barnard, "The Emperor Cult and the origins of the iconoclastic controversy", *Byzantion* 43 (1973) pp. 13–29, and S. Gero, "Byzantine Iconoclasm and the failure of a medieval reformation" in *The Image and the Word*, ed. by J. Gutmann, Missoula, Montana, 1977, p. 50.

so as not only to hear that holy consolation but also to see the form of his body everywhere and receive a double consolation for his absence".[37]

Further evidence is provided by St Gregory of Nyssa, who in his homily *On the Divinity of the Son and the Spirit and on Abraham* relates his personal experience on beholding an icon representing the Sacrifice of Isaac in the following words:

"I often saw a painted icon of the passion and approached the sight not without tears, the artist's skill vividly bringing the story before my eyes".[38]

The Council's comment on this text is sufficiently expressive:

"If the representation benefited such a teacher, how much more should it bring compunction and benefit to the uneducated".[39]

And:

"If St Gregory, who kept a vigilant eye upon divine truths shed tears, which arose at the sight of the icon of Abraham, how more does the depiction of the incarnate economy of our Lord Christ, who became man for us, benefit those who behold it and move them to shed tears".[40]

The definitive conclusion of the Council is formulated immediately afterwards: The icon-painters "present that which Scripture narrates, so that they become advocates of what is written".[41] The "advocacy" of Scripture by the icons constitutes a fundamental argument of the iconophiles in support of their ideas about the icons as bearers and instruments of truth.

The Value of Matter

The basic error of their opponents in this context lies in their theoretical presuppositions which are at least of an Origenist nature if not of purely Greek provenance, according to which matter, found in a "fallen" state and alienated from God, cannot possibly become a means expressive of truth, and especially of saving and divine truth. This confusion is easily pinpointed by the iconophiles:

---

[37] Mansi 13, 8D.
[38] Ibid. 9C.
[39] Ibid. 9E.
[40] Ibid. 12A.
[41] Ibid. 20D.

"What then, taking matter as defiled do they wish to abuse the truth?".[42] They refute it with an apposite example: In the Old Testament there is a reference to sacrifices of material good things which were offered to God but also to the demons. In both cases the "matter" of these sacrifices was absolutely the same. And although when this matter was offered to God, Scripture speaks in terms of praise of "holy sacrifices", when the same "matter" was offered to demons, "although being the same matter it was nevertheless full of defilement".[43] That is to say, the iconophiles did not maintain a position diametrically opposed to that of their opponents. According to the latter, matter was and is defiled, is to be rejected, and is altogether useless for helping to produce divine and sacred results. According to the defenders of the icons, however, matter is not the exact opposite of this, but whether it is honoured or not depends upon its use. Of course essentially matter is "God's creation" and "very good" (Gen. 1:13).[44] It is possible, however, after the Fall for the misuse or abuse of matter to take place for purely Satanic purposes. The iconophiles observe that in these cases matter is truly unable to co-operate in the business of man's salvation and cannot become a means and instrument of expression of truth. Nevertheless, nothing is capable of alienating matter entirely from its original divine provenance and making it essentially "evil". From the Christian point of view such an alienation is absolutely impossible for any being. In conclusion, then, the Fathers of the Seventh Ecumenical Council declare: "The usefulness of matter should not be overlooked just because it is vilified or shown to be base through being used for various contrary purposes". After the Fall, matter is offered as an open potentiality, as much for the adoration of God as for the service of the demons. Its manner of use renders it sometimes "full of every defilement", as in the case of idolatrous sacrifices, and sometimes "full of divine energy and grace", as in the case of the holy icons, the bread of the divine Eucharist, and all ecclesiastical uses in general.[45]

Admittedly, the iconophiles deliver one of their most effective blows against their opponents by associating the infinite possibilities

---

[42] Ibid. 280A.
[43] Ibid. 280B.
[44] John Damascene, *Imag.* 11 (Kotter, p. 104ff); 1, 16 (Kotter, p. 89ff) and 1, 36, 19–22 (Kotter, p. 148): "Although the matter is not to be worshipped in itself, if the person depicted is full of grace, it becomes a partaker of grace in proportion to faith".
[45] John Damascene, *Imag.* 1, 16, 15; 36 (Kotter, p. 88ff, 147ff). The iconophiles asked whether Christian books should be abolished simply because the Greeks celebrated their "gods and daemons in historical books"; (Mansi 13, 280C).

of matter with good — as a result of the evangelisation and salvation of the world — and by taking matter and making it a bearer and herald of Truth: "For being men endowed with senses, we use sensible things to enable us to recognise and remember every divine and pious tradition".[46]

Finally, in their guise as aids for teaching and proclaiming the faith, the icons also provided historical justification for their defenders' claim that throughout the centuries they preserved the truth of the Christian faith in representational form. St Basil the Great is utilised in a telling manner in the iconoclastic period by John Damascene for an incomparable expression of the yearning of the orthodox for the vision of truth.

In a fragment of his discourse on the martyr Gordius, the Archbishop of Caesarea develops in a striking way the significance which the vivid reconstruction of the death of the first martyrs and confessors has for faithful Christians of every period. As a result, the most intimate contact with that saving reality is achieved and the intensity of the impression in the soul of such experiences is not weakened, as happens inevitably when painters, copying pictures in a tradition, distance themselves from their living prototypes. This example is invoked by John Damascene, who transforms it into an argument which stresses the unparalleled contribution which the icons make to knowledge and to the transmission of saving truth, since through these the prototypes are made present:

> "and indeed this is no small thing, accurately to attain to the truth of those who lived before us . . . and how it seems to us to be like that of the painters; for they, because they copy icons from other icons, usually abandon the archetypes; and when we fall short of the actual vision of reality, there is no small danger that the truth will be diminished".[47]

Where truth encounters the "vision of reality", that is to say, in the orthodox icon, there the Church discerns the most exalted form of education.[48]

---

[46] Mansi 13, 280D.

[47] Basil The Great, *Hom.* 19 to Gordius the Martyr, PG 31, 493A. Cf. John Damascene, *Imag.* 1, 39; 11, 35 (Kotter, p. 49ff).

[48] The etymology of the word *anthropos* (from *ano throsko* = I look upwards) permits the additional conclusion that the vision of truth constitutes not simply the ideal education of man but also his appointed end. This is confirmed by the eschatological teaching of the Church, that eternal life will be the ceaseless vision of God for the worthy. As John Chrysostom observes, interpreting Jn 17:24, "that they might see my glory", "every rest is this: to have access to the vision of the Son of God". Doubtless, a foretaste of such a rest of ceaseless vision is provided in the present world by the icons.

CHAPTER FOUR

ICON AND REALITY

The attitude of the iconoclasts to the icon of Christ in particular and of the saints in general betrays a distinctive cosmological point of view, a more or less precise conception of the world of existent things and of matter, in short a polarisation of the relationship between created things and their uncreated Maker. The questions which the sources allow us to put are these:

1. Do the iconoclasts admit a distinction between divine essence and divine energy, and if so, do they allow created things to participate in either of them and in what manner?
2. Are there elements of dualism or Manichaeism in their hostility to the material world?
3. What kind of conception of reality do their views represent?
4. Is there evidence of Jewish or pagan Greek influence on their views?

The Deification of Matter

The scanty information provided by the surviving sources does not allow us to answer these questions easily. Nevertheless, it appears from the iconoclasts' acceptance of the "deification" (*theosis*) of the bread of the Eucharist "as through a certain sanctification by grace" that, unlike their opponents, they do not admit any real distinction between divine essence and divine energy. At the same time they regard matter as generally "ignoble" (*adoxon*) "common and worthless" (*koinen kai atimon*) and, moreover, the hands of the painter as "profane" (*deilous*) and, by extension, his work similarly so to such a degree that it is impossible either for the material or for the work of art produced from it to be sanctified by "sacred prayer".[1] Therein lies the following paradox: Although they accept the "deification" of matter in the unique case of the sanctified bread of the Eucharist, they appear to reject any other possibility of the sanctification of reality. The sources do not permit an exhaustive investigation of the question, but the iconoclasts would seem obliged to recognise the possibility of sanctification at least for the water of baptism and the oil of chrismation. This shows them to contradict

---

[1] Mansi 13, 247E, 264B, 268C, 277D

themselves, since they are unable to determine what receives sanctification in the material world and what does not and why this should be so in either case.

Clearly this hostility of the iconoclasts to matter springs directly from the possibilities for iconic representation inherent in it, which they immediately associate with the pagan manufacture of idols. Moreover, although one would have expected that on the basis of this association the iconoclasts would have rejected anything "Greek" as idolatrous, one is struck by their insistence that "our catholic Church of Christians is situated in between Hellenism and Judaism".[2] The iconophiles will easily refute this paradoxical assertion by stressing the vigorous opposition of the Church to both these orientations in the words of Basil the Great: "Judaism wars with Hellenism and both war with Christianity".[3]

Thus the iconoclasts' conception of reality, in spite of its external reliance of the Jewish aniconic tradition, does not differ very much, on their own admission, from the diametrically opposed Greek tradition. With regard to their arguments concerning the eucharistic bread as alone having the exclusive power to represent Christ, we can clearly discern a totally Greek distinction between "matter" and "shape", or "form", as Aristotle would have said:

> "Just as that which Christ received from us is the matter alone of a human substance perfect in every respect, which does not characterise an individually subsisting person, lest an additional person be admitted into the Godhead, so also the image is offered of special matter, namely, the substance of bread, which does not represent the shape of a man, lest idolatry be introduced".[4]

Idolatry, then, does not arise primarily from the use of matter in itself, but chiefly from the human "shape". Such is their aversion to any representation of "shape" that they even accept the bread of the Eucharist as a representation of Christ precisely because it excludes any "shape", being "shapeless" or "formless".

To be exact, they do not mean that through the eucharistic

---

[2] Mansi 13, 273C.
[3] Basil the Great, *Against Sabellius* 1, PG 31, 600.
[4] Mansi 13, 264ABD. Cf. Tertulian (d. after 220), *On Idolatry*, 3: Igitur omnis forma vel formula idolum se dici exposcit. The source of this distinction is Aristotle, *Metaphysics* VII, 3, 1029a2–4. Of course in Aristotle existents also participate in being by virtue of their form (*Metaphysics*, IX, 8, 1050b2; VIII, 2, 1043a18–20, 1043b1–2). The iconoclasts, of course, have no conscious desire to be taken for Aristotelians, nor do I accept that they represent an Aristotelian philosophical tendency. The distinction which they attempt to make here seeks only to serve their immediate aims in their struggle against the iconophiles.

bread, at least, Christ himself is represented as a real presence, but that only the fact of his incarnation is represented. The sanctified bread is "the true image of the economy of the incarnation of Christ" not of Christ himself.[5]

A Hidden Origenism?

With such a conception of "form" (*morphe*), the iconoclasts depart radically from biblical, especially Pauline, terminology which regards the term "form" as synonymous with "nature" (*physis*) or "substance" (*ousia*) (Phil. 2:6–7). By interpreting the bread as the unique form or type (*typos*) with the power to represent his incarnation, but without the power to represent the actual humanity of his person, the iconoclasts believe that they have found a satisfactory solution to the problem of idolatry, since in their view the problem consists precisely in the worship of "forms", whereas the bread is "formless" (*amorphos*).[6] The fact, then, that the iconoclasts reject specifically the "form" or "shape" and not matter in itself does not permit us to attribute dualistic or Manichaean conceptions to them. The following questions, however, still remain:

1. How do they conceive of created reality in general, since "shapelessness" and "formlessness" do not prevail in the material world?
2. Why in their opinion is matter "worthless", "common" and "ignoble", and not "very good" as it is described in the Bible? (Gen. 1:31)

These two unanswered questions, in conjunction with the tendency of the iconoclasts to use Greek philosophical distinctions, such as that between form and matter, lead us to suspect a hidden Neoplatonism, surviving within an Origenistic system.[7] Is it possible, then that the iconoclasts have been influenced by an Origenistic cosmology?[8] Only an influence of this kind could have justified such views as: "What is this senseless contrivance (*anoetos epinoia*) of the foolish painter ... who pursues the unattainable, which is

---

[5] Mansi 13, 264C.
[6] Mansi 13, 264A.
[7] Cf. Plotinus, *Enneads* II, 4, 5, 6–8.
[8] See J.N.D. Kelly, *Early Christian Doctrines*, London 1977 (5th ed.) pp. 180–2, where it is rightly stressed that according to Origen, "while corporeity can be regarded as the penalty of the fall, it is really an aspect of the diversity belonging to the level of existence to which fallen spirits have been reduced". Cf. *De Prin.* 2, 1, 4.

to form with profane hands that which is believed in the heart and confessed with the mouth?"[9]

There is apparent here an idealism which detests the sensible world of matter and regards the giving of form to the invisible and "unattainable" as profanity. An undertaking of this kind constitutes an invention, a "contrivance" which is utterly "senseless".

For the iconoclasts it is inconceivable that one should transfer "intelligibles", or intelligible reality, to the sensible world and thus make them accessible to the uninitiated and profane. In Origen's eschatology is found the conception that bodies will become "intellects" once again, restored to the primeval state from which they fell to the sensible world and received specific shape and "form". This is also true *a fortiori* of the body of Christ after the Resurrection.[10]

This perhaps explains both (a) the unwillingness of the iconoclasts to reject icons entirely (since they accept the eucharistic bread as an image of the incarnation of the Logos, and the virtues of the saints "as certain animated images" which can be painted inwardly in each believer), and also (b) their attack on lifeless and dumb matter and material colours, since they regarded representation by material and sensible means as a product of idolatrous Hellenism "which became the pioneer and inventor of this abominable workmanship. For not having the hope of resurrection, it contemplated a trifle worthy of it, in order to make that which is not present, present by illusion".[11]

The persistent reference to the resurrection as an argument against icons is strong evidence of the clear influence of an Origenistic eschatology on the iconoclasts: "for it is not lawful for Christians who have acquired hope in the resurrection to adopt the customs of the gentile demon-worshippers and to insult the saints, — who are destined to shine in such glory, — with ignoble and dead matter".[12]

The matter that they keep repeating is lifeless, dead and ignoble reflects their conviction that matter has no place in the resurrection, and will not be glorified in the restoration of all things at the end

---

[9] Mansi 13, 248E. On the significance of the participation of *nous* in the production of a statue or an icon or an ex-voto offering, see E. Bevan, *Holy Images. An Inquiry into Idolatry and Image-Worship in Ancient Paganism and Christianity*, London 1940, pp. 78–80.

[10] Origen, *On Jeremiah*, XV, 6, 18–21: "Although the Saviour witnesses that which he put on was man, even if it was man it is now in no way man; for 'even though we once regarded Christ according to the flesh, we regard him thus no longer' (2 Cor. 5:16)" SC 238, Paris 1977, p. 126. On the eschatology of Origen more generally, see J.N.D. Kelly, op. cit. pp. 470–1.

[11] Mansi 13, 345D, 273D, 276D, 277D.

[12] Mansi 13, 277D.

of the ages. Most probably this is their deepest reason for calling
images "false and spurious" (*pseudonymous kai kakonymous*).[13] Since
neither Christ nor the saints are to have material bodies in the
life to come, it follows that the material likenesses of the iconophiles
are falsely and spuriously called icons of Christ or of the saints.
The iconoclasts are more insistent with regard to the icon of Christ
since Christ has already been resurrected while the saints are still
waiting. It is surprising that the charge of Origenism was not levelled
formally against them. Perhaps this is because the iconophiles
associated the iconoclasts chiefly with Manichaeans, Paulicians,
Cathars, Novatianists and Messalians.

There is however, the clearest hint in the Seventh Ecumenical
Council that the belief of the iconoclasts in the resurrection and
eternal punishment and requital of the dead was openly disputed.[14]
More specifically, the Seventh Ecumenical Council, commenting
on the definition of the iconoclast council of 754 — on the passage:
"if anyone does not confess the resurrection and judgment and
requital of the dead ... and that there is no end to punishment
or to the kingdom of heaven ... let him be anathema" — observed
the following: "This is the confession of the catholic Church and
not of the heretics." Was the Ecumenical Council aware of the
Origenistic tendencies of the iconoclasts? But if such tendencies
indeed existed, why was such an anti-Origenistic clause added to
the definition of faith of Hiereia? Could the iconoclasts have tried
in this way to allay suspicions that they were Origenising? Perhaps
they regarded the goal of securing a condemnation of the icons
as sufficient for the time being, recognising that they would have
undermined their position if they had revealed that their motives
were Origenistic. Or most probably, the broad stance of iconoclasm
and its adoption by a series of emperors did not necessarily
presuppose the adoption or even the general knowledge of such
motives. The question remains open.

The bodies of Christ and the saints are described by the iconoclasts as "not present" (*me paronta*).[15] This may very well have the
eschatological meaning that the time of the parousia has not yet
arrived, when all bodies will appear immaterial and "intellectual"
— they will no longer be "bodies". In this sense one may well look
forward to the resurrection of the dead without implying of necessity

---

[13] Mansi 13, 268C.
[14] Mansi 13, 349D. See also Mansi 12, 1031E; 13, 161B, 168D, 317C; and John
Damascene, *Imag.* II, 13, 2 (Kotter, p. 104).
[15] Mansi 13, 273D.

a resurrection of their bodies. This is perhaps the reason why they explain that

> "the saints who have pleased God and have been honoured by Him with the dignity of sanctity live forever unto God, even when they have departed from this life; he who thinks to raise up images of their bodies in a dead and abhorrent workmanship which has never lived, but has been discovered in vain by the Greeks, our adversaries, proves himself to be a blasphemer".[16]

This passage compels us to ask ourselves if, apart from questions of images, the iconoclasts acknowledge the intercessions of the saints and the possibility of their invocation by the faithful, seeing that the saints are absent from the present world and have no contact with matter or the senses: "They have departed from this life". They themselves appear to accept the mediation of the saints and to refer to it during the Council of Hiereia (754) but the iconophiles accuse some of them of denying it.[17] The important thing for them is that every attempt to "raise up" the material bodies of the saints as icons is blasphemous since such bodies will not exist in the final resurrection. Besides, sanctity is regarded as a "dignity" (*axioma*) and it is clear that this dignity does not refer to an actual participation in the deifying energy of God, but simply to an attainment of a contemplative prelapsarian state of perfection. Yet the saints are considered to be "honourable before God in soul and in body". Whether these already honoured bodies are to be understood as material or immaterial is a question never answered by them.

One understands in consequence why the iconoclasts place Christianity in between Judaism and Hellenism, with the result that they can borrow elements from both in an eclectic way without, however, aligning themselves with either. They know, then, that they are not as hostile to images as is traditional Judaism, since they accept certain images of a spiritual, symbolic and intellectual nature, nor are they as idealistic as the Greeks, since they accept the resurrection, spiritualisation and restoration of the material world, rather than a perpetual cycle as the Greeks did. We are in fact dealing here with a distinctive combination of eschatological elements which are strongly Origenistic, the iconoclasts like Origen understanding as "real" and existing in a proper sense that which

---

[16] Mansi 13, 276D. Cf. Theodore of Studius, *Antir.* I, PG 99, 336B.
[17] Mansi 13, 348E, 345A, Cf. John Damascene, *Imag.* I, 19 (Kotter, pp. 94–5); Nicephorus, *Antir.* II, 6, PG 100, 344B–345B.

is spiritualised or returns to a certain primeval "intellectuality", and as non-existent and evil — almost "non-being" — in a proper sense that which still remains sensible and material, with certain important contradictions, as we have seen. The sanctification of the material world is essentially incompatible with such conceptions, for in a sense that which is sanctified ceases to be material any longer. Sanctification and materialisation are parallel processes and it is almost impossible for the iconoclasts to distinguish between them.

Matter and Evil

Finally, the iconoclasts leave unanswered the questions regarding what matter is in itself, and why it is worthless, common and ignoble.

Against this iconoclast idealism which identifies the real solely with the intellectual, the iconophiles oppose a surprising confidence in and insistence upon that which exists, whether it be material or spiritual. Their conception of reality is genuinely factual. They accept it exactly as it is, as God wanted it to be, as each individual thing originally subsists. Centering themselves on the defence of images, on the vindication of the natural power to represent in art a reality which is enduring and circumscribed, particularly that of bodies, they accept a cosmology which respects the created and honours the positive role of matter with respect to man's salvation. Thus they recognise as real the empirical data of the senses, see no opposition between intellectual and material beings — since the same God is the Creator of both — and believe in the possibility of the sanctification of bodies and of all the material elements which contribute to the realisation of the divine economy: "I do not worship matter; I worship the Creator of matter, who became matter for me and condescended to dwell in matter, and through matter effected my salvation; and I will not cease to venerate the matter through which my salvation was effected".[18]

Strictly speaking, the orthodox believe in the deification of matter in the unique case of the body of Christ by reason of the hypostatic union, and of the saints even before their resurrection by reason of their union by grace with the deifying energy of the Holy Trinity which is the raison d'être for the veneration of holy relics. They do not, however, accept the deification of the eucharistic bread as do the iconoclasts even though they do not doubt that it is the

---

[18] John Damascene, *Imag.* I, 16 (Kotter, p. 89).

body of Christ, which is by nature the source of all uncreated divine energies, and that it communicates to the worthy a proportionate share of those energies.

The insistence of the iconophiles on regarding as existent, absolutely real and "very good" only that which has been created by God is clearly evident in their attitude to matter:

> "Do not vilify matter; it is not worthless. Nothing is worthless which has been brought into being by God; this is the opinion of the Manichaeans. The only thing which is worthless is that which did not take its cause from God but is our own invention by the voluntary inclination and propensity of the will away from that which is according to nature towards that which is contrary to nature, namely, sin".[19]

According to this conception, that which does not exist in reality, which is to say, that which does not have the cause of its existence in God, is evil. "Evil" starts precisely wherever reality is distorted. For that reason it is very naturally considered non-existent or without substance by the Eastern Fathers of the Church, who had understood that one "sins" as soon as one has begun to endow with subsistence "things" which the uncreated will of the Holy Trinity did not create, from the moment when one begins to accept and to live "states" which have no subsistence in the sight of God.[20] And to give subsistence to that which is non-subsistent, is of course a contrivance, an "invention", "Art" which can deflect one from "that which is in accordance with nature to that which is contrary to nature". No product, however, of deflection and apostasy can have equal value with the works of God. Nothing which comes forth from the voluntary "deflection" and "propensity" of any created will is worthy or able to be included within the divinely constructed reality of spiritual or intellectual creation, which "has come into being in accordance with God's will". Every escape from this unique reality, every imagined or "poetic" flight to "worlds" beyond the one that "is very good" (Gen. 1:31) unavoidably entails a fall from

---

[19] John Damascene, *Imag.* I, 16 (Kotter, p. 90) Cf. Mansi 13, 280B.: "Matter is not reproached because it is used in a way contrary to some things; for it to be shown to be disgraceful, one must overlook its usefulness".

[20] See e.g. Maximus The Confessor, *Ambigua*, PG 91, 1332A: "Evil . . . whose being is characterised by non-existence"; Gregory of Nyssa, *Great Cat. Orat.* 5, PG 45, 25A: "Evil is something which in itself has no existence"; Basil the Great, *Against Eunomius* 2, 19, PG 29, 612DC: "Those who have not been united in faith to the God who is have been assimilated to the non-existence of falsehood"; John Damascene, *Against the Manichaeans* 1, 13, PG 94, 1517A: "Evil is a privation of being"; Ibid. 1, 27, PG 94, 1532A: "Therefore evil . . . if entirely evil and entirely a state of corruption will also be self-destructive and self-annihilating".

being and entry into the "total deprivation of essence and existence"
of sin, which the devil's love of self has inaugurated.[21] This insistence
of the iconophiles on reality and its goodness and their confidence
in it, constitutes a realism unrivalled for its immediacy, the chief
characteristics of which we shall attempt to describe in what follows.

Iconophile Realism

The iconophiles, faithful to reality as God desired it and created
it, do not claim to represent that which exists in general, but only
truths which are circumscribed and possess dimensions and are
immediately relevant to man's salvation in Christ. Accordingly they
refuse to represent the first person of the Holy Trinity, the Father,
since he totally transcends every sensory experience: "Why do we
not describe and paint the Father of the Lord Jesus Christ? Because
we do not know who he is, and it is impossible for the nature
of God to be described and painted".[22]

Nothing reveals more clearly the iconophiles' insistence on reality
as God desired it than this point of view. For them sin is properly
one's desire to make possible the impossible — that which is non-
natural and non-existent, that which God has not called into being.
That is why we read repeatedly that the representation of created

---

[21] Maximus the Confessor, *Scholia on the 'Divine Names'*, PG 4, 305B. Cf. the
same author's *Centuries on Theology* I, 49: "Anything that has predicated of it
something of the logos of being is a work of God." On this crucial point for
the understanding of the iconophile arguments as a whole, see the excellent
study of Edwyn Bevan, *Holy Images*, pp. 80–95.
    The fall from being and "total deprivation of essence and existence" is not
to be confused with the "non-being" from which God has created the world.
This "non-being" is good according to the Eastern theological tradition as
expressed by Ps.-Dionysius: see *On the Divine Names* IV, 19, (PG 3, 716D): "Evil
is not a being; for if it were, it would not be totally evil. Nor is it a non-being;
for nothing is completely a non-being, unless it is said to be in the Good in
the sense of beyond-being. For the Good is established far beyond and before
simple being and non-being. Evil, by contrast, is not among the things that have
being nor is it among what is not in being. It has greater non-existence and
otherness from the Good than non-being has" (trans. C. Luibheid). Also striking
is the argument in favour of icons put forward at the Seventh Ecumenical Council
from a story in the *Leimonarion* of John Moschus (mid sixth century) (PG 87,
2900BD). In this story a demon promises an ascetic to deliver him from his
long struggle against the flesh if he ceases to honour the icon of the Theotokos
which he has in his cell (Mansi 13, 60E). Clearly we have here a perception
of evil as something which fights against reality. Cf. Origen, *On Jeremiah* XVI,
9, SC 238, p. 152.
[22] Mansi 12, 963D; 13, 101A. Cf. John Damascene, *Imag.* II, 5, 1: "For if we
had made an icon of the invisible God we would have sinned: for it is impossible
for that which is incorporeal, formless, invisible and uncircumscribed to be
represented pictorially". See also II, 7, 35. Cf. Theodore of Studius, *Antir.* 2,
PG 99, 353D.

sacred realities (e.g. the bodies of the saints or of Christ, the events of sacred history) follows the nature of things, constituting an immediate realism:

"For we do not represent the simple, incomprehensible divine existence in certain forms and shapes; nor have we determined to honour in wax and wood that essence which is beyond essence and before eternity".[23] "On the contrary, we make icons of created men, of the holy embodied servants of God, to mark their memory and honour them, and we do nothing unreasonable in painting them as they were created . . . And when we venerate, we glorify not the icons but the personages indicated in this way by pictorial means. And we do not glorify them as gods — God forbid. I refer to our Lord and Saviour Jesus Christ as he was seen on earth and described by men who met him, and not as God by nature as he is conceived to be; for what likeness or what form belongs to the incorporeal and formless Logos of the Father?"[24] "Who does not know that when the image is dishonoured, the dishonour is inflicted on him whose image it is? This is not only a truth which is self-evident but is also taught by the nature of things. The holy Fathers, moreover, concur with this. St Basil says: 'The honour paid to an image ascends to the prototype'; and Athanasius remarks: 'Therefore he who venerates the image, venerates the emperor it represents'. Chrysostom says similarly: 'Do you not know that if you insult an image of the emperor, you convey the insult to the prototype'? And these Fathers simply followed the nature of things".[25]

Such is their confidence in the natural order of things that even the angels are included within those beings that may be represented, since as "intellectual creatures" they are "not entirely incorporeal and invisible like the divine, on account of which they occupy space and are circumscribed".[26] And although

"they are in reality invisible as far as we are concerned, yet since they have been seen several times in a sensible way by several people in the form of their own bodies — they have been seen by those whose eyes God has opened — they are also proved to be circumscribed by place, not being totally incorporeal like the divine nature. We therefore do not sin when we depict the angels, not as gods but as intellectual

---

[23] Mansi 13, 185C. Cf. Basil the Great, *Hexaemeron* 3, 22: "Since we are taught by Scripture (Sirach 34:5–6), nothing may be imagined by our minds except that which is permitted".

[24] Mansi 13, 164D, 256C. Cf. 188. See, however, John Damascene: "In contemplating the character of Christ we also conceive of the glory of the divinity" (*Imag.* III, 12, 21–30).

[25] Mansi 13, 325D; Cf. Mansi 13, 273AB; Basil the Great, *On the Holy Spirit* 18, 45, PG 32, 149CD; Athanasius, *Against the Arians* III, 5, PG 26, 332A; John Chrysostom, cited by John Damascene, *Imag.* II, 61 (Kotter, p. 163).

[26] Mansi 13, 165B.

creatures who are not strictly speaking incorporeal. Their depiction in human form has come about from their having been thus seen by those to whom they were sent by the only God".[27]

"Sin" for the iconophiles continues resolutely to be whatever is created wilfully or unnaturally by reasonable creatures and hence is totally deprived of real existence. Whatever has existence from God and is visible by whatsoever means, may be and indeed should be represented. The representation of any being, moreover, is to be understood in relation to the absolute presupposition that its existence is appointed by the uncreated will of God.

Inanimate matter, too, wherever and whenever it is sanctified (bread, water, oil etc.) owes its capacity for sanctification equally to the fact that it has its origin in the same uncreated will. It would have been inconceivable for the iconophiles that one should speak of the sanctification of non-existent and non-subsistent "products" of the imagination or of the "deflection" of a created will. Only that which has its existence from God has the capacity, in proportion to what it is, to receive sanctification. And since only the uncreated God remains "entirely incorporeal and invisible", that which has its existence from God is also one way or another, visible. In this way the iconophiles create a theology of sight, of vision, of that which has its existence from God, a theology which strongly fortifies their conception of reality and justifies it in its substance, together with the direct capacity to represent that which truly exists, in absolute contradistinction to that which is "contrary to nature" or in accordance with the "deflection of a created will", which is unlikely, as such, to be sanctified and should not be represented.

The iconophiles, then, "represent those things which are seen and contemplated" primarily "as light" — that is to say, the bodies of Christ and of the saints, which already shine or will shine "like the sun" in accordance with the teaching of the Gospel.[28]

The Sanctifying Vision of the Real

The soteriological character of this "contemplation" will be discussed below, where the iconophiles are shown to deploy strong arguments in this connection: "For if we believe that the people of Israel were

---

[27] Mansi 13, 165C, 404D. Cf. 5E: "All the saints who have been deemed worthy to see angels saw them in human form;" Cf. also 8B. See in addition John Damascene, *Imag*, III, 24, 25, 21, Gregory of Nazianzus, *Theological Oration* 2, 31 (A. J. Mason, p. 354), and Nicephorus, *Antir.* II, PG 100, 345D.

[28] Mansi 12, 967C; cf. Matt. 13:43; 17:2; Acts 26:13; Rev. 1:16, 12:1, 21:23, 22:25.

saved through beholding the bronze serpent, far be it from us to
hesitate, or to depart from the tradition of the holy Fathers, or
to fall away from their teaching".[29] Such is the clarity of their vision
of the real that the Seventh Ecumenical Council appealed to the
example of the Fathers of the Church who shed tears at the sight
of icons: "And Father Asterius, who has just been read, had the
same experience as the most holy Gregory (of Nyssa); for both
became tearful at the sight of the icons".[30]

This matter of tears must not be interpreted as a psychological
excitement, nor simply as an intense function of the power of
recollection, nor as mere visualisation. The iconophiles believe
steadfastly and attempt to prove that there is a mysterious inward
connection and correspondence between the human soul and
whatsoever has come to exist from God, a relationship of duration
between creatures and the Creator, a unity of the whole of created
reality, which is penetrated by the uncreated creative energies of
the Holy Trinity, and has man as its point of reference, as he is
the summit of creation. This, of course, cannot be demonstrated
scientifically, since the uncreated energies elude the human capacity to master them as objects of knowledge. Nevertheless, it cannot
be ignored entirely so as to be thought never to happen at all
to those who receive this experience of the universal presence of
God within His creation. The Fathers who lived before the iconoclastic period had already noted this truth accurately and defended
it with biblical citations:

"I will proclaim to you a word, not mine, neither that of any other
man ... but that which the creation of beings expounds through the
wonders which are within it; the hearer of this becomes the human
eye through the world of phenomena, the wise and skilful Word
resounding in his heart. For the creation cries out before its Maker,
the heavens themselves, as the prophet says (Ps. 18:2), proclaiming
in voices without speech the glory of God. And St Maximus the
Confessor says: 'From the wise contemplation of creation we receive
the word concerning the Holy Trinity ... creation indeed cries out
through the things created within it and, as it were, announces its case
to those able to hear inwardly that which is hymned triadically' ".[31]

---

[29] Mansi 12, 1063D.
[30] Mansi 13, 20B. Cf. 13, 9E, 12A and 12, 963E–966A. On Asterius of Amaseia
see Nicephorus, *Antir.* II, 16, PG 100, 364–365A. On Gregory of Nyssa see *On
the divinity of the Son and the Spirit and on Abraham*, PG 46, 572C.
[31] Gregory of Nyssa, *On the resurrection of the soul* 9, PG 46, 960. Maximus the
Confessor, PG 90, 296B, Cf. PG 91, 1380B; John Damascene, *Imag.* III, 43; Basil
the Great, *On Psalm 28* 3, *On the Eucharist* 2.

The recognition of the uncreated creative energies in creation constitutes the remote cause of compunction in the human soul in its universal but unconfused contact with the Creator. This spiritual condition, which presupposes a person's purification together with correct belief on his or her part, is called in the Orthodox tradition "the contemplation of beings (*theoria ton onton*), or "natural contemplation" (*physike theoria*), and constitutes a fundamental stage in one's perfection and salvation in Christ.[32] We would go so far as to assert that the whole argumentation of the iconophiles is based on this natural power to contemplate all beings. Within this realist framework the iconophiles construct their theology of vision, that is to say, their evaluation of the holy icons: "Through his artifice the good painter always represents real things" (*ta pragmata*).[33] It is this which is the cause of tears at the sight of icons: the recognition and evaluation of real things, of reality as God desired it, created it, provides it. And the direct contact with this reality, that is to say, the beholding of icons, which "through skilfulness" always represent real things", constitutes a moving experience for the spiritually advanced beholder, who is deemed worthy to attain to the "contemplation of beings". It is from this point of view, as we have already said, that the icon constitutes "a door . . . which opens our mind, created in accordance with God, to the likeness of the prototype within", permitting a withdrawal from the illusory and fickle state of non-being and a transition to true reality.[34] Such is the confidence of the iconophiles, in the reality which the icons represent, that the patriarch Tarasius forcefully underlines a phrase of Asterius from the latter's description of the icon of St Euphemia: "It is now time, if you wish, to let me carry out for your sake the painting itself, so that you may observe precisely whether I have not gone too far beyond explicitness".[35] The painting of holy icons is a veritable sacred rite, participation in which initiates the beholder into the truth about real things and permits him to conclude from experience: "The workmanship of the painter is therefore in accordance with true

---

[32] Mansi 13, 12B: "We therefore say that shadow and type are the law and a kind of writing set forth to be viewed by those who perceive reality". See Cyril of Alexandria, *Epistle to Acacius of Melitene on the scapegoat*, PG 77, 217; Maximus the Confessor, *Centuries on Theology* I, 38 and 59.

[33] Mansi 13, 20A. Cf. John Damascene, *Imag. III, 111; Mansi 13, 13A*: "the art of him who draws always contributing to the service of reality" (PG 77, 220); Basil the Great, *Hexaemeron* I, 4; II, 9.

[34] *Life of St Stephen the Younger*, PG 100, 1113A.

[35] Mansi 13, 20B and 17D.

piety" and the icon is greater than the word.[36]

The vision of "real things" initiates the believer more effectively than preaching, since sight is a higher sense than hearing. That is why the iconophiles, faithful to their realism, describe their opponents as blind, precisely because they will not or cannot regard "that which is beheld and contemplated as light".[37]

> "It is characteristic of the blind not to see the light. On account of this they too, being blind in their soul, have lost their power of sight". "For when the eye has been injured it does not see properly; similarly, they have injured and clouded their own mind by the disturbance of evil thoughts and suffer in the same way as madmen, in their hallucinations confusing one thing with another".[38]

Conversely, the iconophiles affirm that "when we see the pictorial representations with our eyes, we are illuminated inwardly" — since "he who looks at the image of the emperor looks at the emperor thus represented"[39] — in order to arrive at a general, systematic defence of this experiential theology of vision:

> "For the holy catholic Church of God . . . hastens to direct all our senses towards the glory of the God who is over all things, and sets them up through hearing and sight before the eyes of those who approach . . . and the constant sight of the pictorial representations becomes a guard and a perpetual reminder, a guard against returning to one's own vomit . . . for when these are set before our eyes, the heart of those who fear the Lord is gladdened, the face comes alive, the despondent soul is turned to cheerfulness, and sings with David, the ancestor of God: 'I remembered God and was gladdened' (Ps. 76:1). Through these we therefore always have remembrance of God; for the reading takes place when there is no singing in the churches: the pictorial representations installed in them narrate to us evening and morning and midday and proclaim the truth of the very deeds that have taken place".[40]

---

[36] Mansi 13, 17D: Cf. PG 78, 408B; Mansi 13, 20C. Cf. Theodore of Studius, *Antir,* III, 1, 2; (PG 99, 392 and 781); also Nicephorus, *Antir,* III, 3 and III, 5 (PG 100, 380 and 384, 748D–749B). Aristotle had already noted the superiority of sight over the other senses; see *De sensu* 437; *Metaph.* A, 1, 980A, 1–24.

[37] Mansi 12, 967C. John Damascene accepts, however, that "the work of the icon and the word is one" (*Imag.* I, 45). Cf. also Theodore of Studius. *Antir.* I, PG 99, 340D: "if you confess the vividness of hearing to be equal to that of sight"; and Nicephorus, *Antir.* III, PG 100, 381C: "These words are icons of things as they really are".

[38] Mansi 13, 185A; 268A.

[39] Mansi 13, 220E; 273A.

[40] Mansi 13, 360–361A. Cf. John Damascene, *Imag.* I, 47 (Kotter, p. 151). See also I.P. Sheldon-Williams, "The Philosophy of Icons" in *The Cambridge History of Later Greek and Early Medieval Philosophy* (ed. A.H. Armstrong) p. 514: "The

The final result of the constant sight of the icons contributes decisively to the "constant remembrance of God" which constitutes a still higher level than the "contemplation of beings" in the perfection and salvation of the faithful.[41]

This sanctifying dimension of beholding the icons is repeatedly emphasised by the Seventh Ecumenical Council:

> "As the faithful, by means of the sense of sight, look at the sacred icon of Christ, and of our Lady and true Mistress, the holy Theotokos, and of the holy angels and all the saints, they are sanctified, and impress their minds with the memory of them, and in their hearts believe in one God, which leads to righteousness, and with their mouths confess him, which leads to salvation. Similarly, when they listen to the Gospel, they fill the sense of hearing with sanctity and Grace". For "'faith comes from the sense of hearing', says the Apostle (Rom. 10:17); but is already stamped in the understanding of those who see through the sense of sight, and by its power they proclaim the mystery that God has been manifested in the flesh and has been believed in the world, a mystery which will be found the most conducive of all to sanctification and salvation".[42]

Precisely because the icons represent saving events from the life of Christ and of the saints, "whose power conserves and saves the human race", they strengthen the conviction of the iconophiles and beholding them proves to be a saving, sanctifying act much more powerful than the corresponding beholding by the Old Testament Hebrews of the bronze serpent.[43] In the final analysis, the defenders of the icons express through these conceptions the truth concerning the special role which the senses of hearing and sight play in the matter of humanity's salvation:

> "that which we have believed to be true through the faculty of hearing, we consolidate through pictorial imitation for our greater assurance. For being compounded of flesh and blood, we are compelled to confirm that which affects our assurance in regard to our souls through the faculty of sight". "For since human beings are endowed with senses, we use sensible things in order to recognise and refer to every divine and holy tradition".[44]

---

images offer to the faithful the tradition and the history of the Faith without mediation, the things themselves as though they were present".

[41] The first to use the expression "remembrance of God" was Philo, who took it from the Old Testament (*De vita contemplativa*, 26). The use of the term is also, of course, encountered in Stoic authors; Zeno, for example, regards the memory as a "treasure-house of images". See von Arnim, *Stoicorum Veterum Fragmenta* 1, p. 19, n. 64.

[42] Mansi 13, 249E; 116A. Cf. 12, 1006A; 13, 220E, 360B–E, 474C; John Damascene, *Imag.* I, 17 (Kotter, p. 93); I, 47 (Kotter, pp. 151–2).

[43] Mansi 12, 1036D.

[44] Mansi 13, 101E; 280D. John Chrysostom makes the striking assertion that

This use of sensible things as a means of ascending to God and to the saints, also makes them a means of communion with the divine, a "contact" which brings about a participation in sanctification:

> "The Church has accepted the composition and execution of icons in order to raise up our minds, and inform them and enable them to participate in sanctification. For if the Holy Gospel produces an impression within us when we hear it read, the icons do the same. And if the martyrologies narrate the suffering of the martyrs, so do the icons".[45]

Participation in sanctification, moreover, is also accomplished through the veneration of sacred vessels, places, images and relics.[46] Fundamental to the understanding of the orthodox realism of the iconophiles is the theological distinction between one nature or essence and three hypostases in God as developed by the Cappadocian Fathers in the course of the Trinitarian conflicts of the fourth century and as accepted by subsequent Fathers, including Augustine and the Ecumenical Councils.[47]

Two Contrasting Ontologies

The iconoclasts seem to rely on the early Alexandrian terminology, which, as in the West, rather than distinguish between nature and hypostases tended to identify them.[48] The iconophiles, by contrast, took as their starting point the difference between nature and

---

"sight" (opsis) and "hearing" (akoe) are the two "entrance-doors" of faith (On Matthew, Hom. 40, 3); Cf. Gregory of Nyssa "the divine is wholly sight and hearing and knowledge" (PG 45, 981A).

[45] Mansi 13, 474CD; Cf. 220E.

[46] Cf. Mansi 13, 364D, 269E; 309D.

[47] Cf. Basil the Great, Epistle 38 to his brother Gregory on the difference between substance and hypostasis, Loeb vol. i. p. 196ff; Gregory of Nazianzus, Oratio 23, 11, PG 35, 1161C; Gregory of Nyssa, Against Eunomius, PG 45, 469AB; Basil the Great, Epistle 231 to Amphilochius, Loeb vol. iii, pp. 400–404; Gregory of Nyssa, On Common Notions, PG 45, 176ff. Cf. J.N.D. Kelly, Early Christian Creeds, pp. 243ff. Augustine followed finally the Cappodocian Trinitarian formula but we do not know to what extent he meant it as clearly as the Eastern Fathers did. However, the only passage from Augustine to be found in the Acta of the Seventh Ecumenical Council (Mansi 12, 1066A) has not been verified in Augustine's works. See on this point L. Wallach, Diplomatic Studies in Latin and Greek Documents from the Carolingian Age, p. 31. See also Augustine's On the Trinity, V 11, 4, 8.

[48] See Athanasius, To the Bishops of Africa, 4, PG 26, 1036; Cyril of Alexandria, Third Epistle to Nestorius, ed. L.R. Wickham, Oxford 1983. Cf. J.N.D. Kelly, Early Christian Doctrines, pp. 136, 224–226; J.S. Romanides, "St Cyril's 'One physis or hypostasis of God the Logos Incarnate' and Chalcedon", in Does Chalcedon divide or unite?, Geneva 1981, pp. 55–59.

hypostasis so as to arrive at a clear distinction between prototype and image and to safeguard with this distinction the possibility and the legitimacy of the imitative representation of reality, that is to say, of existent and circumscribed creatures, as they have been originally willed by their Creator and Saviour.[49]

If, however, behind the views of the iconoclasts is concealed a Platonic ontology or metaphysics, which refuses to recognise in the material world scarcely any right to participation in being and acknowledges only the ideas as the unique and unchanging reality, as the immutable archetypes and truly existent beings, then indeed within such a Platonising perspective (different from that of Athanasius or Cyril) the distinction between nature and hypostasis and even more the distinction between archetype and its imitative image, is without ultimate meaning. The philosophical interpretation of "nature" or substance (essence) as existing of necessity, creates an ontology or metaphysics, which gives priority and ultimate meaning to those beings which are eternal, immutable and impersonal as real existents. For this reason, any attempt to represent corruptible and mutable "beings", which are transitory and change their mode of existence, or which end finally in non-existence, would be regarded as unacceptable. There are indications, as we have seen, that the iconoclasts did not allow a real place within their thinking to the historical bodies of Christ and the saints. When their arguments became christological, they seem to have differed very much as to whether there was a glorified state of the very bodies of Christ and of the saints which could still be depicted in icons. They assumed that to depict such a state, one would have to paint the uncreated divinity or glory of Christ and the saints and apparently only that glory without the glorified bodies themselves.[50]

But such a painting is impossible since the uncreated glory has no similarity to anything created and lies beyond all expressions and concepts. To depict Christ and the saints without their glory, however, would be to proclaim a Christ and saints who do not exist.

That the iconoclasts have made such a strong and lasting point, has become explicit though not clearly mentioned in the sources, from all the icons of Christ and the saints developed in divine uncreated glory, which is beyond expressions and concepts and has no similarity with the creature. Yet this glory is painted usually

---

[49] See Mansi 13, 256E–261A.
[50] This was already Eusebius' point in his letter to Constantia during the 4th century. See Mansi 13, 313 AD.

as a halo in brilliant gold, and depicts no more than the biblical words used to express this same indescribable reality. It is the very existence of such glorified and enduring prototypes, though created ones, that consolidates and justifies the possibility of their representation, assuring the iconophiles that there is no doubt about the place of the material bodies of Christ and of the saints in the life to come.

That is why they insist that "the catholic Church . . . accepts icons as a reminder of the prototypes".[51] We have already noted the important role of the "remembrance of God" in the spiritual ascent of believers. Let us also add here the affection and love of the orthodox for the real and existing prototypes of the persons represented (Christ and the saints), which constitute at the same time both examples of the Christian life and spiritual ideals:

> "In accordance with the affection and love that we have for the Lord and the saints, we set forth their characteristics in icons, showing honour not to the wooden boards and colours but to the persons themselves whose names the icons bear", "making the divine type a reminder of salvation".[52]

The "type" of every icon finds itself in direct communion with the prototype, although it is not actually identified with it.[53] Nevertheless this communion with the prototype constitutes the reality of the icon, its justification, the legitimacy of its existence and at the same time indicates the high esteem of the creation.[54]

> "Therefore we do not call the icon itself God, but we know God who is represented in the icon and whose likeness the icon contains". "For the icon is one thing, and the prototype is another; and anyone who thinks correctly in no way looks for the properties of the prototypes in the icon. For true reason recognises nothing in the icon other than a nominal communion with the icon's subject and not an essential communion".[55]

---

[51] Mansi 12, 1006A. Cf. 13, 474C: "for the elevation and prompting of our mind"; 13, 361A: "for everything which raises us to the remembrance of God is acceptable to him".

[52] Mansi 12, 1063A; 13, 188A. Cf. Nicephorus, *Antir.* I, PG 100, 277B: "Therefore the icon is in this way a likeness and expression of beings and existent things, but the idol is a fabrication of that which has no existence or being"; John Damascene, *Imag.* II, 11 (Kotter, p. 102).

[53] See E. Kitzinger, "On some icons of the seventh century" in *Late Classical and Medieval Studies in Honor of Albert Mathias Friend, Jr.*, ed. K. Weitzmann et al., Princeton 1955, pp. 142–3.

[54] See Theodore of Studius, *Epist. to Nicetas Spatharius*, PG 99, 1504A: "The archetype is revealed by the icon".

[55] Mansi 13, 198D, 256CD, 257D. Besides, the iconoclast argument that the

This last point raises the question whether concealed behind the theology of icons there is a form of nominalism. We can deny this categorically, because the "name" in the biblical and patristic understanding is never in conflict with the reality which it represents.[56] In the text just quoted, the "nominal communion" between prototype and icon constitutes a reality precisely because the prototype exists.

The fact that the icon corresponds to an existent reality (perhaps inaccessible, or unverifiable, or incapable of scientific proof, but nevertheless a reality) determines the realism of orthodox faith: "the conviction of things not seen" (Hebr. 11: 1). By contrast, the mentality of the iconoclasts, who wish to attribute to their opponents the essential identification of the icon with the prototype, is purely Greek and reflects pre-Christian conceptions regarding idols.[57]

It is in an entirely different way that "through the signification of the name we refer the honour paid to the icon to the prototype".[58] And consequently:

> "Just as he who insults the image of the emperor is justly punished, as having in fact dishonoured the emperor, even though the image is nothing other than wood and colours mixed and blended with wax, in the same way he who dishonours the representation of something, conveys the insult to that of which it is a representation. The very nature of real things teaches this, that when the image is dishonoured, the prototype is invariably dishonoured too".[59]

Again we find the same insistence on the real, the same attachment to the "nature of real things", based on the fact that "the very thing of which the image is a representation" exists in reality. In the last analysis the iconoclasts' rejection of images simply signifies "a refusal to follow the nature of real things", a rebellion against the

---

icon of Christ divides his two natures is refuted by the reality of the hypostatic union: "For all clearly proclaim the division of the two natures on the conceptual level and not in reality". See further below, Chapter V.

[56] See Kittel, under onoma, vol. 5, p. 252ff (by Hans Bietenhard). Cf. Mansi 12, 1062C–2067D; J. Barr, "The Symbolism of Name in the Old Testament", *Bulletin of the John Rylands Library*, 52, 1 (1969), pp. 11–29. But compare A.G. Thiselton, "The Supposed Power of Words in the Biblical Writings", *JTS* 25 (1974), pp. 283–99.

[57] Cf. "Greeks through being deceived consider likenesses (in themselves) to be gods" (Mansi 13, 188D); and "producing various ideas and carving forms as they seem" (Mansi 13, 188A).

[58] Mansi 13, 269E, 48C. Cf. John Damascene, *Imag.* I, 56, 26 (Kotter, p. 157), III, 126, 5 (Kotter, pp. 194–195).

[59] Mansi 13, 273A.

Creator of creatures.[60] Thus for the iconophiles the rejection of images, as an indirect rejection of the material world, or at least as a rejection of the possibility of its sanctification, signifies fundamentally the rejection of the very content of the Christian tradition: "Those who find themselves outside this tradition, in which all participated who have become genuine sons by adoption in the catholic Church, are bastards and not sons".[61] In fact the acceptance of the icons as referring to reality, as affirming the possibility of the salvation of rational creatures, has a profound significance not only for this reason but also more specifically for refuting such heresies as docetism:

"The representation in icons of the character of the Lord's outward appearance in the flesh, refutes those foolish heretics who say that he became a man in the imagination and not in reality, and guides those who are not strong enough to ascend to spiritual contemplation".[62]

The last phrase of this passage provides us with a clear hint that icons would not have been necessary if the mass of believers had managed to attain the spiritual level of "theoria" i.e. the unceasing prayer of the Holy Spirit in the heart (Gal. 4:6) which follows the stage of "constant remembrance of God" and from time to time or on special occasions this spiritual level may be replaced by glorification or deification *(theosis)*.[63] There is no reason for those who have attained *theosis*, i.e. the immediate vision of the uncreated glory of Christ and his saints, to use images. Since this is not the case, however, in the Church militant, the icons are judged to be indispensable for the sake of the many, who "also need some bodily means of apprehension for the confirmation of what they have

---

[60] Mansi 13, 273B.
[61] Mansi 13, 361A; Cf. Heb. 12:8; Nicephorus, *Apologeticus pro Sacris Imaginibus*, PG 100, 564.
[62] Mansi 13, 116A.
[63] On spiritual contemplation see Symeon the New Theologian, *Traités théologiques et éthiques*, vol. i (éthique I) ch. 12, 319–451 (SC 122, Paris 1966, pp. 296–304). St Theodore of Studius opposes every division of the members of the Church into the perfect and the imperfect in such a way that the Scriptures are addressed to the perfect and the icons to the imperfect: "Just as it is necessary for every perfect man to be in the book of the gospels, even if he is enrolled in the apostolic dignity, so too (if he is perfect) he should be included in a painted representation of the gospel story" (*Epist. to the monk Nicetas*, PG 99, 1537D). There is no essential disagreement here. St Theodore opposes the division of Church members into perfect and imperfect because this would constitute a judgment for the latter and a danger for the former (ibid. 1537C). Cf. Nicephorus, *Antir.* III, PG 100, 380D.

heard".[64] In proof of this need of the many certain icons are
wonder-working, mainly for the sake of unbelievers, thus underlin-
ing their direct relationship with a reality that lies beyond the
senses.[65]

The consequences, moreover, of the iconoclasts' rejection of the
legitimate use of matter for the benefit of human life are more
far-reaching: "Surely in their madness all science and workmanship
disappears, which has been given by God for His glory and for
the maintenance of our life".

The iconophiles on the other hand, regard as "praiseworthy the
wisdom which has been granted to our nature by the bountiful
God who created us", invoking relevant testimonies from Scripture
and the Fathers, and stressing in conclusion that those "who
disparage and despise the sciences given by God to men align
themselves with the heresy of those who condemn God and are
said to do so".[66]

In all probability there is an allusion here to the Manichaeans.
Apart from this however, the Origenistic cosmological conceptions
also share indirectly in the same tendencies. The Seventh Ecumenical Council does not seem to have taken clear cognisance of this
last point, with the result that it does not mention it in its acts.
Nevertheless sources which are almost contemporary with the Council
are not unaware of it. Thus, for example, although the acts regard
Eusebius of Caesarea simply as an Arian, in the 144th letter of
Photius it is stated explicitly "that he has partaken of Origen's
disease".[67] A natural consequence of the material world, owing to
the existence of a higher, intellectual one, is in fact a rejection
of its use, the withdrawal, in so far as is possible, from all contact
and communion with it. And included in this aversion towards
everything created, material, sensible and corruptible is any possibility of using the skill or the wisdom with which man has been
endowed as the crown, as Scripture says, of creation.[68]

---

[64] Mansi 13, 116A.
[65] Mansi 13, 32AB and 125A: "The chief point with regard to what has been
said is that in various icons God works miracles, which many people wish to
depict in many ways". Cf. John Damascene, *Imag.* I, 56 (Kotter, p. 157); III,
126 (Kotter p. 195); Mansi 13, 48.
[66] Mansi 13, 249B, D.
[67] Mansi 13, 316A. Photius, *Epistulae et Amphilochia*, ed. Laourdas-Westerink,
Leipzig 1983, vol. i, p. 197, Cf. Photius, *Bibliotheca*, Paris (Collection Byzantine)
1960, pp. 90–2; G. Florovsky, "The Iconoclast Controversy" in *Christianity and
Culture*, Belmont 1974; p. 101ff.
[68] Gen. 1:26, cf. Mansi 12, 1062C, 1067D. See also Basil the Great, *Hexaemeron*,
Hom. I, 26–7.

To this practical idealism the iconophiles oppose an orthodox realism:

"No one who thinks correctly disparages craftsmanship if it makes something useful for the necessities of this life. For the purpose and the means must be considered for which the artifices are intended. If they are used for a pious end, they are acceptable; but if for a shameful end, they are abominable and profane". "And if we wish to depict the lives of virtuous men, and the accounts of the triumphs of the martyrs, and the narratives of their sufferings, and the mystery of the economy of our great God and Saviour, and we so make use of the painters' workmanship, we will find ourselves acting very correctly".[69]

Here we have a theory of art and human creativity which flows from the insistence on reality, from the possibility of expressing truth by means of the created and sensible world. We find a surprising application of this view in the distinction which the iconophiles make between icon and idol: "The representation of things which have no being is called idolatrous painting (*eidolike graphe*),[70] which is what the Greek mythologisers shaped out, caricaturing the Creation by bringing non-existent things into existence".[71]

We have here, in the first place, a Christian definition of idols

---

[69] Mansi 13, 241D, 241BC. Cf. the 100th canon of the Quinisext Council, Rhalles-Potles, vol. ii, p. 545.

[70] In Patristic and later Greek the term *graphe* never stands for "painting". For the representation of things without existence and events without substance as supposedly having happened, the word *poietike*, poetry, is used, which as a result is also called "idolatrous writing", corresponding in Greek to *mythopoiia* (*mythopoieo* = I compose fables). There exists in the lexica a unique instance in which the Greek word *graphe* (= writing, written document) means neither "Scripture", nor "edict", nor "indictment, accusation", but "image, picture". The reference is to an ambiguous passage in Justin Martyr (*1 Apology* 24, 2, PG 6, 365A): *oti me... en graphais stephanous kai thysias pheromen*. The two readings *graphais* and *taphais* are equally possible.

[71] Mansi 13, 956CD. Origen was the first to point out this distinction in Scripture in his explanation in Exod. 20:5 of the difference between idol and likeness (PG 12, 353B–354A). By this means, however, he showed the Bible to reject in general every representation of creatures, although clearly the text only concerns the rejection of the worship of representations of beings without rational life. In fact the representation of the cherubim is permitted (Exod. 25:18–20). Cf. also Origen's interpretation of this (PG 14, 948ff) and John Damascene, *Imag.* I, 15 (Kotter, pp. 88–9). Cf. also Mansi 13, 276C: "Evil and its opposite is therefore from us and through us, and not from material objects; for what is an idol? says the apostle; or what is meat sacrificed to idols, if it is not meat sacrificed to demons and not to God?" (1 Cor. 10:19). Among modern scholars E.J. Martin (*A History of the Iconoclastic Controversy*, p. 115) maintains that there was a different understanding of idolatry amongst iconophiles and iconoclasts. The former understood idolatry in a broad way as the endowing

with an insistence on reality as the supreme criterion: idols are
"a representation of things which have no being" — the attempt
to make the non-existent existent. And this attempt, which tries
to bring "non-existent things into existence", abuses and dishonours
art, both as a human creation but also especially as a work of the
Artificer of all things. Consequently, an unlimited potentiality of
artistic creation (chiefly from the human point of view) has no
validity for the iconophiles, for there is the danger that art will
prove to be abused whenever an artist wishes to give substance to
non-being. It is precisely for this reason that every form of aes-
theticism is rigorously excluded from Orthodox art and craftsmanship: The letter of St Neilus to Olympiodorus, which was brought
forward in a falsified version by the iconoclasts, and was accepted
by the Seventh Ecumenical Council in its genuine original form,
although excluding any chasing after voluptuous visual pleasure
("any form displayed for the pleasure of the eyes") and any re-
freshment of the eyes through art ("the deception of the eyes of
believers"), accepts the pictorial representation of reality, which has
a saving power: "By the hand of the excellent painter the church
of the saints should be filled on every side with scenes from the
Old and New Testaments".[72] By contrast, the iconoclasts "did not
distinguish between sacred and profane, giving the same name to
the icon of the Lord and of his saints as to the lifeless statues *(xoana)*
of the satanic idols".[73] In his letter (214) addressed to "Stephen
who has become orthodox" (having renounced iconoclasm) Photius,
the Patriarch of Constantinople (858–867 and 878–886) undertakes
a theological analysis of the difference between icon and idol. The
idols are works "of human hands playing with matter without any
divine influence, shaping whatever occurs to their minds".

That is why idols are

"nothing other than matter which has been abused and the unconsidered
and irrational labour of human hands ... For since their archetypes
are either nothing or wretched and polluted, and their maker (along
with the impious) is even more wretched, and the whole of their

---

of wood and metal with divine properties, while their opponents took it to be
an intellectual condition in which the Creator was replaced by something created.
Although Martin in the same place compares the theses on idolatry of the
Seventh Ecumenical Council with those of Nicephorus of Constantinople, and
although he accepts that the 'broad' understanding was dominant among the
laity, it seems that he has not fully understood the real difference developed
in the council between icon and idol, which renders his distinctions superfluous.
    [72] Mansi 13, 36ABC. Cf. Edwyn Bevan, *Holy Images*, pp. 122–4, where the author
comments on the parallel view of Augustine (*Confess.* X, 34, 53).
    [73] Mansi 13, 376B.

worship is more profane, how will they appropriate to themselves any grace, or glory, or energy, or any certain more dignified calling?".[74]

By contrast, the holy icon

"is formed upon matter, and has a hand, but from above; for it is served by inspirations from above and by thoughts which are intelligent and raised up to pious judgment . . . For from the beginning the divine and infallible proclamation of the Apostolic and Patristic tradition is like a certain living wisdom which dominates matter and, in accordance with its own sacred laws, works it and fashions it and produces a representation and shape, not allowing any element of material disorder or of human curiosity to assert itself in these; but showing and manifesting all its work, it provides us, in a way appropriate to the representation of sacred things, with clear and unadulterated reflections of the prototypes in the holy icons . . . For this reason they are no longer wooden boards . . . or colours bereft of the inherent power and grace which produces form, neither can they be so conceived nor so named; but rather, they are holy and honourable and glorified and venerable. For having come to participate in the energy that comes from above, and in those holy persons, they bear the form and the name and are dedicated, they transport our minds to them and bring us blessings and divine favour from them. They are not indeed named after the material from which the icon is made or after any other property which is incongruous and applies to their opposites. On the contrary it is from those in whom they participate, . . . and whom they serve, and to whom they are dedicated, that they are very rightly known by the true devotees and receive their name".[75]

So realistic a view of icons allowed Theodore of Studius to give the following classic definition: An icon is "a self-manifested vision" (emphasis tes autopsias).[76] It also enabled the Patriarch Nicephorus of Constantinople to say:

"Whenever the falsely-called holy men dare to call the icons of Christ, the great King and God, spurious, they necessarily prove Christ to be himself a spurious Christ and a spurious king, since both Christ himself and each one of his icons are indicative of one another and contain the reflections of one another (kai tas emphaseis allelon kektentai). And even their doctrine of a falsely-called Christ, who by no means exists, will be taught in his icons more clearly if they are in any way spurious; for it is manifestly obvious that falsehood is identical with non-being".[77]

---

[74] Photius, *Epistulae et Amphilochia*, ed. Laourdas-Westerink, Leipzig 1984, vol. 2, pp. 117–19.
[75] Ibid. Cf. Mansi 12, 1067DE.
[76] Theodore of Studius, *Epistle* 36, to his child Naucratius, PG 99, 1220A; Cf. 1288C, 1503A.
[77] Nicephorus Conf. *Refutation et Eversion*, Cod. Paris. Gr. 1250, fol. 223v. 20ff;

Therefore, the only possible solution in which Christ is not to be represented is if he should not exist!

Cf. Mansi 13, 377C. This evident insistence on the truth led the iconophiles not simply to the avoidance of worshipping the icons, although "they possessed the reflections of the prototypes", but to regarding as a primary act of the worship of God the absolute acceptance of the truth, remaining faithful to it and confessing it: "For true worship and veneration of the true God is achieved most precisely in adhering to the holy confessions of faith concerning him and in observing the chief and most cohesive mysteries and laws given by him" (Mansi 13, 109D). It is perhaps for this reason that their most powerful argument against their opponents is that the latter have no relationship with the truth, find themselves outside reality and therefore find it impossible to accept the icons: "Those who have once been led astray are not wholly to be persuaded, since the truth is not in them" (Mansi 13, 124E).

CHAPTER FIVE

ICON AND CHRISTOLOGY

Although the iconoclastic struggle arose from a number of quite different occasions, it developed into a doctrinal, and in particular a christological, controversy. The disagreement between the opposing sides was centred primarily on the icon of the incarnate Logos of God, that is to say, on the legitimacy or otherwise of his pictorial representation.

Iconoclast Objections

The iconoclasts were looking for both of the natures of Christ in his icon. They believed that only the representation of both these natures would satisfy the requirements of a correct representation of the Lord. From another point of view however, the very attempt to represent the two natures was wholly unacceptable and blasphemous, since the divine nature is entirely inconceivable, infinite, indescribable and invisible. But without the possibility of representing this divine nature it was impossible for there to be any question of the representation of Christ, since Christ subsists precisely in these two natures. By representing only one of the natures, i.e. the human nature, the iconoclasts maintained that the one Christ is divided. That which is represented constitutes merely one of the elements of his hypostasis, the human one, entirely cut off from the other, which is the divine. Thus the iconoclasts conclude that "he who venerates the icon divides Christ into two", since although the person represented is worshipped as Christ "in two natures", he does not appear as such in his icon.[1] The acknowledgement of the icon of Christ as the image of Christ himself is therefore unacceptable. That which appears on the icon in no way compensates for the lack of that which is not visible either in the icon or in Christ himself, namely, the divine nature. Thus the iconic depiction of Christ involves essentially his division into two natures. The iconoclasts of course, knew very well that this division had been condemned by all the orthodox councils which dealt with the christological heresies. Consequently, what every attempt to represent Christ achieved was only to divide him according to his

---

[1] Mansi 13, 72B.

natures and never to represent him iconically with both his natures.
It was impossible for anyone to represent the whole Christ and
therefore the attempt was superfluous: "He who beholds the icon
and says or inscribes that this is Christ divides Christ", identifies
him with only one of his natures, and simultaneously deprives him
of the other.[2]

This classic iconoclast thesis is based on the — to them — self-
evident and "reasonable" demand that Christ should coincide with
his icon and be identified absolutely with it "by nature" or "essence".
In the formulation of this demand a decisive influence was exercised by both a Jewish-biblical understanding of the image, which
favours — in the case of man's creation — an immediate relationship between image and subject represented, as well as by a
notion of imitative reference and synonymy, which is a purely Greek
concept.[3]

The natural consequence of this combined attitude is the
characterisation of the icon of Christ by the iconoclasts as an idol.[4]
Arguing from the premises that the icon of Christ is not the Christ
in two natures, they regard the final failure, in their view, of the
attempt to represent Christ as a necessary consequence, and conclude
that the icon is an "idol" — a well-chosen term able to evoke the
abhorrence of those familiar with the history of Christianity, and
especially with the struggles of the martyrs against the worship of
idols in the first three centuries. Whoever understands the icon
of Christ as an idol assumes at once as the reason for its existence
and manufacture the same motive as that which leads to the
manufacture of idols: the adoration of the image, the attribution
to it of divine properties, and its identification with Christ. This
is precisely the conclusion to which the iconoclasts came: they accused
their opponents of being icon-worshippers, creature-worshippers,
wood-shippers, idol-worshippers.[5] They asserted that those who
honoured the icons of Christ called them gods and "worshipped
them as gods . . . placing in them their hopes of salvation . . .
expecting from them the future judgment . . . bestowing on them

---

[2] Mansi 13, 72C. Cf. Christoph von Schonborn, O.P., *L'icône du Christ*, Fribourg,
Suisse 1976, pp. 170–178.

[3] Cf. G. Kittel (ed.), *Theological Dictionary of the New Testament*, vol. ii, p. 391;
W. Eichrodt, *Theologie des Alten Testaments*, Stuttgart 1961, vol. ii, pp. 78–9. Cf.
Constantine V, fragm. 2 in G. Ostrogorsky, *Studien zur Geschichte des byzantinischen
Bilderstreits*, p. 10. On the Greek concept of "icon" see Plato's *Sophist*, 235–236d,
265b–260d; *Republic* 509d–511e. Cf. Kittel op. cit., vol. ii, pp. 389–90.

[4] Mansi 13, 208E, 221D.

[5] Mansi 12, 959D, 966A.

divine reverence".[6] "We find", says the *horos* of the iconoclast council
of 754, "that this unlawful pictorial art blasphemes against the vital
dogma of our salvation, that is, against the dispensation of Christ,
and overturns the six holy, divinely inspired ecumenical councils,
and . . . commends Nestorius, who divided the one Son and Logos
of God, who became incarnate for us, into a pair of sons".[7] The
teaching of Nestorius is successfully exploited and applied to the
icon of Christ as an image which does not succeed in manifesting
his divine nature but only portrays his human nature.[8]

Apart from a Nestorian christological basis to the theology of
the icon of Christ, however, the iconoclasts also discern an equally
applicable but diametrically opposite christological basis, a Eutychian
monophysite one, when they stress that the icon can convey
"confusion": "Indeed there are also Arius and Dioscorus and Eutyches
and Severus, who teach the confusion and jumbling of the two
natures of the one Christ".[9] Nevertheless, on the question of the
confusion of the two natures of Christ through his pictorial representation the iconoclasts do not give satisfactory explanations of
how the confusion takes place. Their opponents will draw attention
to this weakness and will remind them that the heresies which
confuse the two natures are found at the opposite pole to
Nestorianism. How can the painting of icons support both points
of view equally? The iconoclasts most probably mean that if the
iconophiles interpret the icon of Christ as a pictorial representation
not only of the human nature but also of the divine by means
of the human (since both are indissolubly conjoined), they confuse
the two natures:

> "Such a man made an icon, calling it Christ. And this name, Christ,
> is both God and man. It is an icon, then, of both God and man. He
> has therefore by his own vanity either limited, according to appear-
> ances, that aspect of the divinity which cannot be limited, by the
> depiction of the created flesh, or else he has compressed together the
> unconfused union, having fallen into the lawlessness of confusion, and
> has thus joined two blasphemies to the divinity both through limiting
> it and through confusing it. He who venerates such an icon has
> therefore submitted to the same blasphemies, and the "woe" applies

---

[6] Mansi 13, 225A.

[7] Mansi 13, 240C, 241E; Cf. 256B.

[8] On Nestorius' teaching on two persons in Christ, or on two Sons of God,
see J.N.D. Kelly, *Early Christian Doctrines*, pp. 310–343. Jaroslav Pelikan, *The Spirit
of Eastern Christendom* (*The Christian Tradition* Vol. II) pp. 39–49.

[9] Mansi 13, 244D, 248B. On the consequences of confusing the two natures
of Christ in the teaching of Dioscorus, Eutyches and Severus, see also J.N.D.
Kelly op. cit. pp. 331–334 and J. Pelikan op. cit. pp. 50–52.

equally to both groups, for they have been deceived together by Arius and Dioscorus and Eutyches and the heresy of the Akephaloï".[10]

But this conclusion neither relates to the sources, nor does it satisfy, seeing that the iconophiles nowhere appear to support the possibility of representing the divine nature of Christ in his icon. Indeed they deny such a thing explicitly:

"The word 'Christ' is a name signifying both the divinity and the humanity, the two perfect natures of the Saviour. And Christians have been taught to paint his icon in accordance with the nature in which he was seen, but not in accordance with the nature in which he was invisible. For the latter is uncircumscribable, since no one has ever seen God, as the Gospels tell us. Therefore when Christ is painted in his human nature, it is clear, as truth has shown, that Christians confess that the visible icon participates in the name only of the archetype and not by essence".[11]

The last sentence of the above text proves that in fact the two opposing sides have a completely different understanding of "icon". They do not denote the same thing by this word, though both attempt to interpret the same tradition. The iconoclasts, though seemingly committed exclusively and literally to the biblical-Jewish tradition, according to which "image of God" is thought of in a physical sense tending towards identity with its Archetype, they finally found themselves strongly influenced by Plato's philosophical understanding of *eikon*, linking this term with that of *mimesis* (imitation).[12] As it will become apparent in this study, it was from such a philosophical and speculative background that the iconoclasts derived their attitude towards "image worship", considering it in purely Platonic and Neoplatonic terms to be idolatry.

---

[10] Mansi 13, 252A; Cf. 245ABC, 340C.
[11] Mansi 13, 252CD. See also 265B, 101AB, 164E, 185C, 244ABC, 257D, 2253CDE, 261B, 340E.
[12] On this see G. Kittel, op. cit., Vol. IV, pp. 659–66. See also Plato's *Republic* 595A–606D, *Timaeus* 50C; John Damascene, *On the Orthodox Faith*, 90 (Kotter, p. 207): "Moreover, who can make himself an imitation of God, who is invisible, incorporeal and without form? It is indeed extreme folly and impiety to endow the divine with a visible form. It was for this reason that the use of icons was customary in the Old Testament". But according to the same author the icon is already "an imitation of the archetype from which it takes its name" (*Imag.* III, 64, Kotter, p. 170). This is taken, however, from Gregory of Nazianzus' 4th *Theological Oration* (PG 36, 129E, ed. A.J. Mason, p. 424), where it clearly refers to the Son as a natural icon of the Father. It is characteristic that in the theology of the fourth century natural and imitative icons are not only not distinguished but even identified with each other. This identification without doubt proved advantageous to the iconoclasts.

The iconophiles, on the other hand, without excluding the biblical tradition coupled the meaning of *eikon* with the Aristotelian realistic concept of *mimema* as indispensably corresponding to an existing archetype.[13]

The iconoclasts believed that their insistence on the realism of the Bible rendered them theologically superior to the iconophiles, who were, in their view, influenced by pagan Hellenism.[14] This was also confirmed by their emphatic adherence to the dogmatic decisions of all the christological councils and by their persistent attempt to draw arguments against the icons of Christ from the orthodox christology of the six ecumenical councils. This stance was doubtless well calculated. Every attempt at the iconic representation of Christ unavoidably constituted a serious infringement of christological doctrine: "a mode of division or confusion" of the hypostatic union of the two natures.[15] The insistence of the iconoclasts on the consequences of the hypostatic union and their attempt to apply these consequences to iconography is surprising.[16] Their pedantic adherence to both the letter and the spirit of the christological doctrines arms them with new arguments, which as the assertion that the representation of Christ in icons adds "another person to him, the person which they purport to represent", renders his flesh a "hypostasis in itself", and thus "attempts to paint a mere man". In this way "they prove themselves to add a fourth person to the Trinity". Moreover, "by representing that which was assumed by God and deified as undeified . . . they assimilate themselves in this respect to the Nestorian heresy". All these points together tend to prove how great a dogmatic absurdity is perpetuated by "those who make and desire and venerate that which is falsely brought into being and called by them the icon of Christ".[17]

---

[13] See Aristotle, *Poetics* 1448B4–19. Indeed, if it is borne in mind that Aristotle accords a supreme place in the same work to the "imitation of actions" (1449B24), it is possible to draw the conclusion that the icons as "paintings" and "narrative depictions" for the stimulation of the memory of believers clearly seek to be imitations of actions-events and not of abstract metaphysical states. Cf. Mansi 13, 360B–361A. On the different understanding of "imitation" between Plato and Aristotle see: Kathy Eden, *Poetic and legal fiction in the Aristotelian Tradition,* Princeton 1986, pp. 64–75 and Stephen Halliwell, *Aristotle's Poetics,* London 1986, pp. 109–137.

[14] See Mansi 13, 324D: "We unanimously decree that every icon of whatever material made by the base pictorial art of painters is alien and loathsome to the Christian Church and to be rejected". It is striking that Origen uses the term "base art".

[15] Mansi 13, 245E.

[16] Mansi 13, 256E–257A.

[17] Mansi 13, 247E–260B; Cf. 341ADE, 344C.

In spite of all this the iconoclasts did not entirely expunge the term "icon" from their theological teaching. There exists in their view, a single, unique and true icon of Christ,

> "which God, our sacred initiator, having assumed his human substance entirely from us, gave to his initiates at the time of his voluntary passion as a shining type and memorial . . . No other form or type under the sun was chosen by him which could represent his incarnation; behold, therefore, the icon of his life-giving body, performed with reverence and honour". "Just as that which he assumed from us is only the matter of human substance perfect in every respect but not constituting a self-subsistent person that an additional person might not be introduced into the Godhead, so too he commanded an icon consisting of special matter, namely, the substance of bread, to be offered, not forming the shape of a man so as not to allow idolatry a foothold. Therefore, just as the natural body of Christ is holy, since it is deified, so his local body, namely, the icon of his natural body, is equally holy since it is also deified as by grace through a certain sanctification . . . And just as he deified the flesh which he assumed by his own natural sanctification through the union itself, so too he was pleased that the bread of the Eucharist also, as a true icon of the natural flesh, should become a divine body, sanctified by the overshadowing of the Holy Spirit . . . The naturally ensouled flesh of the Lord, endowed with a noetic faculty, was anointed by the Holy Spirit with the divinity.[18] In the very same way the God-given icon of his flesh, the divine bread, along with the cup of the life-bearing blood from his side, was also filled with Holy Spirit. This was therefore shown to be a true icon of the incarnate dispensation of Christ our God, as we have already said, which he, the true life-giving creator of nature, bequeathed to us with his own mouth".[19]

Two important observations may be made on the iconoclasts' understanding of the sanctified bread and wine of the Eucharist as a faithful icon of Christ: first, as we have already noted, it

---

[18] The term "spiritual flesh" in the Greek original is vague and contradictory, since it can mean equally "immaterial flesh" and "flesh endowed with nous", a fact which strongly calls to mind opposition to the opinions of Apollinarius, who, however, had maintained that the soul and not the flesh of Christ was "without nous" or "without logos", since in his opinion its place was taken by the divine Logos lest there should be two *prosopa* or *noes* or *logoi* (see Gregory of Nazianzus, *Epist.* 202,14, PG 37, 333A). Clearly the iconoclasts tried deliberately through a supposedly anti-Apollinarian terminology to introduce the Origenist teaching on immaterial spiritual bodies. Cf. J.A. Munitiz, "Synoptic Greek Accounts of the Seventh Council", *REB* 32 (1974), p. 180, v. 8: "on account of their calling Christ uncircumscribed and incomprehensible as being incorporeal and without flesh". John Damascene, following the earlier Fathers, does not speak of "spiritual flesh" but of "flesh ensouled with a rational and spiritual soul" (*On the Orthodox Faith*, 46), where the "spiritual" element refers obviously only to the soul of Christ.

[19] Mansi 13, 1261E–1264C. In Origen's *Contra Celsum*, VII, 64j and 66m, identical terminology can be identified in his reproaching paganism for "degrading and debasing and abusing the divine worship of God to matter, which has been

strengthens their radical difference from the iconophiles on the meaning of the icon, and secondly — a natural consequence of this difference — it underlines their readiness to accept as an icon an impersonal reality. More specifically, the fundamental criterion of iconoclast theology and christology is found precisely in this: first in the distance they place between icon and person, secondly in their adamant refusal to accept any kind of hypostatic pictorial representation, and thirdly in their final inability to reconcile "pictorial representation" (*eikonizesthai*) with "hypostatisation" (*hyphestanai*). This explains their whole position. They do not object to the icon as such. They do not reject every icon of Christ in itself without exception, but only that which manifests his hypostasis or person. Since the bread and wine of the Eucharist do not manifest anything of this kind, being far removed from every accepted personal pictorial representation, they become acceptable as an icon of Christ precisely because they are impersonal: "only the Christ of the substance". From a purely christological point of view the impersonal icon of the Eucharistic species is equally satisfactory: it includes both natures of Christ on account of the sanctification of the gifts. The iconoclasts thus succeed in attaining an absolutely "pragmatic representation" of Christ which in reality constitutes a nullification of every iconic possibility because it does not actually represent anything pictorial, and thus fulfils the conditions which make it acceptable: the bread and wine are impersonal and at the same time the body and blood of Christ.

In this way the iconoclasts find a solution to the problem of whether the iconic representation of Christ is permissible. Does this solution, however, constitute an essentially theological and christological viewpoint completely independent of the iconoclast controversy, a thesis which somehow or other would have established itself even if icons had never entered into the history of Christianity, or is it simply a historical compromise, a concession — the only one possible — to the iconophiles? Certainly the bread and wine of the Eucharist would have existed, but would they have been viewed as an icon of Christ? This is a question to which a satisfactory answer is unlikely to be found. If we may judge from other Christian confessions which either rejected icons centuries ago or never accepted them in the first place, we see that these did not conceive of the bread and wine of the Eucharist in this way.[20]

---

modelled in such a particular way" and saying that "statues are by no means images of the divine, because they are unable to depict the formless invisible and incorporeal God".

[20] The problem of the iconoclastic understanding of the Eucharist as an icon

In any event, since the iconoclasts had confronted the question of the icon of Christ in this way, they were unable to defend a position on the icons of the Theotokos and the saints on an equally dogmatic level. The only argument which they present against them — if it may be considered an argument — is that since the legitimacy of the icon of Christ cannot be established securely, *a fortiori* the legitimacy of the icons of the Theotokos and the saints cannot be established either.[21] What is evident here is their attempt to base the rejection of icons on a christological foundation, while at the same time, of course, pointing to a pagan influence.[22]

Biblical texts are, of course, invoked, the most important of which from a christological point of view is John 20:29: "Blessed are those who have not seen and yet believe".[23] The iconophiles nevertheless easily refuted such interpretations of Scripture, as will become apparent below. The iconoclasts draw another argument of christological significance from the letter of Eusebius of Caesarea to the Empress Constantia, in which is expressed the impossibility of the representation of Christ even with regard to the human aspect.[24] But again, the iconophiles easily succeeded in refuting this evidence too, since Eusebius held Arianising beliefs and therefore every appeal to him was highly suspect.

It was under the influence of such witnesses that the iconoclasts formulated their anathemas against the iconophiles, appealing to

---

of Christ has been discussed by several scholars. B.N. Giannopoulos in his doctoral dissertation (*Ai Christologikai Antilipseis ton Eikonomachon*, Athens 1975, p. 180ff) argues that for the iconoclasts the bread of the Eucharist is not the body of Christ, nor an icon or type of Christ himself because the divine nature and hypostasis are undepictable. S. Gero, on the other hand, asserts the consubstantiality of the divine Eucharist and the flesh of Christ ("The Eucharistic Doctrine of the Byzantine Iconoclasts", BZ 68 (1975), p. 9). The surviving extracts from the *Peuseis* of Constantine V seem to support Giannopoulos. Fragment 165 refers to "the type of his body", which "through priestly elevation is received as his body properly and truly, even though this happens by participation and convention". Fragment 168 clearly distinguishes between the bread "made with hands" and the resurrected body which is "not made with hands". Giannopoulos's attempt, however, to show that the Synod of Hiereia and Constantine V held contradictory views is not persuasive.

[21] Mansi 13, 272D: "With the first refuted, there is no need of these".
[22] See Mansi 13, 273CD.
[23] Cf. Mansi 13, 280E. Specifically with regard to Jn 10:12, however, the iconoclasts do not seem to have been able to find an irrefutable reply.
[24] See Mansi 13, 313A and the text in H. Hennephof, *Textus Byzantini* pp. 42–4, and H. J. Geischer, *Der byzantinische Bilderstreit*, pp. 15–17, Cf. Mansi 13, 1253A. See the refutation by the iconophiles in Mansi 13, 317CD. Cf. George Florovsky, "The Iconoclastic Controversy" in *Christianity and Culture*, pp. 101–119. See Photius, Epist. 144 (ed. Laourdas-Westerink, Vol. I, p. 197). Cf. Nicephorus, *Antirr*. 12, PG 100, 564C; Antipater of Bozra, *Antirr. against Eusebius' apology "Pro Origene"* PG 85, 1792–1793C.

the spiritual vision of Christ instead of his sensible iconic representation:

> "If anyone attempts to conceive of the divine character of God the Logos after the Incarnation in material colours, and does not venerate him wholeheartedly with spiritual eyes, seated brighter than the sun at the right hand of God in the highest on a throne of glory, let him be anathema".[25]

The demand of the iconoclasts here cannot be a serious one, for it calls for a worship of Christ beyond the powers of fallen man, a worship which is granted to him only when he is purified and illuminated by God, as an experience of *theosis*. The iconoclast perception of Christ "acknowledges him as God, so as to be none the less uncircumscribed", even after the Incarnation, without any fear of docetism.[26] It is at any rate striking that in the definition of the iconoclast council of Hiereia (754) an entirely orthodox understanding of the Theotokos makes its appearance, with the exception of the possibility of her pictorial representation. This comes into conflict with what other sources tell us about the Nestorian beliefs of the Emperors Leo III and Constantine V concerning the Theotokos.[27] Besides this an extreme spiritualism dominates the whole of iconoclast theology and christology — "we all venerate and worship the spiritual Godhead in a spiritual manner"[28] — which inevitably distances them from the historical reality of the incarnation of the Logos.

The Iconophile Case

Against such a spiritualised comprehension of Christianity the iconophiles regarded it as their bounden duty to affirm the iconic representation of Christ, "that the whole of his incarnate dispensation might be known",[29] and they quickly stressed at the outset that all who in the past had falsified or rejected the correct understanding of the incarnate dispensation of Christ had also rejected at the same time the legitimacy of the iconic representation of Christ:

---

[25] Mansi 13, 336E.
[26] Mansi 13, 337C.
[27] Mansi 13, 345A. Cf., however, Theophanes, *Chronographia*, (ed. C. De Boor, vol. i, p. 435).
[28] Mansi 13, 352E–353A.
[29] Mansi 12, 1014D.

"We find Manichaeans not accepting icons, and Marcionites, and those who confuse the two natures of Christ, among whom are Peter the Fuller and Xenias of Hierapolis the heretics, and also Severus".[30] "For having imitated the Jews and the Saracens, the Greeks and the Samaritans,[31] and even the Manichaeans and Fantasists,[32] or the Theopaschites, they desired to banish the holy icons from sight".[33]

The iconophiles were unyielding in their conviction that the opposition to icons was a heresy: "This heresy is a worse evil than all other heresies... because it overturns the economy of the Saviour".[34] It is precisely for this reason that the iconic representation of Christ is judged to be necessary:

"That our mind through the visible character might be caught up into the invisible divinity of his majesty through a spiritual order in accordance with the flesh, which the Son of God deigned to receive for our salvation".[35]

The iconophiles find important corroborative evidence, particularly for the icon of Christ, in the tradition of his pictorial representation as it has always prevailed, and more precisely at it was defined in the eighty-second canon of the Quinisext Ecumenical Council, which says:

"... we decree that the icon of the Lamb who takes away the sin of the world, Christ our God, should be set up in his human character from now instead of the former Lamb, in our appreciation of the depth of the humiliation of the God-Logos, and as a memorial of his dispensation in the flesh and in his passion and the redemption of the world which was brought about through this".[36]

As regards the implication of what was depicted in the icon of Christ, the iconophiles were clear:

---

[30] Mansi 12, 1031E; Cf. 13, 161B, 168D, 317C. See J.N.D. Kelly op. cit. pp. 141–142. J. Pelikan, *The Emergence of the Catholic Tradition*, pp. 75–76, and *The Spririt of Eastern Christendom* pp. 53–57; W.H.C. Friend, *The Rise of the Monophysite Movement*, Cambridge 1972, pp. 167–190, 214–217.
On the Manichaeans, see John Damascene, *Imag.* II, 13, 2 (Kotter, p. 104). Cf. Leslie Barnard, "The Paulicians and Iconoclasm" in *Iconoclasm*, p. 75. For the viewpoint of Severus of Antioch (c. 465–538) see Sebastian Brock, "Iconoclasm and the Monophysites" in *Iconoclasm*, pp. 53, 54 and 56, n. 30. Cf. Mansi 13, 184AB, 253B.
[31] See John Damascene, *Liber de haeresibus*, 9 PG 94, 684–685.
[32] This refers to the followers of Julian of Halicarnassus; see Brock, op. cit., p. 54.
[33] Mansi 13, 157E, 181B, 196E. Cf. 12, 1011A; 13, 253B.
[34] Mansi 12, 1034A.
[35] Mansi 12, 1062B.
[36] Mansi 12, 1126A, 1079B; Cf. 13, 40E, 93E, 220D.

"The icon and portrait bears the character of him who became in-carnate for us and took the form of a servant, and not any character of the divinity which was united indissolubly with the spotless flesh, for the divine nature is invisible and uncircumscribed and free from form. For no one has ever seen God, as the only-begotten himself explained. But we execute the icon of his humanity in pigments and venerate it . . . We venerate the icon of Christ, that is, the person seen by men, not separated from his invisible divinity — God forbid! — but united with it from the moment of his conception . . . He was not only man but also God; and in saying 'I and the Father are one' he does not deny our nature, for these things are spoken by a human mouth and physical tongue".[37]

It is obvious from this passage that the main point of disagreement between the iconoclasts and iconophiles lay not so much in the two natures of Christ as in his one unique person, truly "a contested point", since it existed before his incarnation and was in conse-quence literally divine and uncircumscribed, but now by reason of the incarnation and hypostatic union belongs equally as much to his divine as to his human nature.[38] This extreme realism of the iconophiles with regard to the concrete results of the hypostatic union remained inaccessible to the iconoclasts. And although they too insist, as we have seen, with remarkable fidelity on the outcome of the union of the two natures, they do not seem to have been sufficiently sensitive to the fact that this union has in consequence precisely the identity of a person, the person of Christ. For the iconophiles, however, this identity has an absolute significance, for this alone truly guarantees that the union of the natures has taken place. The true God both before and after his incarnation was and remains a person, and his appearance both before and after the incarnation was and remains personal:

"and Jacob raised a stele to God . . . And God wrestled with him in human form and called him Israel, which interpreted, is 'the intellect seeing God'. And he says: 'I have seen God fact to face and my life has been preserved'. And behold, not only were the spiritual powers seen, but God himself, who is by nature invisible and incorporeal, as it is manifested, was seen in our human countenance".[39]

What seems to escape the attention of the iconoclasts entirely is the experience of the prophets, apostles and saints of the Old and New Testaments, which constitutes the vision of the person of the

---

[37] Mansi 12, 1143D–1146A; Cf. 13, 344E.
[38] Lk 2:34, Cf. Mansi 13, 168A.
[39] Mansi 13, 8B.

Logos in his uncreated glory. This vision, both before and after the incarnation, has always been considered to be the quintessence of the Orthodox tradition, the final end and supreme goal of both Testaments.[40] For this reason the vision of the icons, and especially of the icon of Christ, becomes indispensable:

> "If St Gregory (*of Nyssa*), who was alert to divine truths, shed tears when he beheld the representation of Abraham[41], how much more does the depiction of the incarnate dispensation of our Master, Christ, who for us was made man, urge those who behold it to do good and shed tears? The most holy patriarch said: if we saw an icon depicting the crucified Lord, did we too not shed tears? The holy council said: copiously, for it is precisely in this way that the depth of the humiliation of God who became man for us is properly understood".[42]

The theology of the vision of God in the icon of Christ was founded upon the distinction between archetype and icon, a distinction which nevertheless does not destroy the unity and uniqueness of the person depicted.[43] The iconophiles appealed to the Fathers of past centuries in order to defend this fundamental thesis, which renders the iconographical representation of persons legitimate. Accordingly, they invoked, amongst others, St Basil the Great, who wrote with reference to the christological questions of his time in *Against Sabellians and Arius and Anomoeans*:

> "For where there is one source and one issue, one archetype and one image, the principle of unity is not destroyed. Since the Son is begotten by the Father and naturally 'expresses' the Father in himself, as image or icon he possesses the exact likeness, and as offspring he maintains

---

[40] On this see J. Romanides, *Franks, Romans, Feudalism and Doctrine*, pp. 40–2. Cf. Mansi 13, 225E: "the vision and sight which clearly and unmistakably guides us towards the glory of God".

[41] See Gregory of Nyssa, *On the Divinity of the Son and the Spirit and on Abraham*, PG 46, 572c. Cf. John Damascene, *Imag.* I, 47 (Kotter, p. 151).

[42] Mansi 13, 12A. From the conditional optative of the question addressed by the Patriarch Tarasius to the council, it may perhaps be inferred that the pictorial representation of events from the life and passion of Christ was not yet general. Certainly the confirmation of the council as the Seventh Ecumenical Council contributed decisively to the depiction of the whole of the New Testament. Cf., however, John Damascene, *Imag.* I, 8, 40–75 (Kotter, pp. 82–3); Mansi 13, 45B.

[43] On the contrary, the iconoclasts 'say that there is no difference between icon and prototype, and although these are of different essences they deem them to be of the same essence' (Mansi 13, 252D). Cf. 260E: 'They say that icon and prototype are the same thing and that is why they ascribe confusions or divisions of Christ's two natures to those who depict the narrative of the Gospels'. Cf. also 261A: "They say that the icon of Christ and Christ himself do not differ from each other in essence at all".

the identity of substance. For he who looks at the imperial image in the agora and says that the person in the picture is the emperor does not confess that there are two emperors, i.e. the image and the man who is depicted in it. Nor if he points at the likeness in the picture and says, 'this is the emperor' does he deprive the prototype of his respect for him by such a statement".[44]

In this passage St Basil defends the unity of the triadic God in connection with the homoousion of the Father and the Son. He is clearly replying to the argument of contemporary heretics that if the Son is of the same substance as the Father, then there are two Gods. But what is true, of course, of the relationship between the Father and Son as the natural image of the Father is not true of the relationship between the emperor and his icon, because the icon of the emperor is not natural but imitative. At the same time it was not necessary for such a distinction to be made, because the example was perfectly adequate for the situation for which it was given. In the iconoclastic period, however, when this passage comes to be cited, the distinction is indispensable, for the passage is made to serve entirely different aims from those for which it was originally written. In fact even if it did not happen at once, the Seventh Ecumenical Council made the distinction that in the case of the imitative icon, "the icon is one thing and the prototype another, and no sensible person will look for the properties of the prototype in the icon. For true reasoning recognises nothing in the icon other than participation by name in the subject of the icon, and not by substance", as happens in the case of the Son regarded as a natural icon of the Father. The Seventh Ecumenical Council, however, did not advance further than the latter distinction.[45] Only much later, in Theodore of Studius, for example, is

---

[44] Mansi 13, 72A; PG 31, 600–617. Cf. a parallel passage from Athanasius, Ibid. 69B. Here again we find the imitative and the natural icon treated as identical. Nevertheless, Basil himself, in his treatise *On the Holy Spirit* (PG 32, 149C) is the first to make a distinction between the natural and the imitative icon. He writes in ch. 17: "Because the icon of the emperor is also called '*emperor*' it does not mean that there are two emperors; neither is the power divided nor the glory partitioned. Just as the authority and power which governs is one, our praise is one and not multiple, because honour paid to the icon is transferred to the prototype. Therefore that which the icon is in our case in an imitative mode, the Son is in the divine case in a natural mode. And precisely as in the pictorial craftsmanship the likeness is rendered in the forms, likewise in the case of the divine and uncomposite nature the union lies in the communion of the Godhead". Cf. John Damascene, *Imag.* I, 35; II, 31; III, 48 and Mansi 12 1067D.

[45] Mansi 13, 257D, 244B: "according to the name and according to its application to the members characterised".

it possible to encounter, now with the utmost clarity, the distinction: "the natural icon is one thing, and the imitative icon another".[46]

Thus we can say that the theology of the vision of God through the icon of Jesus Christ simply began but did not come to an end with the Seventh Ecumenical Council. It continued to develop for a long time, even after the definitive victory of the icons (843). The starting-point for this theology, of course, was provided by St Basil who first defined the relationship between archetype and icon and the possibility of the latter's "participation" in the former, a thesis entirely acceptable to the iconoclasts in the case of the natural icon, but inconceivable in the case of the imitative kind.[47]

Prototype and Imitative Icon

It is therefore possible for us to conclude that the iconoclasts adhere to the tendency of the fourth-century Fathers to emphasise the natural icon against the Arians and Eunomians. They are unable to admit, however, that these same Fathers are ready to accept even the imitative icon, and distinguish clearly between this and the natural kind. What they appear to find most difficult to accept is that there should be any relationship between prototype and imitative icon, or that there should be any participation of the one in the other. It is on the capacity for relationship and participation, however, that the iconophiles base their argument:

> "Just as he who does not honour the Son, as the Lord says, does not honour the Father who sent him (Jn 5:23), so too, he who does not honour the icon (of Christ) does not honour the person portrayed either".[48] And "everyone who honours the icon, manifestly honours the

---

[46] Theodore of Studius, IPG 99, 501B. Cf. Euthymius Zigabenus, *Panoply* 22, PG 130, 1164. According to John Damascene, "an imitative mode of icon made by God" is also the creation of man (*Imag.* III, 20, Kotter, p. 128), which means in John's view that "God himself first made an icon and exhibited icons" (*Imag.* II, 20, 15), although John also calls icons "imitations" (*Imag.* II, 58), without employing the adjective *"mimetikos"*.

[47] It should be emphasised at this point that not only Basil (see note 44) but all the Fathers clearly teach that there is absolutely no personal-hypostatic communion and relationship either between the three persons of the Holy Trinity or between consubstantial created hypostases (e.g. angels or men), but that in the case of both the Triadic God and created consubstantial hypostases the only path to communion and relationship is through the common nature of each and its energies. The communion and relationship which exists between prototype and icon cannot be described as "hypostatic" because the icon does not constitute a particular hypostasis but simply belongs to the hypostasis of its prototype.

[48] John Damascene, *Imag.* III, 49 (Kotter, p. 147).

archetype".[49] "For who does not know that when the icon is dishonoured, the dishonour inevitably rubs off on the person portrayed in the icon? This is a fact which truth itself knows and the nature of things teaches. With this the divine Fathers concur, St Basil saying: 'The honour of the icon passes over to the prototype',[50] and Athanasius: 'He therefore who venerates the icon venerates the emperor portrayed in it',[51] and similarly Chrysostom: 'Do you not know that if you insult the icon of the emperor, you transfer the force of the insult to the prototype?[52] And these Fathers followed the nature of things",[53] "with the result that he who venerates the icon and says that this is Christ, the Son of God, does not sin . . . Therefore the Father [i.e. Basil the Great] proved there to be not two venerations but one both of the icon and of the archetype which the icon depicts".[54]

With a christological view of this kind, the only reason that remains for the denial of the iconic representation of Christ is the denial

---

[49] John Damascene, *Imag.* III, 56 (Kotter, p. 169). As one of the Holy Trinity, the Son has the Father as its "archetype". But that which refers to the icon of Christ has Christ himself as its "prototype". In no iconophile text, however, is the thesis presented that anyone who does not honour the icon of Christ insults the Father — evidently not to give rise to the suspicion that in the icon of Christ his divinity is also represented pictorially. Although this was explicitly denied by the iconophiles it was nevertheless something of which the iconoclasts accused them. It is clearly for the same reason that the honour and veneration of the icon of Christ came finally to be characterised as relative and hypostatic. See Euthymius Zygabenus, *Panoply*, PG 13, 1171: "With regard to the icon of Christ, the veneration is relative and equivocal; for in venerating the icon we do not also venerate the Father but only Christ who is represented by it, who as a result of the Incarnation is represented pictorially in accordance with his bodily appearance; this is a veneration which is relative and hypostatic". Cf. Theodore of Studius, *Epist.* 85, PG 99, 1328–29, 1472; but see also Mansi 13, 116C.
[50] *On the Holy Spirit*, PG 32, 149C. Cf. note 45 and Mansi 12, 1146A; 13, 69E, 1273AB, 324C, 93C.
[51] Athanasius, *Against the Arians*, III, 5, PG 26, 332A. Cf. Mansi 13, 69B.
[52] John Chrysostom, cited by John Damascene, *Imag.* II, 61 (Kotter, p.163).
[53] Mansi 13, 325D.
[54] Mansi 13, 72CD and 12, 1067CD. Cf. Euthymius Zygabenus, *Panoply*, PG 130, 1072: "If it is not possible in the case of a body for its shadow to be separated from it, but it always exists alongside it even when it is not visible, neither can the icon of Christ be divided from him . . . and the veneration of these is one because there is a single character in both . . . and for the same reason the icon is identical with its archetype, not with its nature but with its hypostasis". See Theodore of Studius, *Antirr.* 111, PG 99, 405 "In the case of anyone represented pictorially it is not the nature but the hypostasis which is represented . . . Therefore Christ is circumscribed according to his hypostasis (even though he is uncircumscribed in his divinity), but not according to the natures from which he is constituted". See ibid. 99, 349D, 501A. Cf., however, his bold assertion in 99, 344BC: "Thus one may say without necessarily sinning that the divinity is in the icon, since the same is true in the case of the type of the cross and of other dedicated offerings too, but not by natural union — for they are not identical with the deified flesh — but still the divinity is in them by relative participation; because they participate in divinity only by grace and by honour".

of his incarnation: "If the Lord had not become incarnate, his holy icon after the flesh would not have been made".[55] Consequently,

> "by painting the icon of his human character and his human countenance according to the flesh, and not of his incomprehensible and invisible Godhead, we henceforth hasten to set forth the content of faith, showing that he did not unite our nature to himself in an illusory or shadowy way, as some of the ancient heretics have taught in their error, but that he became a man in very fact and in truth, perfect in all things, only without the sin which was shown in us by the enemy. Armed with this understanding of the true faith concerning him, we kiss the character of his sacred flesh when we encounter it in the icons, and we render it every veneration and appropriate honour, for it is by this that we have been brought to the memorial of his divine and life-giving and ineffable incarnation".[56]

For the iconophiles, this insistence on the incarnation, the fundamental fact of Christianity from which all else springs, inevitably involves even its depiction in icons, for iconography constitutes the essential mode in which faith in the incarnation is confessed:

> "True adoration and worship of the true God is performed scrupulously through fidelity to our holy confession of faith about him and through keeping the integral and more cardinal mysteries and laws given by him".[57]

It is striking that the inconophiles give first place to the correct confession of faith as true adoration and worship, which means that in spite of their devotion to icons they were not by any means sacramentalists or legalists, as their opponents showed themselves to be by putting forward the bread and the wine of the Eucharist as the only acceptable icon of Christ worthy of all adoration and worship. At this juncture we should remember that the Orthodox tradition does not honour the body and blood of Christ in the Eucharist with special acts of worship, as the Western Christian tradition does with the service of Benediction.[58] Moreover, not even the icon of Christ is adored as divine in itself by the iconophiles: "We therefore do not call the icon itself God, but we know God, who is depicted in the icon and whose name the icon bears".[59]

---

[55] Mansi 13, 96A.
[56] Mansi 13, 101BC; C. 116AB, 168B, 185DE–188A.
[57] Mansi 13, 109D; C. 124A.
[58] From this observation it is possible for one to conclude that the West, perhaps unconsciously, appears to be the heir to the iconoclast understanding of the Eucharistic gifts as the uniquely acceptable icon of Christ.
[59] Mansi 13, 188D. The difference between veneration and worship is examined at length in the Chapter VI, pp. 117–29.

It is here that we come to an important difference between the icon itself and its material, which has been discussed at length elsewhere. In his funeral oration on Basil the Great, Gregory of Nyssa had already expressed the strong opinion that those heretics who regarded the Logos as a creature and at the same time as God essentially worshipped "the creature instead of the Creator . . . imposing on it the name of Christ".[60] The iconoclasts attempted to transfer these phrases of Gregory to the icon of Christ, since they were unable to conceive of the difference between idol and icon, a situation which flowed naturally from their exclusive insistence on the natural icon and their utter rejection of the imitative icon. The iconophiles, however, rightly opposed them:

"Arius, Eunomius, Eudoxius, Macedonius and the Anomoeans and semi-Arians associated with them, who say that the Son and Logos of the Father is both a creature and our God, worship the creature as God and are therefore rightly called idolaters by him (*Gregory of Nyssa*) and the catholic Church, for they say that he whom they worship has come into being from non-being like the whole order of created things. But the Christians have neither called the holy icons gods, nor have they worshipped them as gods, nor have they placed their hopes of salvation in them".[61]

Furthermore, in order to counter the iconoclasts' accusations that they were thus dividing the two natures of Christ, since they did not represent both of these natures in his icon, nor did they identify his icon with them, the iconophiles appealed to the conceptual distinction (*kat'epinoian*) between the natures of Christ which dated from the time of the christological controversies:

"When the natures are conceptually separated (*tais epinoiais*), the names are also divided, says Gregory the Theologian, and all our holy Fathers, avoiding the confusion of the natures, say that the natures are distinct conceptually by reason of difference, not of division from each other . . . Nestorius divides the natures in reality . . . but the catholic Church confesses the union without confusion and only conceptually divides the natures indivisibly, confessing Emmanuel to be one and the same also after the union".[62]

Thus the conceptual distinction between the natures does not constitute a division of them and may be used in the pictorial representation of Christ according to his human aspect precisely

---

[60] Mansi 13, 224BE–225AC; PG 46, 788–817.
[61] Ibid.
[62] Mansi 13, 248CD, 257C, 261B, 341BC; of *Oration 11 on the Son.*

because it expresses in the best way possible the unconfused union of the two natures of Christ.

While struggling so hard to defend doctrinally the legitimacy of the iconic representation of Christ, the iconophiles decisively reject their adversaries' argument that the unique form of his iconic representation is to be found in the "divine bread" of the holy Eucharist.

> "None of those trumpets of the spirit, the holy Apostles, or of our renowned Fathers has ever called our bloodless sacrifice, which is celebrated as a memorial of the passion of our God and of his whole dispensation, an icon of his body. For they did not receive this manner of speaking or of confessing the faith from the Lord. On the contrary, they hear him saying in the Gospel ... take, eat, this is my body ... He did not say: take, eat the icon of my body".[63] "These gentlemen, in their desire to abolish the vision of the holy icons, introduced another icon which is not an icon but body and blood ... If it is an icon of the body, it cannot be the divine body itself".[64]

Here the deep chasm between the two opposing sides in their understanding of the icon of Christ becomes clearly apparent. With the same ease the iconophiles refute all the biblical testimonies which the iconoclasts adduce to prove the illegitimacy of the iconic representation of Christ:

> "For they have taken the sayings about the invisible and incomprehensible Godhead and applied them to the dispensation according to the flesh ... For what sensible person does not know that the text, 'No one has ever seen God' (Jn 1:18), was written about the divine nature? And that if anyone understands the text, 'We have neither heard his voice nor seen his form' (Jn 5:37), as applying to the humanity, he refutes the whole of the Gospel? ... And the divine adoration and worship (Jn 4:24), which Christians have in themselves as the true and sincere faith, they have likened to a relative and honourary veneration".[65] Moreover, they took the apostolic proclamation that the Son is the express image of God the Father, because of the invariability of essence, and understanding this reciprocally in a perverted way, they applied it to the flesh assumed by the God-Logos and they belch forth a new statement from a deranged mind, saying, 'If anyone attempts

---

[63] Mansi 13, 1264E–265FA.
[64] Mansi 13, 265DE; Cf. 268A.
[65] Mansi 13, 1281CDE; Cf. 284AB. It is worth noting here that the council clearly accepted that the Father could not be represented pictorially. See Mansi 12, 963D; 13, 284AD; Cf. Theodore of Studius, PG 99, 457D: "Therefore if iconic representation had existed before the Incarnation of the Logos, it would not only have been base but most absurd for the non-incarnate Logos to be localised in the flesh".

to understand the divine character of God the Logos in the incarnation through material colours, let him be anathema'. . . But the divine Apostle, wishing to proclaim the identity of the substance of the Son and divine Logos with that of God the Father, found nothing more appropriate and apposite than to proclaim the Son as the character of the hypostasis of the Father".[66]

The Visibility of the Divine

At this juncture we approach what is perhaps the most difficult christological aspect of the iconoclast controversy. Although the iconophiles interpret Scripture correctly on the point at issue, they do not cease to accept that Christ also has a "visible character" and indeed a "circumscribed" character.[67] Even though the term "character" does not always mean a person's external appearance or countenance, nevertheless this is the sense in which the iconophiles use it in this context. The question therefore arises: What is the relationship between this "visible" character and the divine, uncreated hypostasis of God the Logos? Clearly the iconoclasts supposed — and they were perhaps somewhat justified — that both these (*the visible character and the uncreated hypostasis*) were identified with one another by the iconophiles in the imitative icon of Christ if they were not to introduce another person.[68] The reply came later from Theodore of Studius that the visible character of Christ, or "the likeness of Christ, in whatever matter it may be characterised, does not participate in the matter in which it is exhibited but remains in the hypostasis of Christ, of which it is a property".[69] As a result, the answer of St Theodore does not identify the visible character

---

[66] Mansi 13, 337AB.

[67] Mansi 12, 1062B; Cf. 13, 340E and 12, 1143D–1146A and note 54. Theodore of Studius goes even further. In his view every icon "shows in itself in an imitative mode the character of the prototype" (PG 99, 500B). And whereas, as we have already seen, the iconoclasts identified the icon with the archetype with regard to "nature" or "essence", accepting in this way only the natural icon, the iconophiles made a sharp distinction between the two. With regard to the imitative icon, Theodore of Studius arrives at the following valid formulation: "the icon is identical with the archetype through its likeness" (PG 99, 501A).

[68] Cf. Mansi 13, 257E. Strangely, however, some contemporary Orthodox scholars maintain that the presence of a mandorla around the person of Christ in his icons expresses the identity of his uncreated hypostasis with the "visible character" of his human nature. See J. Meyendorff, *Christ in Eastern Christian Thought*, Crestwood 1975, p. 188. But it is precisely the defender of the icons, Theodore of Studius, who rules this out — and rightly too — because then the uncreated hypostasis of the Logos would be visible!

[69] PG 99, 504D–505A. Cf. Ibid. 1640A: "subtracting matter by the logos of the epinoia, from the character represented in it".

with the uncreated hypostasis of Christ, but with a property of this
hypostasis which because of the Incarnation is present also in the
icon and permits a unity between archetype and icon, avoiding
any possibility of division. It has to do, in fact, with the supremely
apophatic element of each person: the uniqueness, exclusiveness
and incomprehensibility of its mode of existence which makes it
"incommunicable" and inaccessible to rational analysis and understanding. We do not really know what "person" or "hypostasis" is,
not only in Christ's case but also in the case of the Father, of the
Holy Spirit and of every human being. We recognise persons,
however, who hypostatise the human nature common to all, thanks
to the natural capacity we possess for marking our natural indi-
viduality wherever and however it may be hypostatised.

The pictorial representation of persons in imitative icons does
not hinder the capacity for recognition which we possess from
operating also in the case of such imitations, as was emphasised
in so masterly a way by Aristotle. Nevertheless, the distinctive
"property" of each hypostasis as depicted on each occasion escapes
us; it continues to be inconceivable, "remaining in the hypostasis
of which it is a property". The potentiality, then, for the iconic
representation of persons or hypostases is not, in the last analysis,
an invention of the iconophiles, but an existent and real capacity
for recognition, which human nature possesses and which functions
naturally amongst all hypostases or persons of the same substance.
Since the Logos became consubstantial with us, a true participant
in our nature, the cognitive function is assuredly operative in his
case too, as regards his humanity and its "visible character", which
does not coincide with his uncreated hypostasis. Consequently, the
iconophiles only "followed the nature of things, while they (*the
iconoclasts*) revolted against both the Church and the truth".[70] The
potentiality for imitative representation lies on the one hand in
human nature and on the other in the hypostasis of the archetype.
Every icon depends absolutely on these two factors, for the icon
is nothing more than "a door . . . which opens our mind created
in accordance with God to the inward likeness of the prototype".[71]

The inability of the iconoclasts to conceive of the imitative icon

---

[70] Mansi 13, 325D. Cf. Theodore of Studius, *Refutation*, PG 99, 444D: "For
nothing else in the properties relating to man is prior to his ability to be represented pictorially; that which cannot be represented pictorially is not a man
but an abortion". See also PG 99, 420A: "The creation of man in the image
(icon) and likeness of God [shows] that the form of icon-making is something
divine".
[71] *Vita Stephani*, PG 100, 1113A.

in this way, and above all to conceive of these two factors on which every imitative representation depends, led them, as we have already seen, to the extreme view of maintaining that Christ is "uncircumscribed even after the incarnation", manifestly on account of the identification on their part of his uncreated hypostasis with his "visible character".[72] This was the cause of their suspicion that the flesh of Christ is represented in icons as "undeified", through being "extracted" in some way from the divine hypostasis, when about to be portrayed, so that its representation can be achieved.[73] The iconophiles, however, refuted this line of reasoning by "following the nature of things":

> "For just as when one draws a man, one does not render him lifeless but he remains alive and the image is said to be his by its likeness, so too when we make an icon of the Lord, we confess that the flesh of the Lord is deified and we know that the icon is nothing other than an icon manifesting an imitation of the prototype . . . and if the image is evidently that of a defiled man or of a demon, it is profane and defiled too, because of its prototype".[74]

Finally, it must be admitted that it is difficult for one to appreciate with the same realism as the iconophiles the immanence of the "incommunicable" hypostasis of the prototype in the imitative icon. It is an immanence which is not proved in any way, yet it does confirm the "ineffability" of the person. The iconophiles appear to be dominated by the certainty of God's undemonstrable yet living immanence "amongst them" (Matt. 18:20) a certainty which in the last analysis coincides with the very essence of the Christian faith, "for if, as they prate, the painting of icons resembles the setting up of idols, the mystery of our redemption is nullified, which the Son of God realised by his very immanence in the flesh so as to conduct himself without sin for our sake".[75]

---

[72] Mansi 13, 337C.
[73] Mansi 13, 341E.
[74] Mansi 13, 344B.
[75] Mansi 13, 409E–412A. Cf. Theodore of Studius, PG 99, 505A.

CHAPTER SIX

ICON AND WORSHIP

The arguments of the iconoclasts relating to the role of the icons in worship are impressive and of fundamental importance. The main point of departure for their hostility was always the suspicion or conviction that for the iconophiles the icons were in themselves objects of worship. The classic formulation of this accusation is that "Christians approach the icons as gods" and consequently the icons are designated "idols" and "the products of human hands".[1] In letting it clearly be understood that "the customs observed by us from ancient times (*viz. of icons*) leads to alienation from God", the iconoclasts expressed themselves forcefully "on the deceptive colourful painting of likenesses, the tearing away of the human mind from the sublime worship that befits God to the lowly and materialistic worship of the creature".[2]

Imageless Prayer

The most significant problem that emerges from this is whether the arguments of the iconoclasts, especially their accusation of idolatry, are sincere, or whether they are put together with the specific intention of furthering the wider aims of iconoclast theology, such as, for example, the affirmation of the enduring nature of inward and spiritual realities in contradistinction to material and corruptible reality. This question, which arises from the iconoclastic theological perspective as a whole, cannot be answered with certainty in the absence of clear indications in the sources. The overall spirituality however, finds biblical support for its defence of a totally immaterial and aniconic Christian worship.

Primary support is provided by St John's Gospel. For the iconoclasts this Gospel constituted the most important source for their conception of imageless worship. Passages such as "God is spirit, and those who worship him must worship in spirit and truth" (Jn 4:24), "No one has ever seen God" (Jn 1:18), "His voice you have never heard, his form you have never seen" (Jn 5:37) and "Blessed

---

[1] Mansi 12, 1010E; 959DE, 966BCD, 1146B; 208E, 216A, 232B, 284D.
[2] Mansi 13, 116D, 229E. Cf. 12, 1054C: "What could be more profane or more abominable than calling Christians idolaters?"

are those who have not seen and yet believe" (Jn 20:29) were mobilised against the icons.[3]

The iconophiles, of course, attempted to counter the iconoclastic interpretation of the Johannine passages, though not always with the same felicity. The problem, however, was not so simple that it could be confined to the hermeneutic level. A whole monastic spiritual tradition, which was already prevalent throughout the Christian East from the fourth century, and was introduced into the West in the same period, was based on the denial of representations and images of the noetic faculty as analogical means of spiritual ascent, though not on the denial of sensible and material means in general. This tradition, found essentially in both the Old and New Testaments, can be traced historically in Eastern monasticism, which through Clement of Alexandria, Origen, Evagrius, and the subsequent monastic and ascetic line of development from Mark the Monk to John Climacus and the later hesychastic tradition, became the main line of Orthodox spirituality. The nucleus of this tradition is the rejection of "intellectual images" (*noerai eikones*), that is to say, of all noetic representations and thoughts without exception, not only of evil but also of good things, in order to attain communion and union with God through prayer. The problem is indeed formidable because, as the history of Eastern Christianity makes abundantly clear, the rejection of "intellectual images" in prayer does not necessarily entail the rejection of the actual visible representations of the sacred personages, Christ and the saints.[4] The defenders of the icons themselves, after the victory over the iconoclasts, continued to fight against noetic representations, and their leaders turned out to be the principal transmitters of Orthodox hesychasm. The sources of monastic literature are truly confused. In Clement of Alexandria and in Origen we find a clear opposition to every kind of image, including no doubt visible representations, which had not yet come into general ecclesiastical use as they did later. Clement openly proclaims "the impossibility

---

[3] Cf. Mansi 13, 280E.

[4] See John Damascene, *Imag.* 111, 12 (Kotter, pp. 123–4): "For since we are twofold, fashioned from soul and body, and our soul is not naked but is hidden as if behind a curtain, it is impossible for us to arrive at intelligibles except through corporeal beings. Just as we hear with corporeal ears by means of sensible words and understand spiritual things, so we come through bodily contemplation to spiritual contemplation. This is why Christ assumed a body and a soul, because man possessed a body and a soul. This is also why baptism is twofold, from water and spirit, and communion, prayer and psalmody are all twofold — both corporeal and spiritual — and also lights and incense". Cf. Gregory of Nazianzus, *Theological Oration* 2, 31 (A.J. Mason, p. 353).

of depicting God" without any reservation with respect to the
consequences of the Incarnation.[5] Origen likewise rejects without
distinction every depiction of the divine.[6]

It is characteristic that in the same period Gnosticism, despite
its partial acceptance of iconic representations showed strong tendencies towards a complete rejection of the depiction of the divine
in at least some of its branches, as Hippolytus of Rome testifies.[7]
Doubtless these phenomena betray a strong Hellenic influence on
early Christianity.[8] Through Evagrius, however, although this influence did not cease entirely, the war against intellectual images and
noetic representations was confined, as a result of the endeavour
to attain union with God through prayer, strictly to the inner world
of man and especially of the monk, or ascetic.[9]

Through Mark the Monk however, and John Climacus, who are
influenced more by the anti-Origenistic current of the sixth century,
the ascetic tradition of the East was delivered decisively from de-
pendence on Greek idealistic philosophy, and remained simply a
practical method of the "discarding of thoughts" for the attainment
of union with God.[10]

It is therefore not by chance that the iconoclasts use arguments
drawn from St John's Gospel. Spiritual and intellectual worship,
without the beholding of any "form" whatsoever, without hearing
any "voice", favours one interpretation more than the other and
perhaps expresses, even if indirectly, a tendency to return to certain
early Christian models which exhibit Hellenistic influences. It is
not certain whether the iconoclasts were always conscious of what
they were aiming at, or of their less immediate motives. The
combatting of idolatry through the rejection of icons was a manifest

---

[5] *Stromateis* 1, 24, PG 8, 909C. Cf. ibid. VI, 76 and *Protrepticus* IV, 50, 53.
[6] See, e.g. *Contra Celsum* III, 76; 111, 40; IV, 26; IV, 31; VII, 65–66; *De Principiis*
1, 1, 4.
[7] Hippolytus, *Contra Haer.* 5, 7 PG 16, 3131C: "Want of form (*aschemosyne*)
is in their view the first and blessed substance, the cause of all forms for whatever
has been endowed with form". Cf. Basil The Great, *Hexaemeron*, Hom. 1, 7; 11,
12. On the different branches of Gnosticism. See Kurt Rudolph, *Gnosis* (trans.
R. McLachlan Wilson) Edinburgh 1983, p. 225f.
[8] On this see C.H. Bigg, *The Christian Platonists of Alexandria*, Oxford 1913,
passim; W.L. Knox, *Some Hellenistic Elements in Primitive Christianity*, London 1944
(esp. Lecture III, p. 55f); C.H. Hodd, *The Bible and the Greeks*, London 1935.
[9] "Blessed is the mind which in the time of prayer has acquired perfect
freedom from form (*amorphian*)", Evagrius Ponticus, *Chapters on Prayer*, Ch. 117,
PG 79, 1193A. Cf. also ibid. chs. 67 and 114; also the same author's *Praktikos*,
ch. 55, PG 40, 1248A.
[10] Mark the Hermit, PG 65, 921D C. ibid. 1064B. John Climacus, *Ladder*, 27,
17, PG 88, 112A.

and conscious rejection of Hellenism. The complete rejection of matter, however, in the name of a spiritual worship, was inescapably a return to Neoplatonism. As regards the former, the rejection was conscious. As regards the latter, was there not even the smallest suspicion of a return?

As this question still remains open, the iconoclasts' precise conception of worship in spirit cannot be clarified completely.

The Veneration of Images

The iconoclasts, of course, did not confine themselves to St John the Evangelist. They also turned to Pauline passages in support of their theses. According to their interpretation, Romans 1:23 — "and they exchanged the glory of the immortal God for images resembling mortal man" — refers to the iconophiles' production of the image of Christ. So too did Romans 1:25 — "They worshipped the creature rather than the Creator". Even more striking and apt is the use of 2 Corinthians 5:16 — "even though we once regarded Christ from a human point of view, we regard him thus no longer" — against the possibility of representing Christ after the resurrection, and also 2 Corinthians 5:7 — "for we walk by faith, not by appearance" — in order to arrive at the assertion: "in serving the invisible Godhead, we all worship in a spiritual manner".[11]

Nevertheless, the testimony of the Seventh Ecumenical Council, that in spite of all this the iconoclasts did not totally reject the legitimacy of the representation of sacred personages but were disposed to agree with the iconophiles on the retention of icons in churches provided they were not venerated, remains important: "They contented themselves with saying that iconic representation should exist only for the purpose of remembrance (*eis anamnesin monon*) and not for veneration (*kai ouchi kai eis aspasmon*).[12]

This iconoclast thesis can indeed be confirmed from a historical point of view if it is borne in mind that iconoclasm originally manifested itself not in the destruction of icons or in their removal from places of worship, but in their being placed higher up in the churches, by order of the emperor Leo III, to prevent their veneration. It appears from this that, originally at least, the fundamental question concerned not the legitimacy or otherwise of the manufacture of icons but the extent to which they should be venerated. This problem continued to be troublesome throughout

---

[11] See Mansi 13, 285C, 352E–353A.
[12] Mansi 13, 364B.

the course of the iconoclastic dispute thus revealing itself to be
the backbone of the conflict.[13] The iconoclasts from the beginning
posed questions concerning the correct worship of God, and the
iconophiles were eager to reply.

The first clarification which the iconophiles made was that there
were two kinds of "manufactured objects" (*cheiropoieta*): "those of
the devil, which are harmful and accursed and which God said
must not be venerated. This refers to the idolaters established in
the promised land who worshipped animals of gold and silver and
wood, and the whole of creation, and all the birds of the air, and
said: these are our gods and there is no other god". But there
are also "manufactured objects" which are intended "for the service
and glory of God . . . God chose two men from the people of Israel
and blessed them and sanctified them so that they might produce
manufactured objects, but to the glory and service of God and as
a memorial to their generations, namely, Bezalel and Oholiab of
the first tribe of Dan".[14]

The second important clarification of the iconophiles was the
distinction between veneration (*proskynesis*) which is relative (*schetike*)
and that which partakes of the nature of worship (*latreutike*).[15] The
first belongs to human life generally, and even to greetings between
people, who bow down before each other as before creatures
created in the image of God.[16] The second, which is worshipful veneration, is given only to the uncreated God.[17] With this clarification

---

[13] Cf. Theodore of Studius, *Antir.* 2, 6, PG 99, 356B.

[14] Mansi 12, 962B–D; Cf. Exod. 35:30–34. See also Mansi 12, 978A, 1070A;
13, 49D, 376B.

[15] Mansi 12, 963C. Cf. 13, 377DE: "It is fitting to render to these (the icons)
salutation and the veneration of honour, but not in keeping with our faith true
worship, which is due to the divine nature alone". Cf. John Damascene, *Imag.*
1, 8, 76, 82; 1, 8, 85f. (Kotter, pp. 80–3).

[16] John Damascene, *Imag.* 111, 33–40 (Kotter, pp. 139–41); 73 (Kotter, 174).
Mansi 12, 1067E; 13, 45E, 48A, 49BC, 53B, 100E–101A, 405AE.

[17] See Mansi 12, 56AB: "Let no one take offence at the meaning of the
veneration . . . of St Anastasius, bishop of Theoupolis; for we venerate both holy
men and holy angels, but we do not worship them. 'For you shall venerate the
Lord your God', says Moses, 'and you shall worship him alone'. And observe
how to the word 'worship' he added 'alone', but to the word 'venerate' he did
not do so at all, so that it is permitted to venerate, veneration being the
manifestation of honour but it is certainly not permitted to worship". Cf. Mansi
13, 100C, and 267B, where a distinction is made between the sacrifice of animals
to God by the righteous of the Old Testament and the sacrifices of idolaters:
"They will therefore condemn Abel and Noah and Abraham, on account of
their offering sacrifices of animals, and Moses and Samuel and David and the
rest of the patriarchs, because even they offered up foreign and Greek sacrifices
to God, even though Scripture bears witness concerning their sacrifice: 'the Lord
smelled the pleasing odour' (Gen. 8:21)".

the iconophiles prove conclusively that neither do they regard the
icons as gods, nor do they worship the icons themselves or, with
the exception of Christ, the persons represented in them.[18]

"I accept the icons and worship them not as gods — God forbid —
but manifesting up to now the relationship and the affection of my
soul which I have always had towards them from the very beginning,
I beseech all of them from the depths of my soul to intercede with
God for me".[19]

That is why the accusation of idolatry which the iconoclasts make
is incomprehensible to the iconophiles:

"What is more profane, or more innovative, than calling Christians
idolaters?"[20] "God forbid that we should deify the icons themselves,
as some gossips say. All our love and affection is focused on affection
for God and his saints. We have the icons, like the books of sacred
Scripture, as reminders of our veneration, preserving the purity our
faith".[21]

The purity of faith is preserved precisely in the clear distinction
between relative veneration and the worship of adoration. The
motive for the production and veneration of icons is not of an
idolatrous nature; it is the love and unquenchable affection which
is felt for the sacred personages represented:

"In accordance with the affection and love which we feel for the Lord
and the saints, we depict their countenance in icons; we venerate not
the boards and colours but the persons themselves whose names the
icons bear".[22]

The fundamental relationship between archetype and image, which
has been discussed elsewhere, contributes decisively to the comprehension of the distinction between iconophiles and idolaters,
and especially that between relative veneration and worship:

"For when imperial portraits and images are brought into a city and
the leading men and the people greet them with acclamations, they
are honouring not a board or a painting of encaustic wax but the

---

[18] Mansi 12, 966B: "We place no hope in these". Cf. 13, 44DE, 104B, 225A.
[19] Mansi 12, 1014B; 13, 104A, 164D.
[20] Mansi 12, 1054C; Cf. 13, 397DE.
[21] Mansi 12, 1062C; 13, 52E, 53A, 101DE, 225A, 361A.
[22] Mansi 12, 1063A; Cf. 1146A: "It is not by bestowing veneration on matter
and colours but by being guided through matter by our spiritual eyes towards
the prototype that we render him honour". See also 13, 57C.

portrait of the emperor. Similarly, creation does not honour that earthly form but hymns the heavenly countenance".[23]

And conversely: "whoever abuses the image of wood and paint is judged to have offended not against lifeless matter but against the emperor himself. For he conveys a twofold insult to the emperor".[24] Every icon made as a representation of the Lord, or of the angels, or of the apostles, or of the martyrs, or of the righteous "is holy".[25] "These we worship with a relative affection . . . clearly assigning our worship and faith to the one and only true God".[26] The referring of the veneration paid to icons to the prototype is indicated with the greatest clarity in the phrases "with a relative affection" and "to the prototype", although at the same time the distinction is proclaimed between this veneration and the worship and faith shown in regard to "the one and only God".[27] "Why, therefore, should we not venerate the holy servants of God and make and set up their icons as a memorial to them, so that they should not be forgotten?".[28]

This appeal to the commemoration of the saints and of Christ as a motive (along with affection and love) lying behind their representation in icons is very characteristic: "It is as memorial that icons of the saints are painted and venerated, since they are servants of God and supplicate and importune the Godhead on our behalf".[29]

At this juncture the following question must be investigated: in the opinion of the iconophiles, to what should we attribute the description of the icons as holy and, above all, the conviction that the icons communicate holiness to their worshippers? From a theological point of view this question has been examined and interpreted on the basis of the relationship between the icons and their prototypes, a relationship which creates a hypostatic identity between them in such a way that contact with the icon constitutes immediate contact with the prototype.[30] The principal liturgical mode of contact with an icon, however, is precisely through its veneration. And it is from this point of view that the question interests us here.

The veneration of an icon was never understood by the iconophiles

---

[23] Mansi 13, 68E. Cf. 12, 1067A; 13, 56E–57A, 69BC.
[24] Mansi 12, 1066E–1067A. Cf. 1146A; 13, 69E, 72A, 56CDE.
[25] Mansi 12, 1067E; 13, 132BE.
[26] Mansi 12, 1086B; 13, 280A, 377DE, 408A.
[27] Mansi 12, 1014A.
[28] Mansi 12, 1070A.
[29] Mansi 12, 1070D. Cf. 996B and 13, 45B 52CD.
[30] See above pp. 172–4.

as a cold fulfilment of an imposed obligation of honour and respect; that is to say, it was not regarded as a dry formality devoid of content. It expresses a basic Christian conception, which was preserved with special intensity in the East, namely, the possibility of a direct relationship and communion of man with God. Nothing confirmed this possibility so vividly and absolutely as the doctrine of the Incarnation. And no other Christian conception drew so much from the doctrine of the Incarnation for its defence as did faith in the veneration of icons as an inviolable means of relating the faithful immediately to Christ and the saints.[31] The icon as a "door" and as a "self-manifested vision" proved to be a real bridge connecting the worshipper with the uncreated energies of Christ and of his saints, an open road linking this world in a unique fashion with a reality transcending it.[32] This being the case, it was completely natural that the icon should be called "holy", that is to say, a permanent vehicle and stable channel of divine grace in so far as it preserves its integrity. That is the explanation of the declarations of the Seventh Ecumenical Council that "the venerable icons have the same status as the sacred vessels" and "they are reckoned as holy along with the saints".[33] Holiness, as the Orthodox understand it, is not a static and incommunicable state. Quite the contrary, uncreated energy suffuses and penetrates every created "environment", transforming visible reality, for the sake of believers, when that reality does not voluntarily oppose the will of God. The "perception" of this completed change of the part of the believer makes the icon an object of affection and love for him. And just as the power of representing created realities is naturally inherent in icons and is not an invention of the iconophiles, so too the demonstration of affection and love for Christ and the saints through their icons constitutes a natural power and not iconolatry:

"Just as true children, when their father is away from home for a while, feel great affection for him from the bottom of their soul, and if they see his staff in the house, or his cloak, kiss them fervently with tears,

---

[31] Cf. John Damascene, *Imag.* 111, 8 (Kotter, pp. 81–3). See also Mansi 13, 45ABE, 101AB, 164E.

[32] *Vita Stephani*, PG 100, 1113A. Theodore of Studius, *Letter to his child Naucratius*, PG 99, 1220A.

[33] Mansi 13, 40BCD. On the contrary, the iconoclasts oppose the assertion that no icon has been accepted "with holy prayer sanctifying it, that as a result it may be transferred from the level of the common to that of the holy" (Mansi 13, 268C). This refers to their characteristic inability to understand the manner in which the icon is rendered a source of holiness without the reading of special prayers. For the communion of the icons with their sanctified prototypes is self-evident.

not venerating these things but showing their love for their father . . . and just as Jacob, when he received from his sons Joseph's coat of many colours stained with blood, kissed it fervently with tears and enveloped it with his own eyes (Cf. Gen. 37:35), not out of love for the garment, but reckoning in this way it was Joseph he was kissing and holding in his arms, so too all Christians, when we handle and kiss the icon of Christ, or of an apostle, or of a martyr outwardly, think inwardly that we are holding Christ himself or his martyr".[34]

And the iconophiles conclude: "In the case of every act of kissing and every act of worship it is the intention which is scrutinised".[35] Consequently, the difference between idolatry and the relative veneration (*as opposed to worship*) of icons can be stated clearly: It is impossible, say the iconophiles, that we should be accused of worshipping idols and at the same time be venerating the martyrs, who abolished the idols. Nor does it make sense that we should be accused of venerating and glorifying wood and stones [i.e. tessellated icons] when we venerate and glorify the martyrs, who abolished wooden idols and destroyed stone images. How could we be idolaters, the iconophiles ask, and at the same time venerate and glorify the Three Children of Babylon who refused to worship the golden image, and raise up churches and dedicate feasts in their honour?[36]

The difference between icon and idol becomes even sharper and more absolute when the divine power of the icon as a source of holiness and purification is compared with the Satanic power of idols:

"Demons are often driven away by the use of the relics and icons of martyrs . . . tell me, how many overshadowings, how many exudations, and often flows of blood too, have come from the icon and relics of martyrs?"[37]

Man as the Priest of Creation

Moreover, the iconophiles not only make fundamental distinctions enabling them to venerate icons, which the iconoclasts are unable to make, but they also reject the dualistic distinctions the iconoclasts make of sensible reality, unable in their turn to make distinctions where the iconoclasts regard distinctions as obligatory. Nothing

---

[34] Mansi 13, 44E–45AC. C. 40AC, 361E.
[35] Mansi 13, 45E.
[36] Mansi 13, 48BD. Cf. Daniel 3:18, Mansi 13, 49C.
[37] Mansi 13, 48C; Cf. 132E; John Damascene, *Imag.* 1, 24, 29 (Kotter, p. 115); 111, 41, 1 (Kotter, p. 141).

proclaims faith in God's "very good material" creation more directly and practically than its use for the glory of God, its employment as a means of ascent to its Creator. This also constitutes the most characteristic justification of matter, its true contribution to the history of salvation, which in practice ostracises all dualistic, Manichaeistic and docetic conceptions.

Basing themselves on the very words of the Old Testament, the iconophiles deny any division of God's creation into sacred and profane "parts". They maintain the primary unity of the works of the substance-forming divine energies by recognising in them an important liturgical role: It is precisely the Scriptures of the Jews which call on "all the works of the Lord" to bless their Lord and Creator — the heavens and the waters, the sun and the moon, the stars and fire and ice, nights and days, light and darkness, lightings and clouds, mountains and all things that grow, the beasts and birds and whales, and of course, men.[38] Scripture also summons us to venerate "his footstool" (Ps. 98:5) and "his holy mountain" (Ps. 86:1). Icons then, are not the only creatures which are venerated. Man alone, however, is the "true worshipper" (Jn 4:23) who draws the whole of creation to worship the true God:

"Know that I too offer veneration and worship only to the Creator and Master and Maker of all things through heaven and earth and sea and wood and stone and relics and churches and the cross and angels and men and through the whole of creation both visible and invisible. For creation does not worship its Maker directly in its own right, but it is through me that 'the heavens declare the glory of God' (Ps. 18:1), through me that the moon venerates God, through me that the stars glory God, through me that the water, rains, dews and the whole of creation venerate and glorify God. When a good emperor makes for himself a crown of precious stones with his own hands, all who pay homage to the emperor in a genuine way kiss and venerate the crown, not thereby venerating the gold or the pearls, but the head of that emperor and his skilful hands which made the crown. Similarly, when Christian people kiss the forms of crosses and icons, they do not render homage to the wood or the stones themselves, or to the gold, or to the corruptible icon, or to the box or to the relics, but through them offer glory and veneration and homage to the God who is the creator of these things and of the whole universe. For the honour paid to his saints ascends to him".[39]

---

[38] See Daniel 3:57–88. Cf. Mansi 13, 285A: "When Moses the faithful servant of God made the tent of witness according to God's command, having shown that all the things in the world are his slaves (*ta sympanta deïkneis doula autou*), he made sensible cherubim in human form, copies in gold of the spiritual cherubim, overshadowing the mercy-seat which prefigured Christ".

[39] Mansi 13, 48E–40B. Cf. 53A: "He who honours the martyr honours God;

An ascent is thus brought about of all things into a single unconfused
unity. Man returns to his primeval liturgical function (Gen. 2:19),
through his own nature offering the created world to God. And
just as it is precisely through man that all things venerate their
Creator, so through the icons, when they are venerated, "the
honour paid to them ascends to him". In spite of the distinction
between prototype and image, which according to the iconophiles
permits the veneration of the latter, the veneration which is paid
does not reach its final goal in the sanctified prototypes/persons
of the saints, but ascends (*anatrechei*) to the uncreated natural
source of holiness, the Trihypostatic God.

Participation in the Uncreated Energies of God

The Seventh Ecumenical Council adopted a notable definition of
veneration which originated with St Anastasius of Antioch: "Veneration is a manifestation of honour".[40] So it is also legitimate for
veneration to be given to creatures, since they are "very good".[41]
Accordingly, the conclusion of the Council, in so far as it relates
to the veneration of icons, that is, to the conferment of honour
upon the sacred persons whom they depict, follows naturally:

"Therefore all who confess that they honour the sacred icons but avoid

---

and he who venerates his mother conveys the honour to God himself; and he
who honours the apostle honours him who sent him". Cf. 13, 100E, 124C; Basil
the Great, *Hexaemeron*, Hom. 111, 45–7.

[40] Mansi 13, 56B. C. 13, 404E, 405CE.

[41] Gen. 1:31, John Damascene, *Imag*. 1, 14. The eschatological conviction of
some modern Russian theologians who have their roots in the Slavophile
movement, that the fact that all creatures without exception are "very good"
and "from God" entails their final deification, is erroneous. Thus one could
conclude that even the devil will not remain outside the scope of deification!
This viewpoint, essentially a revival of Origen's teaching on the apocatastasis
and based on precisely the same rationale, was formally condemned by the Fifth
Ecumenical Council (533). It is strange that some studies of the Orthodox
teaching on icons assume that this theory is implied by the iconophiles' convictions on matter and the created world. On this see I.P. Sheldon-Williams,
"The Philosophy of Icons" in *The Cambridge History of Later Greek and Early Medieval
Philosophy* (ed. A.H. Armstrong), Cambridge, 1980, ch. 33, esp. p. 510: "all things,
including matter, shall in the end be assimilated to their Creator". This view
unfortunately, in spite of its conciliar condemnation, is defended nowadays as
Orthodox chiefly by contemporary Russian theologians. See for example G.
Florovsky, "Tvar i Tvarnost" in *Prvoslavnaya Misl*, Paris 1928, vol. 1 (Greek translation by Meletius Kalamaras, Thessaloniki 1977) and V. Lossky, *The Mystical
Theology of the Eastern Church*, Cambridge and London 1957, p. 109: "It was the
divinely appointed function of the first man, according to St Maximus, to unite
in himself the whole of created being; and at the same time to reach his perfect
union with God and thus grant the state of deification to the whole creation".

their veneration are censured as hypocrites. For in reality, by not accepting veneration which is the sign of honour, they prove themselves guilty of the opposite, which is profanation".[42]

The conferment of honour, however, upon "very good" creatures does not necessarily also signify the veneration of all creatures in general, but only of those which participate in the purifying, illuminating or deifying energies of the Holy Trinity. That is to say, in the last analysis the veneration of creatures presupposes distinctions between the uncreated natural energies of the Holy Trinity which act upon them by grace. The inability to make such distinctions leads to the rejection of veneration. This is the position not only of the iconoclasts, who were unable to differentiate between icon and archetype-bearer of the divine energies and identified these with regard to substance, but also of the Frankish theologians of the Carolingian period who met at Frankfurt (794) and rejected the Seventh Ecumenical Council.

The way the Orthodox distinguish between different uncreated energies may be summarised as follows: The result of the energy which creates and maintains constitutes the natures of substances of beings. Consequently, beings are creatures and as creatures are not venerated. Beings which are creatures, however, participate in the purifying, the illuminating and above all the deifying divine energies, and are venerated precisely because of the abiding indwelling of uncreated divine energy which is supplied to them by grace. The uncreated energy which deifies is supplied by grace from the Triadic God solely to the angels and the saints; the energy which purifies, illuminates and sanctifies is supplied to the icons, and holy Cross, the sacred vessels, holy water, holy oils, etc., and is communicated from these and the Church's sacraments to those who are worthy, not to all in the same way and in the same degree, but in proportion to their spiritual state. Thus, for example, the body and blood of Christ in the divine Eucharist communicated under the sanctified forms of bread and wine operate in a purifying way in those of the faithful who are being cleansed, in an illuminating way in those who are being enlightened, and in a deifying way in those who are being deified. But in those who do not find themselves in any of the above categories it operates for their judgment or condemnation on account of their unworthiness.

In the final analysis, the theological background for the veneration of creatures in the name of God and for his sake, with the

---

[42] Mansi 13, 56C; Cf. 13, 364B.

underlying objective that the veneration paid to them should ascend to him, must be sought in the Orthodox teaching that the Triadic God imparts himself directly to his creatures through his uncreated energies, through which he creates them, guides them providentially, fills them with life, saves them by cleansing and, in proportion to their status, deifies them. It is within this perspective that the assertion of Patriarch Germanus of Constantinople can be understood: "We do not venerate creatures — God forbid — nor do we render the homage due to the divine Master to our fellow servants".[43]

This is so not simply because the veneration paid to the icons of the saints ascends finally to him who alone is holy by nature, but precisely because he who is holy by nature is present by participation in every human saint in such a degree that he becomes a god "by grace" whereas the Trinity is God "by nature".[44] The theological justification then, of the correct approach to the veneration of icons is found ultimately in the teaching of the Eastern Fathers on deification.[45]

---

[43] Mansi 13, 100E, See also 104CD; C. John Damascene, *Imag.* I, 42, 4f (Kotter, p. 150).

[44] Cf. Maximus the Confessor, *Ambigua*, PG 91, 1345C–1349A; John Damascene, *Imag.* I, 19, 27 (Kotter, p. 95); III, 33, 6–36 (Kotter, pp. 137–8). Cf. Mansi 13, 121E.

[45] On this see A. Theodorou, *I peri theoseos didaskalia ton Pateron tis Ekklisias*, Athens 1956; Lars Thunberg, *Microcosm and Mediator*, Lund 1965, pp. 457–8; S.L. Epifanovic, *Prepodobnyi Maksim ispovednik i vizantiskoe bogoslovie*, Kiev 1915, p. 125; L. Contos, *The Concept of Theosis in Gregory Palamas, with a critical text of the 'contra Akindynum'*, 2 vols, Los Angeles 1963, passim. In both the Old and the New Testaments the veneration is permitted of representations of angels or saints and even of Christ himself, precisely because the archetypes of all these venerated representations are deified either by grace, in the case of the angels and saints, or by nature, in the unique case of Jesus Christ. For this reason, moreover, the simple fact that something is represented does not mean that it is also venerated. That is to say, demons and inanimate objects are represented in historical iconographic compositions for the sake of rendering specific events in the divine economy and the lives of the saints. These are not all venerated, of course, nor does their presence in the icons signify the bestowal on them by the Church of any kind of honour, as Theodore of Studius asserts when he makes veneration depend on the presence in the objects venerated of uncreated sanctifying energy: "Every holy thing is to be venerated, even if one is inferior to another in holiness and veneration; for that which is not to be venerated at all is also entirely lacking in holiness" (PG 99, 376B). It is for precisely this reason that objects which are not represented iconically are also honoured and venerated, objects which were used by holy persons either for the working of miracles, or as things of everyday use, such as, for example, the rod of Aaron, the jar of manna, the napkins and aprons and chains of the apostles, the instruments of torture of the martyrs, the instruments of ascetic discipline of the monastic saints, their clothing, shoes and vessels, for the only person who is holy by nature is present by participation in all these in due proportion.

It is not only the saints, therefore, who by grace participate in the natural holiness of God. As already indicated, the icons of the saints also participate in divine holiness by virtue of the hypostatic identity which they maintain with their prototype.[46] They can thus communicate holiness to their venerator and make them partakers of it: "since . . . through them . . . you can ascend to the prototype and participate in holiness".[47] Thus the iconophiles

"behold the icons of the saints with burning zeal and faith, calling to mind their piety. And while venerating they invoke the God of the saints, saying, Blessed art thou, the God of this saint and of all saints, who gave them patience, and made them worthy of thy rule; make us partakers of them and save us by their prayers".[48]

This "perception" of the participation of the icons in the uncreated, purifying and sanctifying energy of God is so intense that the Seventh Ecumenical Council can urge:

"Let us therefore make ourselves worthy of veneration, lest in approaching unworthily we bring on ourselves the punishment of Uzzah. For when he put his hand to the ark, he perished immediately, since he had approached it unworthily; and indeed the ark too was decorated with various designs and was constructed of wood, just like the icons".[49]

The iconophile honour and veneration of icons may be summarised as follows: The uncreated God imparts himself to his creatures in his uncreated glory or energies.[50]

Only the saints and the angels participate in the purifying, sanctifying, illuminating and deifying energies of God. The sanctifying, purifying and illuminating energies (though not the deifying energy) are also participated in through the icon of every saint by virtue of the icon's hypostatic identity with its prototype. Contact/veneration with the icon/vehicle of these divine energies communicates the latter to the venerator himself in proportion to his spiritual state.

This schematic rendering also works in the opposite direction, as follows: Denial of the possibility of participation in divine energies

---

[46] See above, pp. 118–20. Cf. John Damascene, *Imag.* I, 36, 1–4 (Kotter, p. 147): "If the icon of the emperor is emperor, and the icon of Christ is Christ and the icon of a saint is holy, neither is the power divided nor is the glory apportioned, but the glory of the icon becomes that of the subject represented".
[47] Mansi 13, 132E. Cf. 474D. John Damascene, *Imag.* III, 41 (Kotter, p. 141f).
[48] Mansi 13, 168A. Cf. also 13, 301ABC.
[49] Mansi 13, 364AB.
[50] Cf. Nicephorus, *Antir.* II, PG 100, 367ACB.

by means of the veneration of the icons of the saints may very
well mean the rejection of the Church's doctrine on the deification
of the saints. The denial, then, of the veneration of icons indicates
a denial of the possibility of the true and actual existence of the
saints, that is, of the possibility of the sanctification and deification
of human nature.[51] The denial, however, of such a possibility implies
the denial of the divine economy. Furthermore, the denial of the
possibility that through his energies God may be participated in
by his creatures leads to the complete overthrow of Christianity
and to out-and-out atheism.

Whatever is true of the icons with respect to participation in
the divine energies is equally true of the relics of the saints: "We
also kiss their venerable relics in order to participate in their
holiness", proclaims the Seventh Ecumenical Council.[52] And the
Council strongly supports this thesis:

> "Demons are often driven away by use of the relics of martyrs . . . tell
> me, how many overshadowings, how many exudations, and often flows
> of blood too, have come from the icons and relics of martyrs?"[53] "If
> it is impious to venerate the bones, how is it that the bones of Joseph
> were carried from Egypt with the greatest veneration?" (Cf. Gen. 50:25;
> Exod. 13:19). "How did a dead man revive when he touched the bones
> of Elisha? (2 Kgs 13:21). If God works miracles through bones, it is
> obvious that he can do so through icons and stones and many other
> things".[54]

The pious devotion of the iconophiles does indeed reach out "to
many other things" related to the holy places and wonderful events
of sacred history:

> "All of us believers venerate the cross as the staff of Christ, the holy
> sepulchre as his throne and bed, the manger and Bethlehem and the
> rest of his holy dwelling-places as his house . . . We venerate Zion as

---

[51] Cf. John Damascene, *Imag.* I, 21 50–61df (Kotter, p. 109): "Therefore either
abolish the commemorations of the festivals of the saints as things introduced
contrary to the old law, or else allow the icons which, as you say, are against
the law. But it is impossible not to celebrate the commemorations of the saints . . .
seeing that God the Logos became flesh, having become like us in every respect
except sin, and was mingled with what is ours without confusion and deified
the flesh without being subject to change, and that through the unconfused
mutual indwelling of his Godhead and his flesh we have truly been sanctified".
Cf. *Imag.* I, 19 (Kotter, pp. 94–5).

[52] Mansi 13, 364E. Cf. 13, 132C.

[53] Mansi 13, 48C. Cf. 12, 1143C: "Our Master, Christ, has provided us with
the relics of the saints as founts of salvation".

[54] Mansi 13, 52A. Cf. 13, 909 and 12, 720; also Leontius of Neapolis, *Against
the Jews*, PL 93, 1605 and PL 106, 237–8.

his city; we salute Nazareth as his home town; we embrace the Jordan as his divine bath. For wherever he walked, or sat, or appeared, or touched, or cast his shadow, that place we venerate and respect in our fervent and ineffable love for him as the place of God. In doing so, we venerate neither the place, nor the house, nor the town, nor the city, nor the stones, but him who went about in them, and appeared in them, and was recognised in the flesh in them, and delivered us from deceit in them, namely, Christ our God".[55]

The iconophiles are also fond of invoking St Gregory the Theologian, who in his homily on the Nativity of Christ exhorts the faithful with the words: "Respect Bethlehem and venerate the crib".[56]

Despite this, the true worship of God in spirit is not offered by the iconophiles through the veneration of icons, relics, holy places and sacred objects, but through the correct confession of faith and life in him: "For the true worship and veneration of the true God is accomplished with exactitude in the observance of the holy confession of faith in him, and in the keeping of the most essential and capital mysteries and laws given by him".[57] "Therefore the people of Christ have to this day assigned neither the name that is above every name (Phil. 2:10), nor divine reverence nor worship to anyone except the holy and life-giving Trinity".[58] Just as the God whom we worship is one, and faith in him is one, and saving baptism is one,

"so too the worship offered to him by us is one, as has been handed down by the holy apostles and safeguarded: the sacrifice of praise which the divine apostle said is offered through Christ to God the Father, 'that is, the fruit of lips that acknowledge his name' (Heb. 13:15) and the sacred tradition handed down through the life-giving mysteries, which the prophet Malachi foretold (Mal. 1:11) when he said, speaking in the person of God, that 'from the rising of the sun to its setting my name is glorified among the nations, and in every place incense is offered to my name, and a pure offering'", "since we know for certain that there is no hope of salvation for us from any other source than from a devout confession and faith in the only true God who is venerated in Trinity".[59]

---

[55] Mansi 13, 45AB.
[56] Mansi 13, 361D. Cf. 405C: It is very characteristic that even today Christians of all confessions, even of those which centuries ago rejected the use of icons, maintain the tradition of pilgrimage and the veneration of the sacred sites.
[57] Mansi 13, 109D. cf. 280A, 284B, 377DE, 405C.
[58] Mansi 13, 117E.
[59] Mansi 13, 120A. cf. 13, 129E–131A, 185C, 361D, 474D.

CHAPTER SEVEN

THE SIGNIFICANCE OF THE COUNCIL

A Christological Council

Behind the historical circumstances which led to the iconoclastic struggle lies the theological context which enables us to study the fundamental problems which were posed throughout the period of controversy.

Although brought to a head by political events, the essential core of the conflict was theological and as the controversy developed the theological debate came to be centred increasingly on the theandric person of Christ. The iconic representation of the other sacred persons, the Theotokos and the saints, was strictly dependent on the solution to the christological question. This question was primarily one of how the saving uncreated energies of God might become accessible to humanity and be participated by it through the created human nature of Christ himself and his saints. By what means may created beings bear the Uncreated?

Within the context of the earlier phases of the christological controversy the Fathers of the Church had encountered the same problem in a different guise and had dealt with it successfully, endowing it with a soteriological dimension. The achievement of the iconophile Fathers of the Seventh Ecumenical Council consists in the felicitous way in which they applied the theological method of the preceding Ecumenical Councils to the question of icons and drew the necessary conclusions. Consequently, iconoclasm as it developed was strongly coloured by the christological controversy.

The more moderate iconoclasts were disposed, when pressed, to accept iconography as an ecclesiastical tradition "handed down from ancient times" and to accept the paedagogic and narrative role of icons but not their veneration, which they took to be idolatry. Although the iconophiles could well have exploited such a compromise in their opponents, they preferred to prove theologically that iconic representation without veneration of the sacred persons depicted is equivalent to treating them with dishonour, and so they demanded from their opponents the acceptance of veneration too without any reservation.

This must be interpreted not as the result of fanaticism or bigotry but rather as the consequence of theological fidelity to the soteriological implications of the christological doctrine with which the iconophiles linked the whole iconoclast question. It should be noted, of course, that the iconoclasts also attempted in their turn to establish a corresponding link between their arguments and the christology of the six ecumenical councils, but in a partial and fragmentary way without integrating these with the anthropology, cosmology and soteriology of the Fathers so as to form a unified theological position.

A key question, too, was whether the honouring of sanctified creatures and the veneration of their iconic representations constituted a revival of idolatry. In other words, how is the proper worship of the only true and uncreated God to be safeguarded, and how are sanctified creatures to be excluded from this? Is God's material creation receptive of sanctification? If so, how does such a sanctification not require the worship of sanctified creatures?

The Iconoclast Position

For the sake of clarity the arguments of either side may be set out in terms of the theological distinctions and identifications which functioned as criteria for the solution of the questions which arose. Where one side made distinctions, the other usually did not. The iconoclasts, for example, instead of making conceptual (*kat'epinoian*) distinctions often made either sharp divisions or else conflating identifications. The iconophiles, on the other hand, made real distinctions between prototype and imitative icon and between adoration and veneration which the iconoclasts found difficult to accept.

Fundamental to the iconoclast position was a real distinction between the two natures of Christ, human and divine in contrast with the merely conceptual (*kat'epinoian*) distinction made by their opponents and the Eastern Fathers in general. As a result the iconic representation of Christ implied either a division between the two natures, which is Nestorian, or a confusion of natures, which is Monophysite. (Both these points were stressed in opposition to the iconophiles and not independently of the depiction of Christ).

Further distinctions and separations were made between material and spiritual beings, between creatures and the uncreated God and between the iconic representation of Christ and his Incarnation. The separation between creatures and the uncreated God was absolute due to the implicit rejection of the Holy Trinity's uncreated energies, a rejection which lies at the very core of the iconoclast theology. The argument concerning the absolute separation between the iconic representation ("circumscription") of Christ and his Incarnation was absurd, but was maintained against the iconophiles on the strength of a spiritualising theory which saw the Logos as "uncircumscribable" even after the Incarnation, obviously with Origenistic — or even docetic — criteria. Perhaps the phrase "after the Incarnation" signified more specifically "after the resurrection".

The identifications made by the iconoclasts were numerous. First, all true images are taken to be "natural" or consubstantial with their archetypes. From this derives the utter impossibility of distinguishing between "natural" and "imitative" icons. By further consequence, image and archetype or prototype are identified. Consequently, Christ and an icon of Christ must be identified in their essence, that is to say, icon and person represented (prototype) must always be consubstantial. Every icon not identical with the prototype in essence is an idol.

Because the above definition of consubstantiality between prototype and image is never fulfilled in the case of the imitative icon, every non-natural icon must of necessity be an idol. The veneration of such an icon is therefore the veneration of an idol. Every honour rendered to material icons of Christ and his saints signifies veneration of the pictorial representations themselves, and not of the prototype.

Since only natural icons exist and "icon" in general is identified with "archetype", every attempt at the iconic representation of Christ treats his two natures as identical. There is only one "natural" icon of Christ: the sanctified Bread of the divine Eucharist (which is evidently acceptable because it avoids the human form, and not simply because it renders his two natures). Here it is clearly apparent that the problem for the iconoclasts lies not in the iconic representation of the matter itself but of the form.

The sanctification of any created being seems to be conceived of as its spiritualisation. No other sanctification of a creature appears to be acceptable, except that of the bread of the Eucharist and of course, of the "body" of the incarnate Christ. The hesitation, however, of the iconoclasts to accept the existence of uncreated energies leads them to confuse the sanctification of the Bread with "deification". In this way they appear as forerunners of the scholastic teaching on transubstantiation through their wording: "deification of the essence of the Bread by grace". So they obviously suggest that such a deification unavoidably entails the "dematerialisation" or spiritualisation of the Bread.

For the iconoclasts reality was not to be found in the visible world. The real is identified with the spiritual. Only those beings which exist eternally and immutably are true existents. The hypostasis of the divine Logos, however, is identified with "the visible character" of his human nature. This thesis was produced by the need to refute iconophile arguments and was expressed primarily through the axiom that Christ remains "uncircumscribable" even after his Incarnation. Consequently it is not acceptable that Christ — at least after his crucifixion — should any longer have at his disposal a "visible character". The same must hold true for the saints (and for human beings in general) after their death and obviously it is not expected that such a visible character will be acquired again. It is debatable whether the iconoclasts believed in the resurrection of the flesh either of Christ or of men generally, although their council at Hiereia (754) proclaimed its belief in the resurrection of the dead.

The iconoclasts are unable to discern the presence of the uncreated energies of the Holy Trinity in creation apart from the unclear case of the sanctification of the Bread of the Eucharist, which is deified "by grace as through a certain sanctification". The use of "as" *(hos)* shows the difficulty experienced by the iconoclasts in accepting the real presence of uncreated grace in creation. This doubt, however concerning the possibility of the communication of uncreated energies to creatures poses from the beginning the question of how the iconoclasts conceived of the divine economy of the Incarnation, and lends a strongly christological character to the whole iconoclast controversy. Ultimately the unity of the theandric person of Jesus Christ is not seriously taken into account by the iconoclasts. The incarnate Logos appears rather as a Christ who seems to be an almost impersonal sum of two natures.

The Iconophile Response

A number of real distinctions different from those of the iconoclasts, were fundamental to the iconophile position. First was the distinction between nature or essence and hypostasis, from which flows the distinction between kinds of iconic representation. This distinction was of course crucial, for the definition of Trinitarian and christological dogma by all ecumenical councils prior to the Seventh. Second in importance was a distinction between a "natural" iconic representation and a "hypostatic" one. The first enables the icon to be consubstantial with its archetype. (The Son, for example, is a natural icon of his Father both with regard to God and with regard to men). The second excludes this eventuality with the result that on the one hand the icon is an "imitation of an archetype" while on the other it belongs totally, as icon, to the hypostasis of the subject represented.

A distinction between prototype and icon was also of fundamental importance. In the case of natural iconic representation the prototype and its icon are distinguished only according to hypostasis. In the case of hypostatic or imitative representation, the icon is distinguished from its prototype by essence or nature and at the same time participates as icon in the hypostasis of the prototype, while remaining altogether unparticipative "in the matter in which it is manifested". This led to a distinction between adoring worship, which is directed only towards the Trinity (including also the human nature of Christ on account of the hypostatic union of the Logos with the nature), and relative worship (veneration), which is directed towards the icon of Christ or of his saints. It is clear that the distinction between these two different kinds of worship flows from the essential difference between these prototypes and imitative icons. In the case of the prototypes of Christ and his saints we have deification (*theosis*) by nature (Christ) or by grace (the saints). Neither the icons of Christ nor of his saints, however, participate in deifying energy, nor are they deified in themselves as if as a result of this nor do they in consequence impart such energy to their worshippers but communicate only a sanctifying (purifying or illuminating) energy. In spite of all this the deified prototypes of the icons are clearly distinguished on account of their deification from the rest of creation, and those who honour and venerate these and their icons are very far from being worshippers of creatures or idols.

On the level of christology we have a distinction between the visible character of the human nature of Christ and his theandric hypostasis as one of the Trinity. It is obvious that anyone who beholds the visible character of the human nature of Christ in his imitative icon does not of necessity also behold his theandric hypostasis. Conversely, anyone who in a vision of God (*theoptia*) beholds Christ after his Incarnation inevitably beholds his human nature as well in his theandric hypostasis. The visible character of the human nature of Christ belongs inseparably to the theandric hypostasis, and is altogether incommunicable by the matter of the imitative icon which represents him.

The distinction between the two natures of Christ is made on the conceptual (*kat'epinoian*) level alone. They are not divided, in as much as they exist in hypostatic union in the divine Logos. The hypostatic-imitative representation of the visible character of the human nature of Christ expresses the unconfused union of his two natures without in any way dividing them from one another.

A further distinction is made between the icon of Christ and

the Bread of the Eucharist. The Bread of the Eucharist after its
sanctification, although the bearer of uncreated energies, is neither
a natural nor an imitative nor an analogical icon. Indeed it is not
an icon in any sense at all. If it were an icon, it could not be
the body of Christ. It could only represent his body in iconic form.
Clearly the iconophiles suspected that by describing the Bread as
a natural icon of Christ, their opponents denied the reality of the
incarnate Christ's uncreated energies and not only in the divine
Eucharist.

The next distinction is that between imitative icons of which the
type exists and is deified and imitative images of which the archetype does not exist or else does exist but is not deified. Images
which do not represent a deified prototype, or do not even represent an existing prototype, are, or become, reciprocally idols if
honoured. Consequently the matter of imitative images which is
from God and very good of itself is rendered in accordance with
its use either "full of divine grace" in the case of representation
of deified creatures, or else "full of every fulfilment" in the case
of the representation of non-existent or wicked prototypes.

In consequence it is possible that from this "very good" matter
can come equally "manufactured objects made to the glory of God"
and "manufactured objects dedicated to the devil", namely idols.
The icons that are filled with divine grace, even though material,
are partakers and bearers of uncreated (purifying, illuminating,
healing) power communicated to the faithful who venerate them
in a worthy manner in proportion to their spiritual state, while
conversely idols filled with every kind of defilement communicate
demonic influences to those who have any kind of relationship
with them.

Distinctions are also made among several kinds of uncreated
energies, the most important of them being the deifying, the
sanctifying and the creative, which allows the iconophiles to define
clearly which precisely of the uncreated energies all creatures
without exception participate in, which the imitative icons participate in, and which only their prototypes participate in. As a result
the iconophiles are able to connect the question of icons in an
essential manner with the whole of the divine economy and to
pose the question of salvation in Christ to their opponents in a
telling way, reminding them that those who do not participate in
the uncreated divine energies, the natural source of which is the human
nature of Christ, likewise cannot participate in salvation in Christ.

The hypostatic relation between prototype and the visible character of each icon constitutes the warrant for its very existence as

an icon, precisely because it is possible for it to verify (even if not scientifically) its correspondence to a real prototype, which it also represents. The non-existence of a real prototype renders every attempt to make an icon illegitimate, even if such an attempt serves a purely aesthetic aim or an aim irrelevant to Christianity. On this point the iconoclasts do not disagree with their opponents except on the fundamental distinction between real and non-existent prototypes, since either there are no prototypes or all true prototypes are invisible, immaterial and formless. That is why in their understanding all pictorial representations are indistinguishably idolatrous.

The hypostatic relation between prototype and the visible character of each icon helps to make the relationship of the faithful with the icon one of immediate relationship with the icons' prototypes, primarily through relative worship (*veneration*) and honour. Such an immediate relationship with the prototype, particularly in the case of the icon of Christ, becomes feasible because of his Incarnation and is an immediate consequence of it.

Two Different Christologies

There seems to be complete agreement between iconoclasts and iconophiles on the supremely important matter of a connection between icons and christological doctrine. Both sides accept that the two questions are linked with one another. Disagreeing radically, of course, on the manner of evaluating their interdependence, they thus prove that they represent two mutually exclusive traditions of christological teaching. According to the one, "the painters'" art blasphemes the correct doctrine of the economy of Christ". According to the other, opposition to icons is judged "a worse evil than all the heresies, since it denies the economy of the Saviour". Had the opposing parties reached agreement upon the relevant christological issues (i.e. whether Christ is uncircumscribable or not, whether his created body imparts uncreated energies or not to other creatures), they would certainly have been able to do so upon the issue of icons too. Seen from this aspect it would not be wrong to consider the iconoclast controversy the last phase of the formation of christological doctrine of the undivided catholic Church. This endows the Seventh Ecumenical Council with a special value, for it shows how it sets its seal on the completion of christological teaching.

The Soteriological Aspect

Parallel to the opposing christologies of the two sides are two different approaches to salvation. For the iconoclasts only the spiritual was real; the material was no guide at all to what was of lasting value. The immense gulf between the material and the spiritual, the created and the uncreated, could not be bridged by any sanctified matter apart from the Eucharistic body of Christ. This was a highly spiritualised, elitist point of view. The iconophiles, by contrast, were realists with regard to the visible world. For them matter could provide a channel of communication with the divine; it could offer access to God to the ordinary faithful. This was justifiable biblically, because the material world had been created by God and pronounced "very good". It was justifiable philosophically through the participation of the image in its prototype. It was justifiable theologically through the presence in the icon of the uncreated energies of God. If one were to pin the essential difference between iconoclasts and iconophiles on a single doctrine, it would be on their respective attitudes to the uncreated energies of the Holy Trinity. The iconoclasts, by rejecting uncreated energies, were locked into a one-sided doctrine of divine transcendence. The iconophiles' doctrine of the uncreated energies enabled them to postulate a two-way movement: God who is holy by nature is present in every human saint as a deifying energy and in the saint's image as a sanctifying energy. Veneration by the faithful ascends through the icon of the saint or of Christ to the prototype; sanctifying grace descends through the icon to the venerator. The problem of the icons was not a recondite controversy about matters which ultimately were of no practical significance. At its heart lay the question: How does finite man reach up to the infinite God? The answer given by the Seventh Ecumenical Council is that material things filled with uncreated grace — the Eucharist, relics, the saints and the icons — can raise those who are worthy, the uneducated along with the learned, to intimacy with God.

ABBREVIATIONS

AASS	*Acta Sanctorum Bollandiana* (Brussels 1643–)
BZ	*Byzantinische Zeitschrift* (Leipzig 1892–)
CMH	*Cambridge Medieval History* (Cambridge 1913–)
DACL	*Dictionnaire d'archéologie chrétienne et de liturgie* (Paris 1907–1953)
DOP	*Dumbarton Oaks Papers* (Cambridge, Mass, 1941–)
DTC	*Dictionnaire de théologie catholique* (Paris 1905–1950)
EEBS	*Epistimoniki Etaireia Vyzantinon Spoudon* (Athens 1924–)
EO	*Echos d'Orient* (Constantinople and Paris 1897–1942)
GOTR	*Greek Orthodox Theological Review* (Brookline 1954–)
HTR	*Harvard Theological Review* (Cambridge, Mass, 1908–)
JRS	*Journal of Roman Studies* (London 1911–)
JTS	*Journal of Theological Studies* (London 1900–)
PG	*Patrologiae cursus completus, Series graeco-latina*, ed. J.P. Migne (Paris 1857–1866)
RAC	*Reallexikon für Antike und Christentum* (Stuttgart 1950–)
REB	*Revue des études byzantines* (Bucharest and Paris 1946–)
RSR	*Recherches de science réligieuse* (Paris 1914–)
SBN	*Studi Bizantini e Neoellenici* (Rome 1924–)
ZK	*Zeitschrift für Kirchengeschichte* (Stuttgart 1876–)
ZTK	*Zeitschrift für Theologie und Kirche* (Tübingen 1955–)

BIBLIOGRAPHY

I. SOURCES

Acta concilii 815, ed. D. Serruys, *Mélanges d'archéologie et d'histoire publiés par l'Ecole française de Rome*, xxiii (1903) pp. 345–51.

Adversus Constantinum Caballinum, PG 95, 309–344.

DOLGER, F., *Regesten der Kaiserurkunden des ostromischen Reiches*, pt. 1:565–1025, Munich 1924.

——. George of Cyprus, Nouthesia Gerontos peri ton hagion eikonon, ed. B.M. Melioransky, *Georgi Kiprijanin i Ioann Ierusalimlanin, dva mealoizvestnych borca za pravoslavie v VIIIv.*, St Petersburg 1901.

GEORGE THE MONK, *Chronicon*, ed. C. de Boor, Leipzig 1904.

GERMANUS OF CONSTANTINOPLE, *Epistolai* 1) Pros Ioannen Synadon, *PG* 98, 156B–161D; 2) Pros Konstantinon Nakoleias, *PG* 161D–164C; 3) Pros Thoman Klaudioupoleos, *PG* 98, 164–193D. Bios Germanou, ed. A. Papadopoulos-Kerameus, *Maurogordateios Bibliotheke, Anek. hellen.*, suppl. to vol. xvii of the *Hellenikos Philologikos Syllogos of Constantinople* (1886) pp. 1–17 (= *PG* 98, 16–36).

GOUILLARD, J., (ed.) To Synodikon tes Orthodoxias, *Travaux et mémoires*, Paris 1967.

GRUMEL, V., *Les Régestes des Actes du Patriarcat de Constantinople, I: Les Actes des Patriarches, II: 715–1043*, Paris 1936.

HENNEPHOF, H. (ed.) Peuseis Konstantinou, *Textus Byzantini ad Iconomachiam pertinentes*, Leiden 1969, pp. 52–7.

JAFFE, P., *Regesta Pontificum Romanorum ab condita ecclesia ad annum post Christum natum 1198*, Berlin 1851 (2nd ed. Leipzig 1885–8).

JOHN CALIBITES, Bios Ioannou Kalibitou, *PG* 114, 568–582.

JOHN DAMASCENE, Pros tous diaballontas tas hagias eikonas, Logoi III (= Imag.), ed. B. Kotter, *Die Schriften des Johannes von Damaskos*, vol. iii, Berlin-New York 1975 (= *PG* 94 1232A–1420B).

——. *Liber Pontificalis*, ed. L. Duchesne, Paris 1884–92.

MANSI, J.D., *Sacrorum conciliorum nova et amplissima collectio*, Florence and Venice 1759–98, reprinted Paris 1901ff., vol. 12, 951–1154; vol. 13, 1–496.

METHODIUS, Bios Methodiou, *PG* 100, 1244–1261.

NICEPHORUS OF CONSTANTINOPLE, Opera omnia and vita, *PG* 100, 41–1065.

PHOTIUS OF CONSTANTINOPLE, *Epistulae et Amphilochia*, vols. i–iv, ed. B. Laourdas and L.G. Westerink, Leipzig 1983–6.

——. *The Homilies of Photius, Patriarch of Constantinople*, trans. C. Mango, *Dumbarton Oaks Studies* 3, Cambridge Mass. 1958.

POEMS: Eikonomachika poiemata Ioannou, Ignatiou, Sergiou kai Stephanou para Theodoro Stoudite. Elenchoi kai anatrope ton asebon poiematon: *PG* 99, 436–477.

STEPHEN THE YOUNGER, Bios Stephanou Neou, *PG* 100, 1069–1186.

TARASIUS, Bios Tarasiou, ed. I.A. Heikel, *Acta Soc. Fennicae* 17 (1889) (=*PG* 98, 1385–1424).

THEODORE GRAPTOS, Bios Theodorou Graptou, *PG* 116, 653–684.

THEODORE OF STUDIUS, Opera omnia and vita, *PG* 99.

THEOPHANES, Bios Theophanous, *PG* 115, 9–29.

II. MODERN WORKS

AHRWEILER, H.L., *Idéologie politique de l'empire byzantin*, Paris 1975.

——. "L' Asie Mineure et les invasions arabes (VIIe–IXe siècles)", *Revue historique* 461 (1962) pp. 1–32.
——. "The Geography of the Iconoclast World", *Iconoclasm* (edd. Bryer and Herrin), pp. 21–7.
ALEXANDER, P.J., "An Ascetic Sect of Iconoclasts in Seventh Century Armenia", *Late Classical and Mediaeval Studies in Honor of Albert Mathias Friend Jr* (ed. K. Weitzmann). Princeton 1955, pp. 151–60 (reprinted in P.J. Alexander, *Religious and Political History and Thought in the Byzantine Empire*, London 1978, No. VII)
——. *Church Councils and Patristic Authority. The Iconoclastic Councils of Hiereia (754) and St Sophia (813), Harvard Studies in Classical Philosophy* 63, Cambridge, Mass. 1958.
——. "Hypatius of Ephesus: a note on Image-worship in the 6th century", *HTR* 45 (1952) pp. 177–84 (reprinted in *Religious and Political History and Thought in the Byzantine Empire* No. VI).
——. "The Iconoclastic Council of St Sophia (815) and its Definition (Horos)", *DOP* 7 (1953) pp. 35–66 (Reprinted in *Religious and Political History and Thought in the Byzantine Empire*, No. VIII).
——. *The Patriarch Nicephorus of Constantinople. Ecclesiastical Policy and Image Worship in the Byzantine Empire*, Oxford 1958.
ALLCHIN, A.M., (ed.) *Sacrament and Image*, London 1967.
AMANTOU, K., *Istoria tou Vyzantinou Kratous*, vol. i, Athens 1953.
ANASTOS, M., *Ekklisia kai Politeia kata tin periodo tis Eikonomachias, Efcharistirion. Timitikos tomos epi ti 45 etiridi epistimonikis draseos kai ti 35 etiridi taktikis kathigesias Am. S. Alivizatou*, Athens 1958, pp. 8–21.
——. "Iconoclasm and Imperial Rule 717–842", *CMH*, vol. iv, Cambridge 1967, pp. 61–104.
——. "Leo III's Edict against the Images in the year 726–727 and Italo-Byzantine Relations between 726 and 730", *Polychordia: Festschrift Franz Dölger* (ed. P. Wirth) Amsterdam 1968, pp. 5–41.
——. "The Argument for Iconoclasm as presented by the Iconoclastic Council of 754", *Late Class, and Med. Studies in Honor of A.M. Friend*, Princeton 1968, pp.177–88.
——. "The Ethical Theory of Images formulated by the Iconoclasts in 754 and 815", *DOP* 8 (1954) pp. 151–60.
——. "The Transfer of Illyricum, Calabria and Sicily to the Jurisdiction of the Patriarchate of Constantinople in 732–733", *Silloge Byzantina in onore di S.G. Mercati*, pp. 14–31.
ARMSTRONG, A.H., "Some comments on the development of the Theology of Images", *Studia Patristica* 9 (= TU 94) pp. 117–26.
——. "The Philosophy of Icons", *Camb. Hist. Later Greek and Early Med. Phil.* (ed. A.H. Armstrong) Cambridge 1970, pp. 458–60.
BARNARD, L.W., "Byzantium and Islam. The Interaction of two Worlds in the Iconoclastic Era", *Byzantinoslavica* 36 (1975) pp. 25–37.
——. "The Emperor Cult and the Origins of the Iconoclastic Controversy", *Byzantion* 43 (1973) pp.13–29.
——. *The Graeco-Roman and Oriental Background of the Iconoclastic Controversy*, Leiden 1974.
——. "The Theology of Images", *Iconoclasm* (edd. Bryer and Herrin) pp. 7–13.
——. "The Use of the Bible in the Byzantine Iconoclastic Controversy", *Theologische Zeitschrift* 31 (1975) pp. 78–83.
BAUMSTARK, A., "Der in den Akten des siebten allgemeinen Konzils bezeugte angeblische Konstantinische Mozaikzyclus", *Roma e Oriente* 6 (1913) pp. 86–8.
BAYNES, N.H., "Idolatry and the Early Church", in his *Byzantine Studies and Other Essays*, London 1955, pp. 116–43.
——. "The Icons before Iconoclasm", *HTR* 44 (1951) pp. 93–106 (= *Byzantine Studies and Other Essays*, pp. 226–39).
BAYNES, N.H. and H.St.L.B. MOSS, *Byzantium*, Oxford 1948.

BECK, H.-G., "Die Griechische Kirche in Zeitalter des Iconoclasmus", *Handbuch der Kirchengeschichte* (ed. H. Jedin) Freiburg 1966, pp. 31–62.
——. *Die Kirche in ihrer Geschichte. Geschichte der orthodoxen Kirche in byzantinischen Reich. Ein Handbuch* (ed. B. Moeller) Gottingen 1980.
——. *Kirche und theologische Literatur in byzantinischen Reich*, Munich 1959.
BECKER, C.H., *Von Werden und Wesen der islamischen Welt. Islamstudien*, vol. i, Leipzig 1924.
BECKWITH, J., *Early Christian and Byzantine Art*, Harmondsworth 1979.
BELLINGER, A.R., "The Coins and Byzantine Imperial Policy", *Speculum* 31 (1956) pp. 70–81.
BENZ, E., *The Eastern Church. Its Thought and Life*, Garden City NY 1957.
BENZ, F., "Theologie der Icon und das Iconoclasmus", *Kerygma und Mythos* VI, 2 (1964) pp. 75–102.
BERTLEIN, H., *Das Bild als Unterrichsmittel. Fachdidaktische Perspectiven* 46, Munich 1971.
BEVAN, E., *Holy Images. An Inquiry into Idolatry and Image-Worship in Ancient Paganism and Christianity*, London 1940.
——. "Idolatry", *Edinburgh Review* 243 (1926) pp. 253–72.
BONNER, A., "A Story of Iconoclastic Times", *Byzantion* 22 (1952) pp. 237–41.
BREHIER, L., *La querelle des images (VIIIe–IXe siècles)*, Paris 1904.
——. "La querelle des images jusqu'au Concile iconoclaste de 754", *Histoire de l'Eglise* (edd. A. Fliche and V. Martin), Paris 1938, vol. v, pp. 431–70.
BROWN, P., "A Dark Age Crisis: Aspects of the Iconoclastic Controversy", *The English Historical Review* 88 (1973) pp. 1–34 (reprinted with augmented notes in P. Brown, *Society and the Holy in Late Antiquity*, London 1982, pp. 251–301).
——. "The Rise and Function of the Holy Man in Late Antiquity", *JRS* 71 (1971) pp. 80–101 reprinted in *Society and the Holy in Late Antiquity*, pp.103–52.
BRYER, A. and J. HERRIN (edd.) *Iconoclasm* (Ninth Spring Symposium of Byzantine Studies) Birmingham 1977.
BURY, J.B., *History of the Later Roman Empire from Arcadius to Irene (395–800)*, London 1889 (new ed. 395–565, London 1923).
CAMERON, A., *Continuity and Change in Sixth-Century Byzantium*, London 1981.
CAMPENHAUSEN, H. von, "Die Bilderfrage in der Reformation", *ZK* 68 (1957) pp. 96–128.
——. "The Theological Problem of Images in the Early Church", in his *Tradition and Life in the Church*, Philadelphia 1968, pp.171–200.
CASPAR, E., "Papst Gregor II und der Bilderstreit", *ZK* 52 (1933) pp. 29–89.
CAVARNOS, C., *Orthodox Iconography*, Belmont, Mass. 1977.
——. *The Icon. Its Spiritual Basis and Purpose*, Belmont, Mass. 1975.
CLERC, C., *Les théories relatives au culte des images chez des auteurs grecs du deuxième siècle*, Paris 1915.
COBHAM, C.D., *The Patriarchs of Constantinople*, Cambridge 1911.
CORMACK, R., *Writing in Gold: Byzantine Society and its Icons*, London 1985.
CRONE, P., "Islam, Judeao-Christianity and Byzantine Iconoclasm", *Jerusalem Studies in Arabic and Islam* 2 (1980) pp. 59–95.
CROUZEL, H., *Théologie de l'image de Dieu chez Origène*, Paris 1956.
CUTLER, A., *Transfigurations, Studies in the Dynamics of Byzantine Iconography*, Pennsylvania University Park & London 1975.
DALTON, O.M., *Byzantine Art and Archaeology*, Oxford 1911.
DARROUZES, J., "Les listes episcopales du concile de Nicée (787)", *REB* 33 (1975) pp. 5–76.
DIEHL, C., "Leo III and his Isaurian Dynasty (717–802)", *CMH* vol. iv (1923) pp. 1–26.
DOBSCHUETZ, E., von, *Christusbilder. Texte und Untersuchungen zur Geschichte der altchristlichen Literatur*, Leipzig 1899.
DOLGER, F., "Zur Geschichte des Bilderstreits", *Paraspora*, Ettal 1961, pp. 273–92.
DUMEIGE, G., *Nicée II* (vol. 4 of *Histoire des conciles oecuméniques*) Paris 1978.

DVORNIK, F., "The Patriarch Photius and Iconoclasm", *DOP* 7 (1953) pp. 69–97.
——. *The Photian Schism*, Cambridge 1948.
ELIADE, M., *Image et symbole*, Paris 1952.
ELLIGER, W., "Die Stellung der alten Christen zu den Bildern in den ersten vier Jahrhunderten", *Studien über christliche Denkmaler* XX, 2, Leipzig 1930.
——. "Zur bilderfeindlichen Bewegung des achten Jahrhunderts", in *Forschungen zur Kirchengeschichte und zur christlichen Kunst (Mélanges J. Ficker)*, Leipzig 1931, pp. 40–60.
ERNI, R., *Das Christusbild der Ostkirchen*, Luzern-Stuttgart 1963.
EVDOKIMOV, P., *L'art de l'icône, théologie de la beauté*, Paris 1972.
——. "L'art moderne où la Sophia désaffectée", *Contacts*, vol. XII, no. 32, pp. 3–13.
——. *L'Orthodoxie*, Neuchatel 1965.
EVERY, G., *The Byzantine Patriarchate*, London 1962.
FAZZO, V., *La giustificazione delle imagini religiose dalla tard antichita al cristianismo*, Naples 1977.
FELICETTI, W. and W. LIEBENFELS, *Geschichte der byzantinischen Ikonenmalerei*, Olden-Lausanne 1956.
FINK, J., "Die Anfänge der Christusdarstellung", *Theologische Revue* 51 (1955) pp. 241–52.
FLOROVSKY, G., "Origen, Eusebius and the Iconoclastic Controversy", *Church History* 19 (1950) pp. 77–96.
FREY, J.B., "La question des images chez les Juifs à la lumière des dernières découvertes", *Biblica* 15 (1934) pp. 265–300.
FRITZ, G., "Nicée (II Concile de)", *DTC* XI, 1 (1932) cols. 417–41.
GALAVARIS, G., *The Icon in the Life of the Church*, Leiden 1981.
GARDNER, A., "Some Theological Aspects of the Iconoclastic Controversy", *The Hibbert Journal* 2 (1904) pp. 360–74.
GEISCHER, H.-J., *Der byzantinische Bilderstreit. Texte zur Kirchen und Theologiegeschichte*, vol. 9, Gutersloh 1968.
GERO, S., *Byzantine Iconoclasm during the Reign of Leo III, with particular Attention to the Oriental Sources*, Louvain 1973.
——. *Byzantine Iconoclasm during the Reign of Constantine V, with particular Attention to the Oriental Sources*, Louvain 1977.
——. "Notes on Byzantine Iconoclasm in the Eighth Century", *Byzantion* 44 (1974) pp. 23–42.
——. "The Eucharistic Doctrine of the Byzantine Iconoclasts and its Sources", *BZ* 68 (1975) pp. 4–22.
——. "The Libri Carolini and the Image Controversy", *GOTR* 18 (1973) pp. 7–34.
GIANNOPOULOS, B. *Ai Christologikai Antilipseis ton Eikonomachon*, Athens 1975.
GRABAR, A., *L'Art du Moyen Age en Occident. Influences byzantines et orientales*, repr. London 1980.
——. *L'Art paléochrétien et l'art byzantin. Receuil d'études 1967–1977*, London 1979.
——. *Byzantine Painting*, New York 1979.
——. *Byzantium. Byzantine Art in the Middle Ages*, London 1966.
——. *Byzantium. From the Death of Theodosius to the Rise of Islam*, London 1966.
——. *Christian Iconography. A Study of the Origins*, London 1969.
——. *Early Christian Art. From the Rise of Christianity to the Death of Theodosius*, New York 1968.
——. *L'Iconoclasme byzantin. Dossier archéologique*, Paris 1957.
——. *Martyrium. Recherches sur le culte des réliques et l'art chrétien antique*, London 1972.
——. *Les Voies de la création en iconographie chrétienne*, Paris 1979.
GRABAR, O., "Islam and Iconoclasm", *Iconoclasm* (edd. Bryer & Herrin), pp. 45–52.
GREGOIRE, H., "The Byzantine Church", *Byzantium* (edd. Baynes & Moss) pp. 86–135.
GRUMEL, V., "Chronologie des patriarches iconoclastes du IXe siècle", *EO* 34 (1935) pp. 162–6.

———. "L'Iconologie de saint Germain de Constantinople", *EO* 21 (1922) pp. 165–75.

———. "Images (culte des)", *DTC* V, 1 (1916) cols. 776–844.

GRUNEBAUM, G.E., von, "Byzantine Iconoclasm and the Influence of the Islamic Environment", *History of Religions* (1962) pp. 1–10.

GUARDINI, R., "Sacred Images and the Invisible God", *Cross Currents* 10 (1960).

GUTMANN, J., "Deuteronomy: Religious Reformation or Iconoclastic Revolution?" in *The Image and the Word. Confrontations in Judaism, Christianity and Islam* (ed. J. Gutmann), Missoula 1977.

———. *No Graven Images, Studies in Art and the Hebrew Bible* (ed. J. Gutmann), New York 1972.

HADDAD, R.M., "Iconoclasts and Mut 'azila. The Politics of Anthropomorphism", *GOTR* 27 (1982) pp. 287–305.

HALDON, J.F., "Some Remarks on the Background to the Iconoclastic Controversy", *Byzantinoslavica* 38 (1977) pp. 161–84.

HEAD, C., "Who was the real Leo the Isaurian", *Byzantion* 41 (1971) pp. 105–8.

HEFELE, K.J., *A History of the Councils of the Church* (trans. H.N. Oxenham), vols. ii–v reprinted from the 1883–96 edition, New York 1972; vol. i (from the 1894 ed.) reprinted under the title *A History of the Christian Church*.

HENRY, P., "What was the Iconoclastic Controversy About?" *Church History* 35, 1 (1976).

HENRY, J., *The Formation of Christendom*, Oxford 1987.

HODGSON, M.G.S., "Islam and Image", *History of Religions* 3 (1963/4) pp. 220–60.

HOLL, K., "Die Schriften des Epiphanius gegen die Bilderverehrung", in his *Gesammelte Aufsatze zur Kirchengeschichte*, Tübingen 1928, vol. ii, pp. 356–63.

HUSSEY, J.M., *Church and Learning in the Byzantine Empire*, Oxford 1937.

———. *The Byzantine World* (4th edn) London 1970.

———. "The Iconoclast Controversy" in her *The Orthodox Church in the Byzantine Empire*, Oxford 1986, pp. 30–68.

JEFFERY, A., "Text of the Correspondence between Umar I and Leo *III*", HTR 37 (1944) pp. 269–332.

JERPHANION, G. de, "L'image de Jesus-Christ dans l'art chrétien", *Nouvelle Rev. Theol.* 65 (1938) pp. 257–83.

JORGA, N., "Les origines de l'iconoclasme", *Académie Roumaine. Bulletin de la section historique* II, Bucharest 1924, pp. 142–55.

KAEGI, W., "The Byzantine Armies and Iconoclasm", *Byzantinoslavica* 27 (1966) pp. 48–70.

———. "The Byzantine Thematic Armies in the First Iconoclastic Period (728–787)", in his *Byzantine Military Unrest 471–843*, Amsterdam 1981, pp. 209–43.

KALOKYRIS, C.D., *The Essence of Orthodox Iconography*, Brookline, Mass. 1971.

KARMIRIS, I., *Ta Dogmatika kai Symvolika Mnimeia tis Orthodoxou Katholikis Ekklisias*, vol. i, Athens 1960.

KITTEL, G. & KLEINKNECHT, H., "Eikon" in the *Theological Dictionary of the New Testament*, vol. ii, pp. 381–96.

KITZINGER, E., "The Cult of Images in the Age before Iconoclasm", *DOP* 8 (1954) pp. 83–150.

———. "On Some Icons of the Seventh Century", *Late Class. and Med. Studies in Honor of A.M. Friend* (ed. K. Weitzmann), Princeton 1955, pp. 132–50.

———. *The Art of Byzantium and the Mediaeval West. Selected Studies* (ed. W.E. Kleinbauer) Bloomington 1976.

KOCH, H., "Die altchristliche Bilderfrage nach den literarischen Quellen", *Forschungen fur Religion und Literatur des A.u.U.T.*, Gottingen 1919, pp. 3–105.

KOCH, L., "Christusbild-Kaiserbild. Zugleich ein Beitrag zur Losung der Frage nach dem Anteil der byzantinischen Kaiser am griechischen Bilderstreit", *Bened. Monatsschrift* 21 (1939). pp. 85–105. "Zur Theologie der Christusikone", *Bened. Monatsschrift* 19 (1937) pp. 375–87, and 20 (1938) pp. 32–47, 168–75, 281–8 and 437–59.

KOLLWITZ, J., "Bild III (christlich)", *RAC* 2 (1954) cols. 318–41. "Christusbild", *RAC* 3 (1957) cols. 2–24.
——. *Das Christusbild des dritten Jahrhunderts*, Münster 1953.
KORRES, Th., "To Kinima ton 'Elladikon'", *Byzantiaka* 1 (1981) pp. 37–49.
KOUTRAS, D., "I ennoia tis eikonos eis ton Pseudo-Dionysion ton Areopagitin", *EEBS* 35 (1967) pp. 243–58.
LADNER, G.B., "Der Bilderstreit und die Kunstlehren der byzantinischen und abendlandischen Theologie", *ZK* 50 (1931) pp. 1–23.
——. "Eikon", *RAC* 4 (1959) cols. 771–86.
——. "Origin and Significances of the Byzantine Iconoclastic Controversy", *Mediaeval Studies* 2 (1940) pp. 127–49.
——. "The Concept of the Image in the Greek Fathers and the Byzantine Iconoclastic Controversy", *DOP* 7 (1953) pp. 1–31.
LANGE, G., *Bild und Wort. Die katechetischen Functionen des Bildes in der griechischen Theologie des sechsten bis neunten Jahrhunderts*, Wurzburg 1969.
LECLERQ, H., "Images (culte et querelle de)", *DACL* 7, 1 (1926) col. 180f.
LEMERLE, P., *Le premier humanisme byzantin. Notes et remarques sur enseignement et culture à Byzance des Origines au Xe siècle*, Paris 1971.
LOSSKY, V., *In the Image and Likeness of God*, Crestwood 1974.
——. *The Mystical Theology of the Eastern Church*, Cambridge & London 1957.
——. *Vision de Dieu*, Neuchatel 1962.
MAIMBOURG, L., *Histoire et l'hérésie des Iconoclastes, et la translation de l'Empire aux François*, Paris 1686.
MANGO, C., "Historical Introduction", *Iconoclasm* (edd. Bryer & Herrin) pp. 1–6.
——. "The Art of the Byzantine Empire, 312–1483. Sources and Documents", *Sources and Documents in the History of Art* (ed. H.W. Janson) Englewood Cliffs 1972.
MARCAIS, G., "La question des images dans l'art musulmans", *Byzantion* 7 (1932) pp.161–89.
MARTIN, E.J., *History of the Iconoclastic Controversy*, London 1930.
MENGES, H., *Die Bilderlehre des heiligen Johannes von Damaskos*, Münster 1937.
MENDHAM, J., *The Seventh General Council*, London 1849.
MEYENDORFF, J., *Byzantine Theology: Historical Trends and Doctrinal Themes*, London and Oxford 1974, esp. pp. 42–53.
——. *Christ in Eastern Christian Thought*, Washington 1969, esp. pp. 173–92.
MICHAELIS, P.A., "Byzantine Art as a Religious and Didactic Art", *The British Journal of Aesthetics* 7 (1967), pp. 150–7.
MILLET, L.G., "Les iconoclastes et la croix. A propos d'une inscription de Cappadoce", *Bulletin de correspondence héllénique* 34 (1910) pp. 96–109.
MULLER, R., "The Theological Significance of a Critical Attitude in Hagiography", *The Ecumenical Review* 14 (1962) pp. 279–82.
MUNITIZ, J.A., "Synoptic Greek Accounts of the Seventh Council", *REB* 32 (1974) pp. 147–86.
MURRAY, Sr Charles, "Art and the Early Church", *JTS* 28 (1977).
NERSESSIAN, S. Der, "Image Worship in Armenia and its Opponents", *Armenian Quarterly* 1 (1946) pp. 67–81.
——. "Une apologie des images du septième siècle", *Byzantion* 17 (1944/5) pp.58–87.
NYSSEN, W., "Zur Theologie des Bildes", *Handbuch der Ostkirchenkunde*, Dusseldorf 1971, pp. 473–582.
OSTROGORSKY, G., *History of the Byzantine State*, Oxford 1956.
——. "Les débuts de la querelle des images", *Etudes sur l'histoire et sur l'art de Byzance. Mélanges Ch. Diehl*, Paris 1930, vol. i, pp. 235–55.
——. "Rom und Byzanz im Kampfe um die Bilderverehrung", *Seminarium Kondakovianum* 6 (1933) pp. 73–87.
——. *Studien zur Geschichte des byzantinischen Bilderstreites*, Amsterdam 1964.
——. "Uber die vermeintliche Reformatigheit der Isaurier", *BZ* 30 (1929/30) pp. 394–400.

OUSPENSKY, L., *Theology of the Icon*, Crestwood 1978.
OUSPENSKY, L., and V. LOSSKY, *The Meaning of Icons*, Boston 1969.
PAPADOPOULOS, Ch., "Aitia kai genikos charaktir tis Eikonomachias", *Theologia* (1930) pp. 1–16.
PELIKAN, J., *The Spirit of Eastern Christendom (600–1700)* (vol. ii of *the Christian Tradition. A History of the Development of Doctrine*) Chicago 1974.
———. *Imago Dei: The Byzantine Apologia for Icons*, New Haven and London 1990.
PUTMAN, G.E. "The Image as Sacramental", *Sacrament and Image* (ed. A.M. Allchin) pp. 12–16.
RESNICK, I., "Idols and Images: Early Definitions and Controversies", *Sobornost* 7 (1985) pp. 35–51.
RICE, D. Talbot, *Art of the Byzantine Era*, London 1963.
———. *Byzantine Art*, Harmondsworth 1962.
———. *Byzantine Painting. The Last Phase*, New York 1968.
———. *The Appreciation of Byzantine Art*, London 1972.
RICE, D. Talbot and Tamara Talbot Rice, *Icons and their Dating*, London 1974.
RILEY, A., "The Doctrine of the Holy Images", *The Christian East* 1 (1920) pp. 30–5.
ROMANIDES J., *Franks, Romans, Feudalism and Doctrine*, Brookline 1981.
ROUAN, M. -F., "Une lecture 'iconoclaste' de la Vie d'Etienne le Jeune", *Travaux et Mémoires* 8 (1981) pp. 415–36.
RUNCIMAN, S., *Byzantine Style and Civilization*, Harmondsworth 1975.
———. "Some Remarks on the Images of Edessa", *Camb. Hist. Journal* 3 (1931) pp. 238–52
SAHAS, D., *Icon and Logos*, Toronto 1987.
SAVRAMIS, D., "Bilderverehrung, Bilderstreitigheiten", *Weltkirchlexicon*, Stuttgart 1960, pp. 161–3.
———. "Der abergläubische Missbrauch der Bilder in Byzanz", *Ostkirchliche Studien* 9 (1960) pp. 174–92.
———. "Die Kirchenpolitik Kaiser Leons III", *Sudostforschungen* 20 (1961) pp. 1–22.
SCHAFERDIEK, K., "Zu Verfasserschaft und Situation der epistula ad Constantiam de imagine Christi", *ZK* 91 (1980) pp.177–86.
SCHEBESTA, B., "Bild", *Lexikon für Theologie und Kirche* II, Freiburg 1958.
SCHODEMAN, J.B., "'Eikon' in den Schriften des h1. Athanasius", *Scholastik* 16 (1941) p. 335ff.
SCHONBORN, C. von, *L'icône du Christ: Fondements théologiques élaborés entre le Ier et le IIe concile de Nicée (325–787)*, Fribourg 1976.
SCHUG-WILLE, C., *Art of the Byzantine World*, New York 1969.
SCHWARZLOSE, K., *Der Bilderstreit: Ein Kampf der griechischen Kirche um ihre Eigenart und ihre Freiheit*, Gotha 1890.
SCOUTERIS, C., "Never as gods: Icons and their Veneration", *Sobornost* 6 (1984) pp. 6–18.
SENDLER, E., *L'icône: image de l'invisible*, Paris 1981.
SPECK, P., *Kaiser Konstantin VI*, Munich 1978.
STAKEMEIER, E., "Das 7. oikumenische Konzil: Bilderkult und Einheit der Kirche" *Unio Christianorum (Mélanges L. Jaeger)*, Paderborn 1972, pp. 243–61.
STANILOAE, D., *Theology and the Church*, Crestwood 1980.
STIERNON, D., "Images (culte des)", *Catholicisme* V, Paris 1960, pp. 1250–8.
STEIN, D., *Der Beginn des byzantinischen Bilderstreites und seine Entwicklung bis in die 40er Jahre des 8. Jahrhunderts*, Munich 1980.
THEODOROU, A., *Opseis tines tis peri kakou, theoseos tou anthropou kai hieron eikonon didaskalias tou agiou Ioannou tou Damaskinou*, offprint from *Theologia*, Athens 1972.
TSELENGIDES, D., *I theologia tis eikonas kai i anthropologiki simasia tis*, Thessaloniki 1984.
VASILIEV, A.A., *History of the Byzantine Empire 324–1453*, Madison and Milwaukee 1964.
———. "The Iconoclastic Edict of the Caliph Yazid II, A.D. 721", *DOP* 9/10 (1955/56) pp. 25–47.

VEN, P. van den, "La patristique et l'hagiographie du Concile de Nicée de 787", *Byzantion* 25/27 (1955/57) pp. 325–62.

VISSER, W.J.A., *Die Entwicklung des Christusbildes in Literatur um Kunst in der fruhchristlichen und fruhbyzantinischen Zeit*, Bonn 1934.

WALLACH, L., *Diplomatic Studies in Latin and Greek Documents from the Carolingian Age*, Ithaca and London 1977.

WENDT, C.H.W., "Bilderlehre und Ikonenverehrung. Ein Beitrag zum Verstandnis der alten Ikonenmalerie", *Zeitschr. für Rel. und Geist.* 2 (1949/50) pp. 23–33.

WARE, Kallistos (Timothy), *The Orthodox Church*, Harmondsworth 1959.

——. "The Transfiguration of the Body", *Sacrament and Image* (ed. A.M. Allchin) pp. 17–32.

——. "The value of the Material Creation", *Sobornost* 6 (1971) pp. 154–65.

WALTER, C., *Art and Ritual of the Byzantine Church*, London 1982.

WEBER, G., *Die Bildhaftigheit der christlichen Verkundigung*, Paderborn 1958.

WILLMS, H., Eikon. *Eine begriffsgeschichtlich Untersuchung zum Platonismus*, vol. i: *Philon von Alexandrien*, Münster 1935.

ZAKYTHINOS, D., *Skepseis tines peri Eikonomachias*, Athens 1975.

INDEX OF NAMES AND PLACES

INDEX OF SUBJECTS

Studies in the History
of Christian Thought

EDITED BY HEIKO A. OBERMAN

50. HOENEN, M. J. F. M. *Marsilius of Inghen*. Divine Knowledge in Late Medieval Thought. 1993
51. O'MALLEY, J. W., IZBICKI, T. M. and CHRISTIANSON, G. (eds.) *Humanity and Divinity in Renaissance and Reformation*. Essays in Honor of Charles Trinkaus. 1993
52. REEVE, A. (ed.) and SCREECH, M. A. (introd.) *Erasmus' Annotations on the New Testament*. Galatians to the Apocalypse. 1993
53. STUMP, Ph. H. *The Reforms of the Council of Constance (1414-1418)*. 1994
54. GIAKALIS, A. *Images of the Divine*. The Theology of Icons at the Seventh Ecumenical Council. With a Foreword by Henry Chadwick. 1994

Prospectus available on request

E. J. BRILL — P.O.B. 9000 — 2300 PA LEIDEN — THE NETHERLANDS

DATE DUE